D0989333

By the Same Authors

Heroic Clients, Heroic Agencies: Partners for Change, *Barry Duncan, Jacqueline Sparks*

The Heart and Soul of Change: What Works in Therapy, *Mark Hubble, Barry Duncan, Scott Miller*

Escape from Babel: Toward a Unifying Language for Psychotherapy, *Scott Miller, Barry Duncan, Mark Hubble*

Psychotherapy with "Impossible" Cases: The Efficient Treatment of Therapy Veterans, *Barry Duncan, Mark Hubble, Scott Miller*

Brief Intervention for School Problems: Collaborating for Practical Solutions, *John Murphy, Barry Duncan*

Handbook of Solution-Focused Brief Therapy: Theory, Research, and Practice, *Scott Miller, Mark Hubble, Barry Duncan*

Changing the Rules: A Client-Directed Approach to Therapy, *Barry Duncan, Andrew Solovey, Greg Rusk*

Working with the Problem Drinker: A Solution-Focused Approach, *Insoo Berg, Scott Miller*

Self-Help

Staying on Top and Keeping the Sand Out of Your Pants, *Scott Miller, Mark Hubble, Seth Houdeshell*

"Let's Face It, Men Are &$$%\¢$": What Women Can Do About It, *Joseph Rock, Barry Duncan*

The Miracle Method: A Radically New Approach to Problem Drinking, *Scott Miller, Insoo Berg*

Overcoming Relationship Impasses: Ways to Initiate Change When Your Partner Won't Help, *Barry Duncan, Joseph Rock*

The Heroic Client

Barry L. Duncan

Scott D. Miller

Jacqueline A. Sparks

The Heroic Client

A Revolutionary Way to
Improve Effectiveness Through
Client-Directed, Outcome-Informed
Therapy

Revised Edition

JOSSEY-BASS
A Wiley Imprint
www.josseybass.com

Published by Jossey-Bass
A Wiley Imprint
989 Market Street, San Francisco, CA 94103-1741   www.josseybass.com

Jossey-Bass books and products are available through most bookstores. To contact Jossey-Bass directly, call our Customer Care Department within the U.S. at 800-956-7739 or outside the U.S. at 317-572-3986, or fax to 317-572-4002.

Jossey-Bass also publishes its books in a variety of electronic formats. Some content that appears in print may not be available in electronic books.

Excerpts from "The psychology of mental illness: The consumers/survivors/ex-mental patients' perspective" by Ronald Bassman from *Psychotherapy Bulletin*, *34*(1), Winter 1999, 14–16. Reprinted with permission of *Psychotherapy Bulletin*.

Figure 4.1 from *American Psychologist*, *41*(2), 1986, 159–164, copyright © 1986 by the American Psychological Association. Reprinted with permission.

Library of Congress Cataloging-in-Publication Data

Duncan, Barry L.
   The heroic client : a revolutionary way to improve effectiveness through client-directed, outcome-informed therapy / Barry L. Duncan, Scott D. Miller, Jacqueline A. Sparks.— Rev. ed.
      p. cm.
"First edition."
Includes bibliographical references and index.
   ISBN 0-7879-7240-1 (alk. paper)
   1. Client-centered psychotherapy.   I. Miller, Scott D.   II. Sparks, Jacqueline. III. Title.
   RC481.D86   2004
   616.89′14—dc22   2003018314

Printed in the United States of America
REVISED EDITION

PB Printing   10 9 8 7 6 5 4 3 2 1

Contents

Foreword to the Revised Edition   ix
Bruce E. Wampold

Foreword to the First Edition   xii
Larry E. Beutler

Preface   xvii

1   Therapy at the Crossroads   1

2   The Myth of the Medical Model   21

3   Becoming Client Directed   49

4   Becoming Outcome Informed   81
with Lynn Johnson, Jeb Brown, and Morten Anker

5   The Client's Theory of Change   119
with Susanne Coleman, Lisa Kelledy, and Steven Kopp

6   The Myth of the Magic Pill   147
*with Grace Jackson, Roger P. Greenberg,
and Karen Kinchin*

7   Planet Mental Health   178

Epilogue: A Tale of Two Therapies   201

Appendixes

I   A First-Person Account of Mental Health Services   213
Ronald Bassman

II   Consumer/Survivor/Ex-Patient Resource Information   217
Ronald Bassman

III   Five Questions About Psychotherapy   219

110100

IV Outcome Rating Scale and Session Rating Scale;   221
     Experimental Versions for Children

References   229

About the Authors   249

Name Index   254

Subject Index   261

──— Foreword to the Revised Edition

Every society, historical or contemporary, has a culturally embedded set of healing practices. These practices are so ingrained into people's thinking that they go unquestioned. Receiving acupuncture as part of Chinese care would not be astonishing to a Chinese person living in the culture. To an ancient Greek, the acupuncture ritual would be all wrong: the idea of *chi* would be foreign, but temple rituals based on mythical gods would be comfortable and accepted. Simply, we do not question the predominant healing models of our culture.

The predominant healing practice in our culture is modern medicine. We may question a particular diagnosis or procedure, but most Westerners unquestioningly accept the basic premise that disease is caused by some physiochemical abnormality that can be corrected through the administration of medicine or physical procedure. In the most simple example, bacteria causes pneumonia; antibiotics kill the bacteria; and the pneumonia is cured. Sufficient evidence exists that bacteria are real (we can see them with a microscope) and that antibiotics are effective. Modern medicine has a distinct distaste for healing practices that have "strange" explanations (that is, involve processes not verifiable by scientific means) such as those involving animal magnetism (the basis of Mesmer's treatments), *chi*, spirits, and so forth, whether or not the healing practices are effective.

Barry Duncan, Scott Miller, and Jacqueline Sparks have cogently examined the research on psychotherapy and concluded that the medical model does not apply to this healing practice (see Chapter Two). This conclusion is controversial, not because it is not supported by the research but because it challenges the predominant cultural understanding. There is convincing evidence that psychotherapy does not act specifically on disorders in the way in which medicine is purported to work. It is not the cognitive interventions in cognitive therapy that make it effective; more likely, the benefits are due to the explanation given to the clients; the rituals consistent with that explanation, which remoralize the client; the relationship between the therapist and the client; the skill of the therapist; the healing context; the client's expectation and hope; and so forth. Indeed, as Duncan, Miller, and Sparks explain, all psychotherapies competently administered are equally effective. People benefit from psychotherapy in ways that are not easily explained by a medical model. It is not surprising, therefore, that pharmacological treatments are not particularly effective and may work primarily through means other than the specific effects on the brain. Chapter Six (coauthored with Grace Jackson, Roger P. Greenberg, and Karen Kinchin) is a stunning indictment of drug treatments for most conditions that we label as mental disorders.

It is important to note, as Duncan, Miller, and Sparks have, that the medical model permeates the treatment of clients. Television is saturated with advertisements for medicines for physical ailments (e.g., allergies, constipation, diarrhea, heartburn, chemotherapy-induced nausea) as well as mental disorders (e.g., depression and anxiety). Psychotropic medications are among the most widely sold drugs in the United States. However, the helping professions have shared in applying the medical model to assisting clients, partly from the pressures of managed care, partly from competition from biological psychiatry, and partly from our reverence of science and the medical model. We diagnose clients; we formulate treatment plans; we administer diagnostics (e.g., personality tests); we maintain medical charts; and we think of ourselves as the agents of change. Our leaders in academia are busy developing empirically supported treatments so as to establish our treatment authority. Duncan, Miller, and Sparks have cogently and refreshingly presented an alternative: client-directed and outcome-informed therapy.

The Heroic Client is not simply an humanistic tilting at the medical-model windmill. Duncan, Miller, and Sparks's contribution may be thought of as proposing a scientific alternative to the medical model. One of the distinguishing features of modern medicine is that it has resulted in treatments that are demonstrably effective. Over the history of the world, the effectiveness of thousands of healing practices adopted by various cultures has not been established. Although it is not clear whether or not such practices have been beneficial, there is no doubt that some have been harmful (see Duncan, Miller, and Sparks's description of the iatrogenic effects of George Washington's physicians' treatments of his respiratory disorder in Chapter One).

Psychotherapy has been scientifically established as a remarkably effective practice, more effective than many accepted medical treatments. Duncan, Miller, and Sparks take a further and vital step down the empirical road by demonstrating the usefulness of monitoring client progress. Monitoring client outcomes is such an obviously important activity that knowing it has not been standard practice since the inception of talk cures boggles the mind. We have for decades attempted, albeit unsuccessfully, to identify the characteristics of successful therapists—Duncan, Miller, and Sparks propose the eminently reasonable solution that we evaluate the effectiveness of therapy based on the outcome and not on the adherence of the therapist to a treatment protocol, an expectation of a supervisor, or other implicit aspects of the therapy.

The final recommendation of *The Heroic Client* is to listen to the client to guide the therapy. The notion of client-directed therapy hits indeed at a central tenet of the medical model, which always proposes an external explanation for a disorder, located in scientific understanding. Client-directed therapy requires that we therapists give up our notion of "expertness," a proposition that is difficult to assimilate after the years of training we have endured in order to achieve our status. I suspect that many clients present to us because of the perceived expertness as well. However, Duncan, Miller, and Sparks make a convincing case that the humility required to become a client-directed therapist is worth the effort because of the benefit that clients will experience by participating in a healing practice that recognizes their wisdom and respects their understanding of themselves.

Duncan, Miller, and Sparks have it exactly right, to my mind, by focusing on effectiveness as well as respect. They have shown the courage to break free of the shackles of the medical model without sacrificing the values (and value) of science and evidence. It is not only the clients who are heroic—Duncan, Miller, and Sparks are heroic, as are the therapists who resist the temptation to conform to a medical model and thus assist clients in effective and respectful ways.

BRUCE E. WAMPOLD
University of Wisconsin-Madison

~~~ Foreword to the First Edition

Name a psychiatric condition, and it is likely that a document from one or another mental health agency or interest group maintains that this condition is "seriously underdiagnosed and unrecognized" in society. Often, it is asserted that it is underdiagnosed because it is malignantly asymptomatic (without symptoms), but if the truth were known, we are told, it would be revealed that this condition has reached epidemic proportions. And of course, all of these conditions require the services of an expert clinician, a magic pill, and months or even years of expensive treatment.

Factually, it is quite uncertain that the clusters of symptoms that we bind together under discrete diagnostic labels really represent discrete conditions or disease processes at all, and even more uncertain that even highly trained clinicians can identify them reliably or treat them discriminately when they are recognized. Diagnostic descriptors are proliferating at a much faster rate than the accumulation of supportive research or the expansion and growth of new symptoms, with every new edition of the *Diagnostic and Statistical Manual of Mental Disorders* adding new diseases to our vocabulary. The accumulation of these diseases, some might add, are more responsive to the vote of the American Psychiatric Association than to the findings from the research laboratory. Applications of democracy to eradicating disease, as done in psychiatry, should certainly be tried by those who treat cancer and heart disease.

In view of this, one has to wonder why and how both diagnoses and treatment approaches have proliferated so widely, there now being more than 400 of each. As one inspects the peculiarly strong correlation between the number of new diagnoses and the number of professionals being trained to treat these disorders, he or she may secretly wonder, which came first—the diseases or the healers? Conventional wisdom portrays a struggling mental health system that is overrun by an ever expanding epidemic, straining under the press of emerging disorders—a system whose scientists are uncovering, daily, new sicknesses and problems, and whose weak efforts to amass an army to fight these diseases is inadequate to stem the tide.

But there is another view, one that suggests that new diseases have been manufactured in order to feed a social system that prefers to think of "diseases" needing treatment than of choices that imply personal responsibility and vulnerability. This latter view suggests that the expanding diagnostic system was created in order to support the needs of a growing array of mental health professionals and a burgeoning pharmaceutical industry—make it into a disease and you imply that it requires an expert, a pill, and a specialized treatment to fix it.

The evidence for this alternative perspective is compelling, as Barry Duncan and Scott Miller document. For example, in spite of an exponential increase in the number of new and novel theories of change, psychopathology, and treatment, it remains that even skilled professionals cannot agree on when a given condition is present. Even if they do agree, moreover, they assign different treatments. And finally, the treatments they assign, while different in assumed mechanism and form—both chemical and psychological—are nonspecific. That is, they produce similar effects, and most of the effects take place early in treatment. It seems that every new practitioner develops his or her own theory of how behavior develops and changes, which often is no more than a rationale for why his or her special skills are needed. The evidence available indicates that factors that are incidental to most of these theories account for most of the benefits of the treatments. Most of the factors that help people are inherent to the patient and involve his or her resources, expectancies, and faith. What change is not accounted for by these qualities of the person who seeks treatment is largely accounted for by how well the therapist can relate to the patient. Indeed, in this day of trying to identify empirically supported treatments, the treatment that has earned the strongest research support is any specific one in which therapist and client/patient collaborate, the therapist is supportive and caring, and both or all participants share a perspective of where they are going. A therapy that capitalizes on creating this type of environment is what is advocated and described by Duncan and Miller in espousing "client-directed, outcome informed" therapy.

Considering contemporary literature about the contributors to effective amelioration of problems in living and personal discomfort, one would be hard pressed to imagine that client-directed therapy would be ill advised for anyone. It is an approach that respects the patient and stimulates collaboration toward patient-initiated goals. And it addresses the area about which we know the most regarding how to maximize the effects of psychotherapeutic efforts, the therapeutic relationship. It acknowledges the importance of patient preparation, of session-by-session evaluation, of early change events, and of monitoring and correcting the quality of the therapeutic alliance.

Duncan and Miller and I agree about the problems of diagnosis, the fallacy of the magic pill, the importance of early change, and the value of working through the treatment relationship to construct a treatment plan. At this juncture, however, we also have some divergent views. The snag is in the question of whether improvement beyond the relationship can be achieved by the use of specific techniques in any way that will allow pretreatment and presession planning. Duncan and Miller argue that specific procedures applied on the basis of group algorithms add little to treatment benefit and that any implementation of specific procedures should be decided in response to immediate feedback from patients about the relationship, their expectations, their wants, and their progress. They critique those like me who advocate adding to the relationship enhancement processes a prescriptive or preplanned intervention, tailored to patient qualities. Duncan and Miller fear, with some justification, that such preplanning places too much faith in the skill of the therapist and introduces a status rift into the relationship. I, on the other hand, fear that patients may, just as therapists clearly do, come to reify beliefs and theories to their disadvantage. There are instances, I believe, such as that of Stacey (Chapter Five) in which working from only the patient's theory tacitly reinforces the tendency to assume that one's memories, especially those induced by treatment, are accurate representations of real events from the past, and freezes our views of what is real. I believe that a therapist's responsibility is partially to provide a check against reification of memories and cementing of constructed theories that are or may be damaging to people and relationships in the long run.

But the differences in our views represent hypotheses that are in need of further test. Science will eventually reveal the path to follow. But whatever we ultimately determine the effect to be of specific psychotherapeutic interventions based on diagnosed disorders, I am convinced that we will continue to find that they are of lesser importance than those things whose objectives are to enhance and facilitate the quality of the relationship between client and clinician. This relationship is enhanced when the therapist is able to move within the patient's view and world. It is these things that this book addresses most completely and thoroughly. It is the descriptions of how to treat a "patient" as an equal, how to facilitate the quality of the relationship, and how to establish collaboration and cooperation that are the most valuable and enduring facts. And in this, one cannot go wrong by following Duncan and Miller's lead. But more, you can do much that will be good and helpful.

LARRY E. BEUTLER
University of California, Santa Barbara

To

The memory of Lee Duncan—

Who taught Barry about Heroism

─⁓─ Preface

About twenty-four years ago, I (Barry Duncan) began my mental health career at a state hospital. I experienced firsthand the facial grimaces and tongue wagging that characterize the neurological damage (tardive dyskinesia) caused by antipsychotics and sadly realized that these young adults would be forever branded as grotesquely different, as "mental patients." I witnessed the dehumanization of people reduced to drooling, shuffling zombies, spoken to like children and treated like cattle. I barely kept my head above water as hopelessness flooded the halls of the hospital, drowning staff and clients alike in an ocean of lost causes.

Shortly thereafter, I began working in a residential treatment center for troubled adolescents. So "disturbed" were these kids that every one "required" at least two psychotropic medications and a minimum of two diagnoses. One time when the psychiatrist was on vacation and the center director was unable to cover him, a sixteen-year-old, Ann, was admitted to the center. I was assigned her case and saw her every day in individual therapy as well as in the groups I conducted. Ann was like many of the kids, abused in all ways imaginable, drop-kicked from one foster home to another, with periodic suicide attempts and trips to hospitals and runaway shelters. In spite of all that, Ann was a pure delight—creative, funny, and hopeful for a future far different than her childhood. The therapy went great: we hit it off famously, and Ann settled in and started attending high school for the first time in several months.

Three weeks later, the psychiatrist returned and prescribed an antidepressant and lithium for Ann. She adamantly opposed taking the medication—she said she had been down that path already. But her voice went unheard. More accurately, she had no voice at all in her own treatment. I protested to the psychiatrist, citing evidence of how well she was doing, but to no avail. I was only a mental health grunt and a student to boot. I argued that forcing meds on Ann could be harmful, but he did not listen. And it was.

Ann became a different person—sullen, hostile, and combative. She soon ran away and went on a three-day binge of alcohol and drugs. A carload of men picked her up while she was hitchhiking and ended the ride with a gang rape. Adding insult to injury, Ann was forcefully injected with an antipsychotic when the police brought her back to the center. When Ann described this experience, she saw the horror on my face and reassured me that she had suffered far worse indignities than being forcefully tranquilized. It was little solace for either of us.

When Ann persisted in her ardent protests against the medication, I encouraged her to talk to the center director. Rather than listening, however, the director admonished me for putting ideas into Ann's head and told me to drop it. Instead, I spent days researching the literature. What I found surprised me. In contrast to what most clients were told, little was known about how psychotropic drugs actually worked. Drugs like cocaine, for example, blocked the reuptake of the brain chemicals believed critical to depression in exactly the same way as antidepressants but did not have any so-called therapeutic effect. Furthermore, although increases in these supposedly critical neurotransmitters were present within hours of the first dose, they did not result in any therapeutic benefit for four to six weeks! Moreover, there was no empirical support for prescribing these drugs to children—let alone multiple drugs.

Finally, I was shocked to find that the very helpfulness of medication was suspect. I discovered a 1974 review (Morris & Beck, 1974) of ninety-one studies that showed antidepressants to be no more effective than a sugar pill in one-third of the published reports. This finding is particularly noteworthy because the studies eliminated participants who showed rapid improvement to the fake pill (called placebo responders). Furthermore, because research with negative results is less likely to be published, this review likely underestimated the extent of the placebo response rate.

Simply put, I had unexpectedly discovered that the emperor had no clothes. What did I get when I challenged the psychiatrist with these facts? Fired. Ann survived as usual, resisting when she could, and unfortunately viewed this experience as just another cog in her wheel of abuse from her "helpers." I left demoralized but determined never to be in the dark again, complicit by virtue of ignorance. Later, Ann wrote me and thanked me for supporting her resistance. Ann's resilience gave me hope.

These many years later, the same practices that diminished and excluded Ann, as well as dictated her options, still thrive. This book seeks to undermine those practices that oppress clients and provide therapists with the information necessary to question the mental health status quo. Consequently, this book is decidedly political. We critically examine and slaughter the sacred cows of the medical model as it applies to the human dilemmas clients and therapists routinely face.

But that is not enough. Therapists have whined about the mental health system for many years. More important, we also suggest an alternative that we believe fits therapist's values more and releases therapists and clients alike from practices in which they do not believe. At the core of our proposal is the heroic client. This book recasts the drama of therapy and places clients in their rightful role as heroes and heroines of the therapeutic stage.

We argue that attending to clients' centrality to change by monitoring the client's view of progress and fit dramatically improves effectiveness and makes psychotherapy accountable to both consumers and payers. We call this approach "client directed and outcome informed."

We, however, are not laying the cornerstone of a new model or concocting a tag line for selling a new and improved brand of therapy. Any therapy can be client directed and outcome informed; the only requirement is that ongoing client perceptions about the fit and progress of therapy direct options and provide the ultimate litmus test for success. Consequently, we dictate no fixed techniques, no certainties or invariant patterns in therapeutic process, and offer no insightful explanations for the concerns that bring folks to therapy. We are certain that you have "been there, done that." Instead, we suggest principles that therapists of any orientation can consider to enhance those factors identified by research to account for successful outcome—but only the client can determine the benefit of any particular application. Therefore, we suggest a way that therapists of any theoretical preference can elicit clients' "real-time" feedback about the benefit of the services received to inform and modify their work—not only to improve effectiveness but also to form an identity separate from the medical model.

In this revision of *The Heroic Client,* we intended at first to change only two chapters substantially to reflect the evolution of our thinking and simply update the others. But as Jacqueline Sparks, our new third author, commented, once you repaint one room in the house, suddenly all the rooms look in need of a coat of paint. Consequently, readers familiar with the first edition will notice many changes in addition to updated references. The new version is decidedly more user friendly, replete with several more client examples to illustrate our points. This edition offers a more practical discussion of the most radical of our ideas: partnering with clients to change the way mental health services are delivered and funded. We lay out the details of becoming outcome informed to encourage not only more insurrection against those practices that marginalize clients but also to provide enough foundation for readers to begin an outcome project in their settings. Those desiring to implement these ideas can find support at our listserv, http://www.heroicagencies.org. We have also expanded our arguments about evidence-based treatments and psychotropic medication to enable the informed therapist to thoughtfully consider the controversies at hand.

Finally, we changed the subtitle to "A Revolutionary Way to Improve Effectiveness." These are strong words. We mean "revolutionary way" to reflect two themes central to this book. One is our revolutionary desire to overthrow mental health practices that do not promote a partnership with clients in all decisions that affect their well being. The second theme is the revolutionary improvements that recent research about outcome feedback has demonstrated—using client-based outcome feedback increases effectiveness by an incredible 65 percent in real clinical settings. Such results, when taken in combination with the field's obvious failure to discover and systematize therapeutic process in a manner that reliably improves success, have led us to conclude that the best hope for improving effectiveness will be found in outcome management.

—⁓—

Any project of this kind reflects contributions by many, and to them we are deeply grateful. We remain indebted to our clients, who continue to teach us to do good work by depending on them. Several people deserve special mention. In addition to the influences mentioned in our previous publications, we would like to acknowledge the inspiration provided by therapists and leaders around the world who implement the ideas described in this book in the places that really matter, in the day-to-day world with clients in distress—Wenche

BrunnLien, Dave Claud, Daniil Danilopoulos, Morten Hammer, Mary Susan Haynes, Tove and Andy Huggins, Bill Plum, Geir Skauli, Dave Stadler, Anne-Grethe Tuseth, and Jim Walt to mention just a few—and whose willingness to challenge the status of the emperor's fashions provide models for us all to emulate. We are grateful to Rita Benasutti, Joan Katz, Sara Klug, and Joe Rock for their feedback and ongoing support; and to the heroicagencies listserv, too many names to mention, for continued lively conversation and the inspiration to try to make a difference. Finally, we feel especially indebted to Alan Rinzler, executive editor at Jossey-Bass, for recognizing our passions and encouraging them to become manifest.

BARRY L. DUNCAN
SCOTT D. MILLER
JACQUELINE A. SPARKS

CHAPTER ONE

Therapy at the Crossroads
The Challenges of the Twenty-First Century

. . . every man his greatest, and, as it were, his own executioner.

—*Sir Thomas Browne,* Religio Medici

O ne day, the ancient fable by Aesop goes, the mighty oaks were complaining to the god Jupiter. "What good is it," they asked him bitterly, "to have come to this Earth, struggled to survive through harsh winters and strong fall winds, only to end up under the woodcutter's axe?" Jupiter would hear nothing of their complaints, however, and scolded them sternly. "Are you not responsible for your own misfortunes, as you yourselves provide the handles for those axes?" The sixth-century C.E. storyteller ends the tale with a moral: "It is the same for men: they absurdly reproach the gods for the misfortunes that they owe to no one but themselves" (Duriez, 1999, p. 1).

Though removed by some 2,600 years, the perilous situation of the oaks described in Aesop's fable is not unlike that of the field of therapy today. Indeed, changes in virtually every aspect of the profession over the last ten years have left mental health practitioners with much to feel uncertain and unhappy about. Where once therapists were the complete and total masters of their domain, their power to make even the smallest of decisions regarding clinical practice has dwindled to nearly nothing. A recent survey found that a staggering 80 percent of practitioners felt they had lost complete control over aspects of "care and treatment they as clinicians *should* control" (e.g., type and length of treatment, and so on; Rabasca, 1999, p. 11, emphasis added).

Of course, the loss of control does not mean there has been a corresponding decrease in the workload of the average mental health professional. Rather, in place of the responsibility therapists used to have are a host of activities implemented under the guise of improving effectiveness and efficiency. For example, where in the past a simple, single-page HCFA 1500 form would suffice, clinicians must now contend with preauthorization, lengthy intake and diagnostic forms, extensive treatment plans, medication evaluations, and external case management to qualify for an ever decreasing amount of reimbursement and funding for a continually shrinking number of sessions and services. The paperwork and phone calls these activities require make it difficult to imagine how they could ever save time, money, or increase the effectiveness of the provided services.

As far as income is concerned, the reality is that the average practitioner has watched the bottom line drop by as much as 50 percent over the last ten years (Rabasca, 1999)! Berman (1998), for example, found that the net income of doctoral-level psychologists in solo practice after taxes averaged $24,000—a salary that hardly seems to merit an average investment of six years of postgraduate education and a minimum of $30,000 in tuition costs (Norcross, Hanych, & Terranova, 1996). On the public side of things, case managers and other bachelor-level providers render more and more services, reducing the value and therefore salaries of master's-trained mental health professionals.

Furthermore, several studies have found that the field has twice as many practitioners as are needed to meet current demand for services (Brown, Dreis, & Nace, 1999). Indeed, since the mid-1980s there has been a whopping 275 percent increase in the number of mental health professionals (Hubble, Duncan, & Miller, 1999a). Consumers can now choose among psychiatrists, psychologists, social workers, marriage and family therapists, clinical nurse specialists, professional counselors, pastoral counselors, alcohol and drug addiction counselors, and a host of other providers advertising virtually indistinguishable services under different job titles and descriptions (Hubble et al., 1999a). The reality is, as former American Psychological Association (APA) president Nicholas Cummings (1986, p. 426) predicted, that nonmedical helping professionals have become "poorly paid and little respected employees of giant health care corporations."

In truth, those seeking mental health services have not fared any better than the professionals themselves. Consider a recent study that found that in spite of the dramatic increase in the number of practitioners between 1988 and 1998, actual mental health care benefits decreased by 54 percent during the same time period (Hay Group, 1999). This decrease, the research further shows, is not part of an across-the-board cut in general health care benefits. During the same period that outpatient mental health encounters fell by 10 percent, office visits to physicians increased by nearly a third. In addition, those seeking mental health services face a number of obstacles not present for health care in general (e.g., different limits, caps, deductions, etc.).

Moreover, most third-party payers now require the practitioner to provide information once deemed privileged and confidential before they will reimburse for mental health services (Johnson & Shaha, 1997; Sanchez & Turner, 2003). Unlike cost and numbers of visits, the impact of such obstacles is more difficult to assess. Nonetheless, in an exploratory study, Kremer and Gesten (1998) found that clients and potential clients showed less willingness to disclose when there was external oversight and reporting requirements than under standard confidentiality conditions.

Clearly, the future of mental health practice is uncertain. More troubling, however, like the mighty oaks in Aesop's cautionary tale, the field itself may be providing the very handle—not the ax head, mind you, but the handle—that delivers the cutting blows to the profession.

THE FUTURE OF MENTAL HEALTH

The greatest enemy of the truth is not the lie—deliberate, contrived, and dishonest—but the myth—persistent, pervasive, and unrealistic.

—*John F. Kennedy,* Commencement Address,
Yale University

Imagine a future in which the arbitrary distinction between mental and physical health has been obliterated; a future with a health care system so radically revamped that it addresses the needs of the whole person—medical, psychological, and relational. In this system of integrated care, mental health professionals collaborate regularly with M.D.'s, and clients are helped to feel that experiencing depression is no more a reflection on their character than is catching the flu. This new world will be ultraconvenient: people will be able to take care of all their health needs under one roof—a medical superstore of services. Therapists will have a world of information at their fingertips, merely opening a computer file to learn the patient's complete history of treatment, including familial predispositions, as well as compliance issues or other red flags.

Now imagine a future in which every medical, psychological, or relational intervention in a "patient's" life is a matter of quasi-public record, part of an integrated database. Here, therapy is tightly scripted, and only a limited number of approved treatments are eligible for reimbursement. In this brave new world, integrated care actually means a more thoroughly medicalized health care system into which therapy has been subsumed. Yes, counselors will work alongside medical doctors but as junior partners, following treatment plans taken directly from authorized, standardized manuals. Mental health services will be dispensed like a medication, an intervention that a presiding physician orders at the first sign of "mental illness" detected during a routine visit or perusal of an integrated database.

These are not two different systems; rather, they are polarized descriptions of the same future, one that draws nearer every day. Noted psychologist Charles Kiesler (2000)—who in the mid-1980s predicted that fledgling managed care organizations would dominate the U.S. health care industry—predicts that mental health services will soon be integrated into medical patient care and administered accordingly. The reason for this coming change, of course, is the tremendous pressure on health care administrators to reduce spiraling costs. Many health care prognosticators believe that the cost-cutting measures of managed care have already realized all possible benefits and only a total reconfiguration will bring the critical savings required (Strosahl, 2001). Integrated care is a product of this realization.

And it is not hard to see their point. Over the last four decades, studies have repeatedly shown that as many as 60 to 70 percent of physician visits stem from psychological distress or are at least exacerbated by psychological or behavioral factors. In addition, those diagnosed with mental "disorders" have traditionally overutilized general medical care and have incurred the highest medical costs (Tomiak, Berthelot, & Mustard, 1998). Combine these well-known facts with the rather extensive evidence that the delivery of psychological services offsets the cost of medical care (Sanchez & Turner, 2003)—and voilà, integrated care is the greatest thing since sliced bread. Cummings (2000) suggested that a mere 10 percent reduction in medical and surgical care resulting from behavioral care intervention would exceed the entire mental health care insurance budget! Bottom line: according to its supporters, integrated care increases collaboration, improves care, and makes psychotherapy more central to health care—and of course, saves insurance companies and public funders a ton of money.

What the proposed advantages obscure is the inevitability that, in the name of integration, psychotherapy will become ever more dominated by the assumptions and practices of the medical model; that much like an overpowered civilization in the sci-fi adventure *Star Trek,* we will be assimilated into the medical Borg. The mental health professional of the coming integrated care era, Kiesler (2000) predicts, will be a specialist in treating specific disorders with highly standardized, scientifically proven interventions. At issue here are not the advantages of greater collaboration with health care professionals or of bringing a psychological or systemic perspective to bear on medical conditions. Rather, at issue is whether we will lose our autonomy as a profession by becoming immersed in the powerful culture of biomedicine, breaking the already tenuous connection to our nonmedical, relational identity.

The resulting influx of potential mental health clients into the primary care setting will further promote the conceptualization of mental "disorders" as biologically based and increase current trends toward medication solutions. Indeed, a recent large national survey of primary care physicians revealed that antidepressants were the treatment of choice for depression 72 percent of the time, compared to only 38 percent for mental health referrals (Williams et al., 1999). This is a disturbing trend, especially given what is known about the relative merits of antidepressants (see Chapter Six). Parenthetically, physicians typically diagnose depression in a thirteen-minute visit in which they discuss with patients an average of six problems (Schappert, 1994).

In this nightmarish vision of the future, the woodcutter in the Aesop fable has already cut us down into fireplace-sized pieces, hauled us off, and neatly stacked us for consumption in the fires of the medical model of integrated care. And what is so bad about the medical model? Nothing when it is applied to medical conditions and nothing as one among many options to address the concerns that clients bring to our doorsteps. But as a privileged or mandated practice in mental health, it is a myth, "persistent, pervasive, and unrealistic." The medical model works with the following equation:

$$\text{PROPER DIAGNOSIS} + \text{PRESCRIPTIVE INTERVENTION} = \text{EFFECTIVE TREATMENT}$$

Or

$$\text{TARGETED DIAGNOSTIC GROUPS} + \text{EVIDENCE-BASED TREATMENTS} = \text{SYMPTOM REDUCTION}$$

Consider the left side of the first equation: proper diagnosis and prescriptive intervention. A cursory review of professional publications and training offerings strongly suggests that the medical model of mental health already rules, that integrated care will only add icing to a cake of foregone conclusions. For example, of all the continuing education workshops to appear in a recent ad for the American Healthcare Institute (2003)—one of the nation's largest sponsors of training for therapists—nearly 90 percent were organized around a psychiatric diagnosis. Of these, 70 percent taught specific treatments for specific disorders as defined in the *DSM-IV* (American Psychiatric Association, 1994). As another example, consider that nearly two-thirds of the articles appearing in the prestigious *Journal of Consulting and Clinical Psychology* during 2002 were organized around a psychiatric diagnosis, and more than a quarter reported on specific treatments for specific *DSM* disorders. In fact, funding for studies not related to a specific *DSM* diagnosis dropped nearly 200 percent from the late 1980s to 1990 (Wolfe, 1993), and the trend continues. The bottom line: the medical model of mental health prevails and is so much a part of professional discourse that we do not notice its insidious influence.

Further, on a national level, mental health professional organizations, drug manufacturers, and hospital corporations design and support campaigns aimed at informing the public about the nature of psychiatric illness and benefits of professional treatment. National Anxiety and Depression Awareness Day is a good example. Advertising on radio, on TV, and in print lay out the signs and symptoms of these two "common colds" of mental health and then tell people where they can go to be evaluated and speak with a professional. At least one study found that more than 50 percent of those who are screened end up in some form of treatment—a considerable return on the investment of a single day (APA, 1998a)! In truth, diagnosis and psychopathology are now part of the American vernacular. Almost everyone knows, thanks to the Zoloft television ad and that cute happy face guy, that depression is a serious medical condition caused by an imbalance of chemicals in the brain.

Concurrently, evidence-based practice has become the buzz word du jour. They represent those treatments that have been shown, through randomized clinical trials, to be efficacious over placebo or no treatment (or in psychiatry's case, via research review and clinical consensus). Hardly a day goes by without some publication crossing therapists' desks announcing the latest in evidence-based fashion. Consider the opening line in a recent guide to evidence-based practices: "Good clinicians understand that medical care must be based on the skillful use of scientifically valid and evidence-based information" (McGuire, 2002, p. i). Such pronouncements are not only a part of the everyday information barrage but also have become institutionalized in training programs and licensing boards. For example, APA's executive director for education, Cynthia Belar, asserts: "Health professionals must learn evidence-based practice. Although APA accreditation criteria require this in training, psychologists must also develop the capability to deliver evidence-based care throughout their careers" (Belar, 2003, p. 38). Such statements imply that you will be left at the station if you don't jump on board the evidence-based train. They play on our desires to be good clinicians as well as on our fears about surviving financially in an era that promises that insurance or public funds will reimburse only such treatments.

Among physicians, the concept of evidence-based practice has tremendous appeal. For example, an editorial in the *New England Journal of Medicine* advised physicians to refer patients to therapists proficient at manualized cognitive-behavioral therapy (Scott, 2000), the crown prince of psychology, for chronic depression. The integrated care system will only increase evidence-based treatment because primary care doctors will be the ultimate gatekeepers. Physicians, of course, are not at fault here. Unfortunately, we have not educated the health care system that success depends far less on the type of treatment provided than on the strengths and resources that the client brings and the quality of the alliance the client forms with the therapist.

The development of evidence-based therapies has in fact become a growth industry, paralleling the growth of therapies in general. Since the mid-1960s, the number of talk therapy approaches has mushroomed from 60 to more than 250 at last count (Hubble et al., 1999a). Similarly, since the birth of evidence-based treatments in the early

1990s, these have expanded to well over 100, depending on whose "evidence" from which professional organization you include. Ironically, the effectiveness of psychotherapy has not improved one scintilla, not one percentage point, despite this exponential growth of new treatment technologies and the purported advantages of the so-called scientifically validated approaches. In truth, therapy is no more effective now than it was in the 1960s.

Trying to adjust to yet another fad, mental health agencies and individual professionals spend thousands of dollars on workshops, conferences, and books to learn designer diagnostics and brand-name miracles purportedly based on empirical science. Stepping back, we see that this process differs little from the rush to be brief when managed care first appeared or the stampede to learn about the infamous borderline personality disorder when it first frightened the mental health scene. Unfortunately, similar to all the prior claims of the latest and greatest approaches, the promised advantages always seem just out of reach for most of us, even with those models that supposedly have scientific, valid, and evidence-based information. Why won't the powerful evidence-based sword slay the dragon of misery of the client in my office now? Why doesn't the state-mandated empirically supported treatment work in our agency as its proponents insist?

At this point, one might reasonably wonder what could possibly be wrong with the medical model applied to mental health. What's so bad, for example, about a day of psychoeducation aimed at informing people about the nature of mental illness and helping them overcome the stigma and natural resistance to treatment? For that matter, what's wrong with diagnosis and an emphasis on pathology? After all, people don't go to therapy when they are doing well! Doesn't it just make sense that to help a person, the therapist must first figure out what's wrong with that person? And isn't interest and growth in medication treatment and the number of available therapy approaches a useful development in the field? For far too long, the mental health professions were dominated by the one-size-fits-all approach based on the thinking and techniques of Sigmund Freud. And finally, doesn't the fact that there is more and more demand for treatments that have demonstrated their effectiveness represent a bold step forward from the days of "anything goes" as long as somebody will pay for it? Doesn't the push for evidence-based treatments indicate that the field of mental health has finally arrived as a credible scientific profession?

The problem with the common beliefs and practices of the medical model shoehorned into mental health emerges when we examine them in the light of empirical research. Data from over forty years of increasingly sophisticated research shows little support for

- The utility of psychiatric diagnosis in either selecting the course or predicting the outcome of therapy (the myth of diagnosis)
- The superiority of any therapeutic approach over any other (the myth of the silver-bullet cure)
- The superiority of pharmacological treatment for emotional complaints (the myth of the magic pill)

In fact, as Chapter Two will detail, diagnosis, via the *DSM*, has notoriously poor reliability and has yet to prove any substantial validity. A closer look at evidence-based practice shows that a psychotherapy model claiming superiority over placebo is not front-page news and should not be taken to mean that the approach is better than any other, especially not over the client's own sensibilities of what is helpful. Finally, surprisingly sparse support exists, as Chapter Six will detail, for the widespread use of medication for client complaints, especially children's, arguing for a balance of options for the clients we serve.

The research literature is clear: therapists can assign diagnoses, use the latest evidence-based treatments, and dispense all the new varieties of psychoactive drugs from now until doomsday; and the overall effectiveness and efficiency of therapy will not improve in the least (Hubble, Duncan, & Miller, 1999b). These factors are simply not critical to the outcome of therapy. Importantly, this does not mean that therapy doesn't work. Indeed, available research provides strong evidence for the overall effectiveness of therapy. Most studies, for example, find the average treated person is better off than 80 percent of those without the benefit of therapy (Asay & Lambert, 1999; Wampold, 2001). Daily, clinicians can see the difference our work makes in people's lives.

The lack of empirical support for the medical model is especially disconcerting because it is now enforced by government funding agencies and managed care entities. As early as 1982, Parloff warned the field about the consequences of policymakers misusing such practices. Now, virtually no third party will pay for services without a qualifying

DSM-IV diagnosis. Many will not pay unless the person being served agrees to take medication (e.g., stimulant drugs for children with attention problems, antidepressants for those suffering with depression) or at least submits to evaluation for medication. Finally, several managed care companies and public funds distributors explicitly dictate the treatment approach that clinicians or agencies must use to qualify for reimbursement (e.g., cognitive-behavioral treatment for anxiety disorders, dialectical behavior therapy for borderline personality disorder, multifamily group and psychoeducation for schizophrenia).

Despite this movie trailer setup, replete with the husky voice-over promising a classic struggle of good versus evil, the medical model is not evil. Captain Picard is not really battling the Borg in this tale of Starship Psychotherapy. The medical model is a viable way, among many, of understanding and helping human suffering. The medical model, then, is not the problem. Privileging the medical model over clients and the data is the problem.

To ensure quality mental health services for clients and to be treated as valued professionals, therapists must lead the way and provide alternatives to the medical model. In particular, leadership entails abandoning the empirically vacuous practices of the field's past and directing attention to what works. Furthermore, taking the helm of the good ship mental health requires a full recognition of who is really the captain of the vessel.

BECOMING CLIENT DIRECTED

To exchange one orthodoxy for another is not necessarily an advance. The enemy is the gramophone mind, whether or not one agrees with the record that is being played at the moment.

—*George Orwell*, Inside the Whale and Other Essays

During the 1980s, the attention of the field was riveted on psychiatrist Milton H. Erickson. Clinicians couldn't seem to get enough information about the hypnosis pioneer whose intriguing methods defied conventional practice and seemed to work with the most intractable cases. Learning to do what Erickson did was not an easy task, however, because he steadfastly resisted the temptation to develop an organizing theory for his work. He summed up his reason for this, saying, "I think any theoretically-based psychotherapy is mistaken because each person is different" (Zeig, 1980, p. 131). Curiously, this did not stop Erickson's students from attempting to understand the magical mysteries underlying his work. Indeed, in the years immediately following his death, a plethora of books and articles were published, each purporting to have deciphered the secret code.

Unsatisfied with available theories and caught up in the excitement of the time, a group led by the brief therapist Steve de Shazer made its own attempt at figuring out how Erickson did what he did (de Shazer, 1994). After gathering as many case reports as possible, the group began sorting them into piles based on characteristics each shared. Eventually, they organized all the cases into six different piles—five of which contained cases sharing a basic pattern that enabled the team to replicate Erickson's interventions. The sixth—known as "miscellaneous"— was for "unusual interventions" (p. 247), clever things Erickson did one time and never repeated. These cases did not share any identifiable characteristic with each other or with those in the other five piles. Unfortunately, no matter how the group sorted the cases, this motley pile ended up with the largest number! Fearing they were not clever enough to discern the real patterns in Erickson's work, the group members abandoned the project.

Over a decade would pass before de Shazer discovered the fatal flaw in the earlier project, something so obvious he later wondered how they had missed it. In studying Erickson's cases, they had focused on the wrong person in the therapeutic dyad—namely, Erickson. They had, like everyone else trying to crack the secret code, left the client out of the equation! In truth, the case reports convey little information about the people in them. Rather, the individuals are largely two-dimensional figures whose primary purpose in the unfolding drama seems to be playing a supporting role to Erickson's lead (Sparks, 2000).

Recognizing this gross oversight led de Shazer to a new conclusion, "Most of the ideas for 'unusual interventions' in the miscellaneous pile came from the clients themselves!" (1994, p. 249). In other words, in the majority of his work, Erickson was not the more clever one in the therapeutic dyad. Rather, it was the client. Most of the time, Erickson simply listened carefully and then did what his clients told him to do. Alas, this seems to have been his message all along. "What is needed is the development of a therapeutic situation permitting the patient to use his own thinking, his own understandings, his own emotions in the way that fits him in his scheme of . . . life" (Erickson, 1980, p. 223).

Research on outcome in psychotherapy suggests that Erickson's observations were right on target. Indeed, data from forty years of outcome research provide strong empirical support for privileging the client's role in the change process (Hubble et al., 1999b). In short, clients, not therapists, make therapy work. As a result, therapy should be organized around their resources, perceptions, experiences, and ideas. There need be no a priori assumptions about client problems or solutions, no special questions that are best to ask, and no invariant methodology to follow in order to achieve success. Rather, as the chapters that follow will illustrate through multiple client examples, therapists need only take direction from clients: following their lead; adopting their language, worldview, goals, and ideas about the problem; and acknowledging their experiences with, and inclinations about, the change process.

Just as earlier theorists left the client out of understandings of Erickson's work, the most potent factor of successful outcome, the client and his or her own propensities for change, are conspicuously absent from the medical model equation. Given the data presented in this book, which reflects the importance of the client's strengths and perceptions of therapy, it is time to recast the client as not only the hero or heroine of the therapy drama but also the director of the change endeavor.

Becoming client directed, however, will not be enough to ensure clients' rightful place on the therapeutic stage or the vitality of the field. Mental health professionals must also be capable of proving that their work is effective and efficient. Traditionally, the effectiveness of therapy (symptom reduction or cure) has been left up to the judgment of the provider of the treatment. We will propose something very different: proof of effectiveness can emerge from the systematic recruitment of the client's perception and experience of outcome as a routine part of therapy—enlisting the client as a full partner in both the therapeutic and accountability process.

BECOMING OUTCOME INFORMED

The dogmas of the quiet past are inadequate to the stormy present.

—*Abraham Lincoln,* Annual Message to Congress, 1862

On a cold, blustery December day in 1799, the sixty-seven-year-old former president of the United States, George Washington, returned to his mansion from his usual morning ride on the grounds of his Mount Vernon estate. The day continued in normal fashion. The former president and first lady read newspapers together in the parlor while the household staff performed the usual duties. As the day wore on, however, a minor sore throat the president had experienced since his morning ride worsened. By early the next morning, his condition was so grave that a doctor was summoned.

The doctor—along with two other physicians who eventually made it through the snowy weather to Mount Vernon—skillfully and competently administered the accepted therapy of the day. Observing no results, the three agreed that more of the same treatment was indicated. Several hours and two additional treatments later, the president was dead. The cause of death? Whatever course the disease might have taken, historians agree that the treatment Washington received while in an already weakened state likely hastened his demise. This intervention, of course, was the accepted "standard of care" for late eighteenth-century medicine—bloodletting (Flexner, 1974).

Although it might be tempting to believe that the modern healing arts have evolved beyond such primitive practices, strong evidence exists that the very same forces that led Washington's physicians to administer (and then readminister) an ineffective (and ultimately lethal) treatment continue to guide the practice of therapy—specifically, an emphasis on the competence of service delivery rather than the effectiveness of the services delivered. Nowhere is this more evident than in the ethical codes of the three largest mental health provider organizations: National Association of Social Workers (NASW), APA, and the American Association for Marriage and Family Therapy (AAMFT). None of these existing codes explicitly require social workers, psychologists, or marriage and family therapists to practice effective therapy. Neither do they require therapists to subject their practices to any systematic assessment of outcome. Rather, the codes mandate only that therapists practice, "within the boundaries of their *competence* based on their education, training, supervised experience, consultation, or professional experience" (APA, 2002, [Principle A], p. 1063 [principle 2.01a], emphasis added; NASW, 1999 [Principle 1.04]; AAMFT, 2001 [Principle 3.6]). A refreshing exception can be found in the American Counseling Association (ACA) ethical code, which states: "Counselors continually monitor their *effectiveness* as professionals and take steps to improve when necessary" (ACA, 1995 [Section C2d], emphasis added).

Conventional wisdom suggests that competence engenders, if not equals, effectiveness. As the death of George Washington illustrates, however, competence is no guarantee of effectiveness because providers can use even ineffective or dangerous treatments competently. More important, perhaps, the story shows that having no systematic method for evaluating the outcome of an approach may create an illusion of success that blinds practitioners to corrective feedback.

As just one example of the conflation of competence with effectiveness in mental health, consider the continuing education workshops therapists must attend to maintain their professional licenses. In theory, the continuing education requirement is designed to ensure that clinicians stay abreast of developments that enhance treatment outcome. In practice, however, the vast majority of approaches taught at these workshops do not include any systematic method for evaluating the effectiveness of the approach. Rather, workshop leaders place sole emphasis on the attendees becoming proficient at using the skills or techniques of a particular brand or style of treatment. In the world of continuing education, competency is king.

Far from benign, this emphasis on competence versus outcome decreases effectiveness and efficiency, and it limits the growth of individual therapists. For example, although most would say their clinical ability has improved with experience, a sizable body of research finds little or no relationship between the experience level and effectiveness of therapists (Clement, 1994). If anything, the data indicate that increasing the amount and type of training and experience that most therapists receive may lessen therapeutic effectiveness (Lambert & Ogles, 2004).

Consider a study on the qualities of effective therapists (Hiatt & Hargrave, 1995). Using client self-report and peer ratings, researchers successfully distinguished between least and most effective therapists (as determined by outcome). In brief, they found that therapists in the low-effectiveness group tended to have been in practice for more years than those in the high-effectiveness group (18.2 versus 12.9 years, respectively). More distressing, however, was their finding that the ineffective therapists were unaware that they were ineffective. Even worse, they considered themselves as effective as the truly helpful therapists in the study!

Although these findings are discouraging, awareness of them affords frontline practitioners a critical window of opportunity. Chapter Four will show that therapists can improve the quality of their therapy while simultaneously proving the value of their work by becoming outcome informed. They can be more effective by gathering valid and reliable feedback about the process and outcome of their clinical work and then using that data to inform therapy. Studies now show that providing therapists with such feedback affects outcome, with improvement rates up to 65 percent (Miller, Duncan, Brown, Sorrell, & Chalk, in press; Whipple et al., 2003).

As is news to no one, third-party payers are increasingly cost-conscious and are now stridently insisting that therapists must substantiate the effectiveness of their services before they will be paid. This interest in outcome is not specific to any particular professional discipline (e.g., mental health versus medicine) or type of payment system (e.g., managed care versus public funds) but is rather part of a worldwide trend (Lambert, Okiishi, Finch, & Johnson, 1998; Sanderson, Riley, & Eshun, 1997).

As we will demonstrate, clients benefit from an alternative to the present system. First and foremost, using client feedback to inform the therapy would finally invite the users of our services to be full and equal participants in virtually all aspects of therapy. Giving clients the perspective of the driver's seat instead of the back of the bus may also enable consumers to gain confidence that a positive outcome is just down the road. Consider recent surveys that found that next to lack of insurance and cost, 76 percent of people identified low confidence in the outcome of therapy as the major reason for not seeking treatment (APA, 1998b). Indeed, the "no confidence" vote was far more important than variables traditionally thought to deter people from seeing a therapist (e.g., stigma, 53 percent; length of treatment, 59 percent; lack of knowledge, 47 percent).

Finally, the availability of outcome data could eliminate the need to assign pathological labels or transmit sensitive, personal information to third-party payers in order to qualify for reimbursement. Such information simply wouldn't be needed because third-party payers could tell from the measures of outcome whether the therapy was beneficial or not to the individual client. As Chapter Four will demonstrate, outcome management has the propensity, and has already started, to revolutionize mental health care.

In this book we advocate routine and systematic assessment of the client's perceptions of progress and fit so that the clinician can empirically tailor the therapy to the client's individual needs and characteristics. We therefore argue for practice-based evidence rather than evidence-based practice. Such a process of becoming outcome informed, we believe, fits with how most therapists prefer to think of themselves: sensitive to client feedback and interested in results. Becoming outcome informed not only amplifies the client's voice but also offers the most viable, research-tested method to improve clinical effectiveness.

MARIA: A PREVIEW

Not long ago, Maria, a woman in her late thirties, came into therapy, searching for an identity that she believed that she had lost. All her life, Maria had wanted to be a police officer. As a teenager, she rode with state troopers; and as a young woman, she became the first female to graduate from the police academy.

Maria lived her dream as an officer for several years, until a car accident plunged her into a coma that lasted for two years. In a triumph of biomedicine, an experimental drug revived her, although it left her with some brain damage and seizures that made it impossible to work as a police officer. Without the identity she had devoted her life to achieving, she was no longer certain who she was.

Our first contact with Maria was founded not in just giving lip service to being respectful of clients and collaborative with them but in using the set of empirically supported findings that we will cover in this book. As we will see in Chapter Four, in all the research literature, perhaps the most clinically relevant finding is that the client's improvement early in therapy is one of the best predictors of successful outcome. So instead of regarding the first few sessions as a warm-up period or a chance to try out the latest technique, it is crucial to be accountable in the very first contact with clients. And given all we know about the importance of the therapeutic alliance, discussed in Chapter Three, such initial sessions offer a chance to discover how to make the best possible match with clients. Clients monitor the burgeoning alliance through session-by-session evaluations of their satisfaction with and progress in counseling. The guiding principle behind our work with clients is recognizing that all decisions must be directed by clients' engagement in the therapy process, their view of the quality of the therapeutic relationship, their theories of change, and—the gold standard—their assessment of whether change occurs.

When Maria came for her first appointment, she was intrigued by the therapist's comments that her perceptions were to be the light that guided the coming process. She filled out a brief form about how she felt she was progressing individually, interpersonally, and socially. She then explained that she felt at a dead end in her life. Having recovered enough to go back to work of some kind, she could not even imagine a backup dream now that her career in police work seemed over. To complicate matters, Maria was also wrestling with the idea of being "disabled," a word she despised but that others suggested that she accept so that she could move on. She recognized that she had some limitations and could not perform the strenuous duties she had once dispatched with ease. Still, the word stuck in her craw. As she intimated her experience of her path to recovery, the therapist was amazed by her courage, resilience, and wisdom. Here was a woman who had it all and lost it—who defied others' expectations of what she could and could not do many times: early on when she became the first female to graduate from the academy and then the first to make detective; when she unexpectedly came out of a coma; and now once again. Despite her problems with seizures, vision, and balance, she was fighting the expectations of her "disabled" label. She knew there was much more to her than any description of her disability could begin to capture, as anyone who spent any time getting to know her would know. The therapist told Maria that one of the things he liked most about her was her refusal to accept her disability. She liked that comment very much.

A few minutes before the end of the meeting, the counselor again asked Maria to fill out a short form, evaluating the therapy and the therapist. Here, the key information was that she felt that the therapist was taking her problems and ideas seriously and that his approach seemed like a good fit. Maria indicated on the form that indeed things were on the right track. Checking the form with Maria and reflecting on how impressed he had been by her, the therapist jokingly asked her if she had ever thought about pursuing a career as a motivational speaker. It was an offhand tribute to the power of her story, but it struck a deep chord. Just as the conversation was about to end, Maria declared that it had occurred to her that she might pursue a career teaching police officers.

That pronouncement was a key step in Maria's journey toward reclaiming her life. She did not end up as a training officer but was able to reestablish her relationship with the work she loved by becoming a dispatcher. This satisfied her itch for reconnecting with police work, which, for her, was crucial to a meaningful life. She reported improvement on the outcome measure, and therapy ended a few sessions later.

How might a medical model address Maria's concerns? Although her quest for a new identity does not neatly fit into *DSM* categories or evidence-based treatments, there is a good possibility that Maria would be abridged to a collection of symptoms and interventions. She might well be diagnosed as depressed and prescribed cognitive-behavioral therapy and an antidepressant, along with additional skills training for deficits left by her brain injury. In this process, the fullness of Maria as a person could easily be lost, as well as her voice about treatment choices—reducing her to a description of an illness and its formulaic solutions.

We present Maria's case not as an example of a therapeutic miracle but just the reverse. In fact, the ordinariness of this kind of interaction addresses the core of what we have to offer as mental health professionals. The therapist offered Maria no irresistibly powerful interventions, just a relationship structured around her goals and values, one that showcased her talents and fortitude. And her therapist's repeated requests to tell him whether the therapy was serving her needs involved a kind of accountability that is very different from the accountability that managed care and government funders have traditionally demanded from therapists and the kind that we may expect even more of under the assimilation into the medical model. Partnering with clients to make our work effective and accountable stands in sharp contrast to a decision-making process predicated on psychiatric diagnoses and evidence-based treatments. It offers a viable alternative for revamping mental health services to reduce runaway costs.

THE TERRITORY AHEAD

Cautious, careful people, always casting about to preserve their reputation and social standing, never can bring about a reform. Those who are really in earnest must be willing to be anything or nothing in the world's estimation, and publicly and privately, in season and out, avow their sympathy with despised and persecuted ideas and their advocates, and bear the consequences.

—*Susan B. Anthony,* In Decisions

Let's confront the unpleasant reality and say it out loud, "The field of therapy is in trouble." More distressing but less obvious, popular clinical beliefs and practices are in large part responsible for the mess in which therapists presently find themselves. They have been reified into reality through the institutionalization of the medical model into mental health. But there are alternative visions of the twenty-first century.

Our vision subscribes to a relational rather than medical model, embraces change that is client directed rather than theory driven, and commits itself to successful outcome instead of competent service delivery (Duncan, 2002; Duncan & Sparks, 2002; Duncan, Miller, & Sparks, 2003; Miller, Duncan, & Hubble, 2004). In Chapter Two we challenge the medical model as it applies to mental health, those practices that cast clients as extras and exclude them from their own change efforts. No longer emphasizing exclusive and expert-derived theory as a basis for practice, Chapter Three proposes instead to invest in client ideas of change, client-initiated topics, and client priorities; to elevate, without reservation, local client theories over all those that the therapeutic community previously held sacrosanct. Chapter Three spotlights the heroic client's dramatic contribution to positive outcome and presents guidelines for tapping into the client's star power.

The medicalized milieu of present-day practice increasingly defines *service* as the appropriate application of empirically supported treatments. Instead, we argue for practice-based evidence as an alternative to evidence-based practice. Chapter Four shows the nuts and bolts of a surprisingly simple process of partnering with clients to make therapy both beneficial and accountable—how using client feedback in the form of reliable outcome and process tools makes it possible for therapists to improve their effectiveness.

Chapter Five explores the idea of the client's theory of change and illustrates the integration of diverse approaches through the client's inclinations about change. Given the meteoric rise in psychotropic prescriptions, particularly with children, Chapter Six addresses the thorny issue of medication. We explode the myth of the magic pill while simultaneously honoring client choices to be helped by them. We examine the controversy surrounding drug treatments to encourage reflection about the options offered to clients. In Chapter Seven we address commonly asked questions about our ideas but also deconstruct the unspoken assumptions and practices underlying those questions. We invite the reader to take an alien's look at the talk of "mental health" and its implications. Finally, and appropriately, we end our discussion with a client's own words. The Epilogue highlights the advantages of an outcome-informed approach with a client who is not experiencing change. The client provides important commentary enabling an understanding usually missing in accounts of therapeutic stalemate and change.

If the surprises we encountered in our journey of the past eleven years are any indication of the terrain ahead, there are likely to be both pitfalls and opportunities as the field struggles to establish an identity based on empirical fact and client partnership rather than myth. As Hamlet says, however, we cannot let this undiscovered country "make us rather bear those ills we have than fly to others that we know not of" (3.1.24–27).

CHAPTER TWO

The Myth of the Medical Model

Dethroning Diagnosis and Best Practice

The great tragedy of science—the slaying of a beautiful hypothesis by an ugly fact.

—*Thomas Henry Huxley*,
Presidential Address to the British
Association for the Advancement of Science

The medical model, emphasizing diagnostic classification and evidence-based practice, has been transplanted wholesale into the field of human problems. Psychotherapy is almost exclusively described, researched, taught, practiced, and regulated in terms of the medical model's assumptions and practices. But how did we get here?

Psychologist George Albee (2000) suggests that psychology made a Faustian deal with the medical model over fifty years ago when it uncritically accepted the call to provide psychiatric services to returning veterans of World War II. The medical model was perhaps permanently stamped, however, at the famed Boulder conference in 1949, where psychology's bible of training was developed, under protest by many, with an acceptance of medical language and the concept of "mental disease."

Later, with the passing of freedom of choice legislation guaranteeing parity with psychiatrists, psychologists learned to treat clients in private offices and collect from third-party payers requiring only a psychiatric diagnosis for reimbursement. The other mental health professions soon followed suit—all vying to get a slice of the pie, not thinking about the long-term consequences of a high-fat, high-carbohydrate diet. Soon thereafter, in the mid-1980s, the rising tide of the medical model reached dangerous levels of influence. Drowning any possibilities for other ways of understanding human challenges, the National Institute of Mental Health (NIMH), the leading source of research funding for psychotherapy, decided to apply the same methodology used in drug research to evaluate psychotherapy—the randomized clinical trial (RCT).

Adopting the RCT for evaluating psychotherapy had profound ramifications. It meant that a study must include manualized therapies (to approximate drug protocols) and *DSM*-defined disorders to be eligible for an NIMH-sponsored grant. Funding for studies not related to specific treatments for specific disorders precipitously dropped as both research and psychotherapy itself became more and more medicalized.

The result: the medical model rules. Ask therapists why they talk about diagnosis of mental disorders and prescriptive treatments, and they reply much like the tragic heroine attempting to flee gender oppression by passing as a boy played by Hilary Swank in *Boys Don't Cry*. When asked why he allowed himself to be dragged on the ground behind a pickup truck, she said, "I thought that's what boys did around these parts."

This chapter suggests that we stop allowing ourselves to be dragged behind the medical-model truck. Using the research literature to autopsy ideas that have long since died, we show that the fixation with nomenclature, categories, and diagnostic groupings is largely a waste of time. Instead of growing orderly and yielding a nourishing bounty, diagnosing mental disorders has multiplied like a weed. They choke and smother alternative, hopeful ways of understanding and encouraging change and are based more on political and economic factors than science.

Further, we debunk evidence-based treatments and their alleged scientific superiority. We challenge the myth of the silver-bullet approach and demonstrate that change in therapy does not come about from the special powers of any particular treatment. Rather, change principally results from the client's preexisting abilities and participation—the client is the star of the therapeutic drama. In this chapter we seek to hold the feet of practice as usual to the empirical fire so that we may propose an alternative in the chapters that follow.

THE MYTH OF PSYCHIATRIC DIAGNOSES

*Seek facts and classify them and you will be the workmen
of science. Conceive or accept theories and you will be their
politicians.*

—*Nicolas Maurice Arthus,* De l'anaphylaxie à l'immunité

In medical endeavors a diagnosis names a problem and specifies the
treatment. For example, a diagnosis of diabetes allows the physician
to prescribe a proper balance of diet, exercise, and insulin. On the
other hand, if you are talking about mental health diagnoses, the truth
is that labeling a mental disorder is not especially useful in determining what treatment to offer. In the end consumers receive the treatment in which the clinician is experienced or entrenched, regardless
of diagnosis.

Outside of mental health, medical practitioners work with definitions of disease based on deviations from a known, healthy starting
point. For instance, a known range of glucose levels in the blood indicates the presence or absence of diabetes. In the mental health arena,
it is just the opposite (Watzlawick, 1976): disease is considered the
known factor, while normality is impossible to define. Such a backward arrangement creates a situation ripe for self-promotion and
manipulation of the so-called facts.

Diagnostic Disorder

Sigmund Freud (1990, p. 56) once said, "I have found little that is good
about human beings. In my experience, most of them are trash." Surprising commentary from our founding parent! But the field still finds
little that is good about human beings. The only difference is that it
has cataloged that "trash" into hundreds of specific types in the professional digest of human disasters, the *DSM-IV* (APA, 1994).

First, we want to mention a couple of qualifiers: criticizing diagnosis in no way diminishes the deviancy or weirdness of some behaviors or the distress that many individuals endure. Most agree that
sexual abuse is socially deviant and hearing voices is peculiar. Many
people are also troubled by experiences of depression or anxiety. Further, our diatribe against diagnosis does not mean that some individuals do not find comfort or help in viewing themselves in diagnostic
ways. Rather, the issue is whether diagnosis is useful or necessary for

people to resolve problems and whether it is as scientifically sound as its overwhelming dominance suggests. The fact is that diagnosis doesn't deliver.

DIAGNOSIS LACKS RELIABILITY. Even those flying the banner of diagnosis must agree about which diagnosis is accurate, if it is to be useful at all. This is called reliability. Mental health diagnoses are remarkably unreliable, although most professionals consider reliability a problem long since solved by the so-called advances of the *DSM-III* (APA, 1980; Carson, 1997; Kirk & Kutchins, 1992). In truth, it is far from solved.

Consider a major study conducted by some of the authors (Williams et al., 1992) of the *DSM-III* (APA, 1980). This large-scale multisite study extensively trained clinicians to make accurate diagnoses using the much-touted new and improved version of the *DSM*. Following elaborate training and supervision by the researchers, pairs of clinicians interviewed six hundred clients to see if they could agree on a diagnosis. The study defined *agreement* as diagnoses that fell in the same *class* of disorders, not the specific *type*. Overall agreement for these specially trained clinicians ranged from .68 to .72 for Axis I, and .56 to .64 for Axis II. Individual reliability ratings on specific disorders were as low as .26! In these field trials, one clinician could diagnose an individual with dysthymic disorder and panic disorder, and another might diagnose major depressive disorder and obsessive compulsive disorder: both diagnoses would still be considered in agreement, because they fall within the same class of disorders. You be the judge of how much reliability this agreement reflects. Imagine the reliability on a specific disorder by a regular Jane or Joe mental health professional in a typical clinical setting.

To give the devil his due, proponents believe that with the publication of *DSM-IIIR* (APA, 1987), the field has obtained acceptable levels of reliability (Garb, 1998). So-called good reliability, though, has mysteriously shrunk over the years. Before *DSM-III*, agreement on the specific category was considered important. After the *DSM-III* field trials, 70 percent agreement within a *general* category was reframed as good. Now, an even lower standard is suggested. According to Garb, reliability is said to be poor if values are less than .40, fair between .40 and .59, *good* between .60 and .74, and excellent above .75.

Twenty-some years after the reliability problem has been declared solved (by lowering standards and only comparing general classes), not one major study has replicated the field trials or shown that regular mental health professionals can routinely use the *DSM* with high reliability (Kutchins & Kirk, 1997). However, even if we accept that diagnosis can fall within the good range under specialized conditions (if 60 percent agreement on a general category can be considered good), it doesn't matter—because diagnosis does not stand up to the test of validity.

DIAGNOSIS LACKS VALIDITY. Even among diagnosis advocates within psychiatry, the lack of validity is abundantly realized. Kendell and Zablansky (2003, p. 7), writing in the *American Journal of Psychiatry*, conclude that "At present there is little evidence that most contemporary psychiatric diagnoses are valid, because they are still defined by syndromes that have not been demonstrated to have natural boundaries." They make the significant point that psychiatric symptoms are continuous with normal human experience and do not coalesce into well-defined clusters. According to Kendell and Zablansky, a diagnostic category can be described as valid only if its defining characteristics are separated from neighboring syndromes and normality; or if the category is defined by a physiological, anatomical, histological, chromosomal, or molecular abnormality showing clear differences. These criteria yield only a few examples of valid diagnosis, such as Down's syndrome and so on. Of course, these authors are only repeating what has been known and reported for years: there is no empirical standard to distinguish the hypothesized pathological states from normal human variation to the problems of life. The result is a set of murky overinclusive criteria for an ever growing list of disorders.

The *DSM* makes no claim of achieving a valid classification system. But most professionals in the field take for granted that it is valid. Why? Because everything about it shouts validity: the voluminous size; the hundreds of expert contributors; the NIMH funding; the extensive literature reviews, committees, and conferences devoted to its construction; and the ongoing discussion about its science and database. This impressive display of scientific prowess and medical authority exudes an aura of validity where none exists.

Another way to evaluate the validity of diagnosis is to examine its utility. In this light, validity asks the question: How useful is diagnosis to treatment? Consider borderline personality disorder (BPD), the mental health equivalent of "the thing" in horror movies. The prevailing diagnostic guide provides 126 possible ways to arrive at a diagnosis. All it takes is to meet five out of nine criteria. If one can be diagnosed as BPD in 126 possible ways, how distinctive or valuable can such a diagnosis be?

Further and more specifically, diagnosis does not select a remedy for individuals, nor does it predict how they will succeed in treatment. If a diagnosis fails to prescribe a particular treatment and is not linked to a person's success or failure with a given treatment, it has little value (Garfield, 1986). Let's take the selection issue first. If a diagnosis, for example, of depression is truly analogous to a diagnosis of diabetes, then it would allow a therapist to select the proper treatment for that specific disorder. The problem is that no approach has demonstrated superiority over another for any disorder! They all work about the same.

For example, consider the Treatment of Depression Collaborative Research Project (TDCRP) (Elkin et al., 1989). This landmark NIMH project, considered to be the most methodologically sophisticated study ever done, involved psychiatrists and psychologists in multiple cities. It randomly assigned 250 participants to four groups: cognitive-behavioral therapy (CBT); interpersonal therapy; antidepressant treatment; and finally, a placebo pill and clinical management condition. Overall, the four treatments—including the placebo—worked with about the same effectiveness! As in other studies of other disorders, there were no differences in overall effectiveness between the different treatment conditions. Despite the claims of snake oil peddlers and model maniacs, no winner has emerged for depression or any other disorder. Diagnoses do not help in treatment planning or selection. Selection of options requires a collaborative conversation with clients about the particulars of their specific circumstances and their own sensibilities about how they may be helped.

The prediction of outcome is even more empirically unsound than the selection issue. If diagnosis actually predicted how well people did in therapy or whether they would even benefit at all, then diagnosis could be argued to have some redeeming value. It doesn't. There is no correlation between diagnosis and outcome nor between diagnosis and length of treatment (Brown et al., 1999; Beutler & Clarkin, 1990). Bottom line: there are no diagnostic-specific benefits to psychotherapy. Diagnoses lack validity (Garfield, 1986). In mental health, naming a problem with a diagnostic moniker neither explains it nor solves it. Other factors, we shall see, are far more predictive of success than these limited descriptions of client experiences.

DIAGNOSIS PAINTS AN IRRELEVANT AND UGLY PICTURE. A diagnosis provides a flat and colorless picture that highlights weaknesses at the expense of resources, an unrepresentative story tantamount to reading one page out of a book or watching one scene from a movie. Recall Maria and how a diagnosis of depression, although arguably correct, told a very limited story about her, leaving out her miraculous resilience. Central to treatment planning and implementation is enlisting the strengths that people bring to address the concerns they present. Moreover, knowledge of a person's unique circumstance and goals for therapy are better indicators of what approach to apply than a diagnosis (Beutler & Clarkin, 1990).

Complicating things even more, diagnosis does not capture most of the problems that people seeking help from a therapist bring (Beutler & Clarkin, 1990). Relational difficulties and the situational distress of everyday life are the most common presenting concerns. How do you diagnose a marital problem, a family conflict, or a concern of not meeting one's potential?

Diagnoses brand people with labels that carry blame, hopelessness, and helplessness. It is no wonder that a stigma still exists for seeking counseling despite all the public relations work conveying it is OK to have a mental illness. Once a label has been attached, it sticks like glue. Although many advocates of proper diagnosis warn against equating the label with the total person, it is impossible to avoid this extension. We call this "attribution creep" (Duncan, Hubble, & Miller, 1997). A diagnosis, once set in motion, creates an expectancy of hard going or poor outcome that is surprisingly resilient (Salovey & Turk, 1991). Left unchecked, the expectation becomes the person. Should this occur, observers (nonprofessionals and clinicians alike) unwittingly distort information to conform to their expectations. (See Rosenhan's classic experiment published in *Science* in 1973.)

Consider the king of all diagnoses, schizophrenia. Many, if not most, accept that schizophrenia is a lifelong struggle with mental illness only made somewhat manageable with medication—a catastrophic, if not hopeless, life of turmoil and destitution. Many, if not most, have never heard of the Harding study (Harding, Zubin, & Strauss, 1987). Harding tracked down 269 clients who were admitted to Vermont hospitals with a diagnosis of schizophrenia—an average of thirty-two years after their first admission. She found that about two-thirds of these former back ward patients showed no signs at all of schizophrenia and had long since stopped their medications! The "recovery" rate is astounding, considering the images that the label of schizophrenic typically brings to mind. Moreover, the clients reported the key to recovery had been finding a safe, decent place to live, and having a mentor, someone they trusted, who cared. Client perspectives, like these comments, can undermine the attribution creep accompanying "schizophrenia" (see Appendix I for a moving account of the despair that accompanies the label of schizophrenia).

Despite our awareness of attribution creep, diagnoses continue to direct impression formation and undermine critical thinking. Therapists—armed with the *DSM* required in their training, reinforced in licensure, and enforced by third-party payers—selectively listen to information that people present and focus on the very behaviors that confirm their expectations. Clients accept diagnosis as medical fact and become enslaved by its implications. As the extant literature proves, this process is robust, operates outside the range of awareness, and erodes the curative elements of therapy (Duncan et al., 1997).

Money, Power, Fashion, and Cultural Bias

The rise of mental health diagnosis to its status today is particularly ironic given the traditional hesitancy of most therapists to label clients. Eighty-seven percent of a national sample of social workers, for example, indicated they used a less serious diagnosis to avoid the adverse impact of labeling (Kirk & Kutchins, 1988). Most therapists view it as a white lie for good purpose, a fiscal formality unrelated to treatment. In a survey of psychologists (Miller, Bergstrom, Cross, & Grube, 1981), 86.1 percent said they used diagnosis because it was required for payment; only 2.8 percent considered it reliable and valid! We cite these old surveys because many new mental health professionals do not know how much diagnosis has been resisted historically. Unfortunately, even fewer know of its long-standing poor reliability and validity since it has become a mainstay in clinical training programs, required by state licensing and credentialing boards. Diagnosis is far more accepted now than ever before.

Given this acceptance, a recent large survey of psychologists, arguably a profession wholeheartedly embracing a medical-model perspective, is even more telling. Murphy, DeBernardo, and Shoemaker (1998) found that 63 percent of those surveyed indicated that psychologists alter diagnoses to protect client confidentiality, future employment, or medical insurance. Sixty-one percent believed that psychologists submit the lowest level of diagnosis that is reimbursable and leave off Axis II diagnoses. If diagnosis is scientifically sound and helpful to the suffering masses, why do so many, even of the converted, seek to soften its impact?

The number of categories of the American Psychiatric Association's *DSM* jumped from sixty-six in the first edition (1952) to well over three hundred in its current rendition. Apparently, we are sick and getting sicker by the minute. Renowned psychiatrist Jerome Frank's ironic observation (1973) is being borne out—psychotherapy may be the only treatment that creates the illness it treats. Kutchins and Kirk (1997) speak to the economic side of Frank's observation and argue that the *DSM* transforms ordinary reactions to life stress into billable pathology. Everyone becomes a potential patient. Witness recent reports (for example, the president's New Freedom Commission of Mental Health) suggesting that 30 percent of adults and 20 percent of children suffer from a diagnosable mental disorder (Holloway, 2003). Who benefits from these statistics? How many times do we hear of new diagnoses that have been tragically underreported and now demand treatment on a large scale?

Diagnoses change as our social tolerances and preferences do (Beutler & Clarkin, 1990). Consider the most famous example, homosexuality, which, unbelievably, was once regarded as a mental disorder. Homosexuality was "cured" by a vote of the American Psychiatric Association when gay activists protested being identified as sick. And the story continues: Kutchins and Kirk (1997) present an eye-opening account of the voting for and against different disorders, and they convincingly show how diagnostic inclusion is based far more in politics and economics than science. They provocatively suggest that the *DSM*'s language of mental illness is a self-serving political instrument rooted in psychiatrists' striving for credibility among their medical brethren.

David Healy (1997) persuasively argues in *The Antidepressant Era* that drug companies are as much in the business of selling psychiatric diagnoses as they are of selling psychotropic drugs, because obviously one promotes the other. In doing so, they capitalize on the public's propensity for believing medical authority. Healy raises disturbing questions about how much the medical science of diagnosis is governed by financial interest.

Finally, consider that diagnosis does not include contextual factors. A diagnosis describes only individual behavior; it ignores relational, environmental, and cultural influences. Classifying only individual behavior as abnormal implies that when someone does not fit smoothly into his or her prescribed cultural role, it is that person who is at fault. The result is that diagnoses often reinforce male-female inequalities and codify racial and cultural prejudice (Kutchins & Kirk, 1997). Women, not surprisingly, come out on the short end of the diagnostic stick. They compose the majority of people diagnosed as BPD and fill the ranks of many other diagnoses. As further evidence, a recent study (Zito, Safer, dosReis, & Riddle, 1998) found that both race and social status of children influenced the diagnoses and treatment they received. Children who were culturally different than their helpers received more serious diagnoses and more drugs and were less likely to receive therapy.

Diagnostic Disorder: An Underreported Illness That Demands Treatment on a Large Scale

To recap: psychiatric diagnosis represents a flawed extension of the medical model. It maintains a medical mystique around problems that diminishes clients and obscures more hopeful avenues of addressing troubling situations. Diagnosis has questionable reliability at best and is worthless in terms of treatment planning and the prediction of outcome. It can engender harmful attributions by the labeled individual, his or her family, and helping professionals. Most therapists dislike it, actively lie to protect clients from its implications, and report that it does not inform their day-to-day work. Finally, diagnosis is culturally biased and changes like the tide, depending on the prevailing currents of politics and the gravitational pull of the marketplace.

It is time to dethrone diagnosis as the pharaoh of mental health and stop using the excuse that we must diagnose to get paid. The only reason we must use it for reimbursement is because we haven't articulated the pitfalls of diagnosis to funding sources, nor have we offered anything different. In this book we offer an alternative based in the outcome or benefit of the services therapists provide. Imagine if the whole upcoming generation of mental health professionals challenged diagnosis and explored alternatives. Imagine these possibilities flourishing into more and more credible and humanistic ways of understanding human behavior.

THE MYTH OF EVIDENCE-BASED PRACTICE: THE SILVER BULLET

I admire those who search for the truth. I avoid those who find it.

—*French motto*

When psychotherapy is portrayed in workshops and books, it is easy to form the impression that it operates with technological precision. The illusion is that the all-knowing therapist assigns the proper diagnosis and then selects the right treatment for the particular disorder at hand. The therapist sizes up the demon that plagues the hapless client, loads the silver bullet into the psychotherapy revolver, and shoots the psychic werewolf terrorizing the client. This section shines the light of an empirical understanding on this mythic tale and hopefully debunks it once and for all.

Research has led to an unarguable conclusion that is good news for both mental health professionals and clients alike: psychotherapy is effective in helping human problems. The good news of therapy's usefulness, however, has been accompanied by a rabbitlike propagation of different models. Over the years new schools of therapy arrived with the regularity of the Book-of-the-Month Club's main selection. Most professed to have captured the true essence of psychological dysfunction as well as the best remedies.

In the hopes of proving their pet approaches superior, a generation of investigators ushered in the age of comparative clinical trials. Winners and losers were to be had. Thus, behavior, psychoanalytic, client-centered or humanistic, rational-emotive, cognitive, time-limited, time-unlimited, and other therapies were pitted against each other in a great battle of the brands. Nonetheless, all this sound and fury produced an unexpected bonfire of the vanities (Hubble et al., 1999a). Put another way, reiterating Huxley's epigraph introducing this chapter, science slew a beautiful hypothesis with an ugly fact. The underlying premise of the comparative studies, that one (or more) therapies would prove superior to others, received virtually no support. Besides the occasional significant finding for a particular therapy, the critical mass of data revealed no differences in effectiveness between the various treatments for psychological distress. Despite the Herculean efforts of legions of model worshipers, no one succeeded in declaring any religion to be the best.

These findings have been creatively summarized by quoting the dodo bird from *Alice's Adventures in Wonderland,* who said, "Everybody has won and all must have prizes" (Carroll, 1962). In his remarkable seminal articulation of a common factors perspective, Saul Rosenzweig (1936, p. 412) first invoked the dodo's words to illustrate his prophetic observation of the equivalent success of diverse psychotherapies (Duncan, 2002). Almost forty years later, Luborsky, Singer, and Luborsky (1975) empirically validated Rosenzweig's conclusion in their now classic review of comparative clinical trials. They dubbed their findings of no differences among models the "dodo bird verdict" (p. 1003). It has proven to be the most replicated finding in the literature.

Confirming the notion that all models are created equal is the landmark TDCRP mentioned earlier (Elkin et al., 1989). After all the effort that went into designing a study that represented the state of the art in outcome research, the investigators were stunned by their own findings. Recall that, overall, the four treatments—including placebo—worked with about the same effectiveness. Recent advancements in statistical methodology, particularly meta-analytic studies, which allow researchers to comb through the vast clinical literature and draw conclusions from huge collections of data, lend even further credence to the dodo bird verdict. In a comprehensive 1997 review of the outcome literature, psychotherapy researcher Bruce Wampold and colleagues analyzed some 277 studies conducted from 1970 to 1995 to determine which therapeutic models have yielded the most robust results (Wampold et al., 1997). This review once again verified that no approach has reliably demonstrated superiority over any other. Other recent meta-analytic studies also confirm the wisdom of the dodo bird. "Why," Wampold asks (p. 211), "[do] researchers persist in attempts to find treatment differences, when they know that these effects are small? . . ."

Punctuating this point is an enormous study conducted by Human Affairs International of over two thousand therapists and twenty thousand clients. This real-world study of effectiveness (compared to controlled efficacy studies) revealed no differences in outcome among thirteen approaches, including family therapy and medication (Brown et al., 1999). Although a handful of studies have found differences, the number is far less than would be attributable to chance (Wampold, 1997). For example, Wampold (2001) reveals that, of the over three thousand dependent variable comparisons of CBT with other forms of therapy, only fifteen have found CBT to be superior.

Despite extraordinary efforts, the preponderance of the data indicates that no one can declare any approach superior to any other. The fact that the dodo bird verdict emerged by accident—while researchers were trying to prove the superiority of their own models—makes it particularly worthy to consider. It is a finding remarkably free of researcher bias. But what does it mean? As Rosenzweig amazingly said in 1936 (and legions have since, e.g., Frank, 1973), because all approaches appear equal in effectiveness, there must be pantheoretical factors in operation that overshadow any perceived or presumed differences among approaches. Therapy works, but our understanding of how it works cannot be found in the insular explanations of the different theoretical orientations; rather, we must seek it in the factors common to all approaches.

If therapies work, but this has nothing to do with their bells and whistles, what are the common factors of change? Our recent book, *The Heart and Soul of Change* (Hubble, Duncan, & Miller, 1999c) empirically answers that question. We assembled leading outcome researchers to review four decades of investigation and reveal its implications for practice. Figure 2.1 depicts the four factors of change and their percentage contribution to a positive outcome regardless of the therapist's theoretical orientation or professional discipline (Asay & Lambert, 1999).

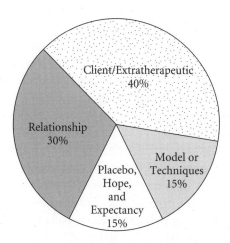

Figure 2.1. Factors Accounting for Change in Therapy.
Source: Asay & Lambert, 1999.

The common factors provide the empirical backdrop for client-directed, outcome-informed ways of working with clients. A client-directed, outcome-informed approach contains no fixed techniques, invariant patterns in therapeutic process, or causal theory regarding the concerns that bring people to therapy. Any interaction with a client can be client directed and outcome informed. This comes about when counselors partner with clients for three purposes: (1) to enhance the factors across theories that account for successful outcome (Chapter Three), (2) to use the client's theory of change to guide choice of technique and model (Chapters Three and Six), and (3) to inform the therapy with valid and reliable measures of the client's experience of process and outcome (Chapter Four).

Since the publication of *The Heart and Soul of Change* and the first edition of this book, Bruce Wampold (2001) published his meta-analytic review of the psychotherapy outcome research. Not only has it bolstered our perspective of the common factors, but it has significantly broadened our understanding. To our surprise Lambert's delineation of the common factors actually overattributed importance to technique and underrated the importance of client and alliance factors.

Client Factors

Clients have long been portrayed as the unactualized message bearers of family dysfunction, the manufacturers of resistance, and in most traditions, the targets for the presumably all-important intervention. Rarely is the client cast in the role of the chief agent of change or even mentioned in advertisements announcing the newest line of fashions in the therapy boutique of techniques. Tallman and Bohart's review (1999) of the research makes clear, however, that the client is actually the single most potent contributor to outcome in psychotherapy—the resources clients bring into the therapy room and the influences on their lives outside it (Miller, Duncan, & Hubble, 1997). These factors might include persistence, openness, faith, optimism, a supportive grandmother, or membership in a religious community—all factors operative in a client's life before he or she enters therapy. They also include serendipitous interactions between such inner strengths and happenstance, such as a new job or a crisis successfully negotiated. Asay and Lambert (1999) ascribe 40 percent of improvement during psychotherapy to client factors. Wampold's meta-analysis (2001) attributes a whopping 87 percent to these so-called extratherapeutic factors, leaving only 13 percent of the variance accounted for by the impact of therapy. This perspective about how change occurs suggests a radical revision of our ideas about clients and about what therapy should look like.

Consequently, the carefully acquired and much ballyhooed silver bullets are not the defining factors of change. Clients are the main characters, the heroes and heroines of the therapeutic stage. Using this information, Chapter Three flies in the face of the killer *D*s of client desecration—diagnosis, deficits, disorders, diseases, disabilities, and dysfunction—and instead suggests ways to enlist client factors in service of client goals.

Alliance Factors

Bachelor and Horvath (1999) convincingly argue that next to what the client brings to therapy, the client's perceptions of the therapeutic relationship are responsible for most of the gains resulting from therapy. Relationship factors account for 30 percent of successful outcome (Asay & Lambert, 1999).

In a study examining client perceptions of the relationship, Bachelor (1995) found three different types of relationship that clients valued. Nearly one-half of clients described a good relationship in terms of therapist respect, empathic understanding, and attentive listening; this often included a friendly relationship with the therapist. For another 40 percent, improved self-understanding, gained through therapist clarification of client material, characterized a positive relationship. Finally, a smaller proportion of clients viewed the relationship in terms of collaboration. The collaborative-type client acknowledged that the work of therapy was not exclusively the therapist's responsibility and that each partner contributes. Thus, it appears that, from the client's perspective, there is no single, invariably facilitative, type of relationship. Some clients want a friendship; some, expert advice; and some, a collaborative endeavor. Bachelor's work suggests that a flexible repertoire of relational stances that suit different clients is important to the efficacy of therapy.

Seeking a more satisfying description of the interpersonal dynamics involved between client and therapist, researchers have expanded the relationship into a broader concept known as the alliance. The alliance emphasizes a partnership between the client and therapist to achieve the client's goals (Bordin, 1979). Research repeatedly finds that a positive alliance is one of the best predictors of outcome (Horvath & Symonds, 1991). For example, Krupnick et al. (1996) analyzed data from the TDCRP and found that the alliance was predictive of success for all conditions (recall that the treatment model was not). In another large study of diverse therapies for alcoholism, the alliance was also significantly predictive of success (sobriety), even at one-year follow-up (Connors, DiClemente, Carroll, Longabaugh, & Donovan, 1997). Furthermore, client ratings of the alliance are far better predictors of outcome than are therapist ratings (Bachelor & Horvath, 1999). Clearly, then, it is critical for therapists to attend closely to the alliance they develop with clients and to monitor its quality regularly.

If you are not convinced that the alliance should be central to your ideas about change, consider the Wampold meta-analytic perspective (2001) of the alliance. He portions 54 percent of the variance attributed to the impact of therapy to the alliance. (Recall that he attributes only 13 percent of the overall variance to the therapy. Don't worry about Wampold's figures adding up to 100 percent; the reported figures are always in comparison to technique and model effects.) Putting this into perspective, the amount of change attributable to the alliance is about seven times that of the amount attributable to a specific model or technique.

Research on the power of the alliance reflects over a thousand findings and counting (Orlinsky, Grawe, & Parks, 1994; Orlinsky, Ronnestad, & Willutzki, 2004). Orlinsky and colleagues (1994, p. 361) boil down their extensive review of the alliance to one word, *participation,* and conclude:

> The quality of the patient's participation in therapy stands out as the most important determinant of outcome. . . . The therapist contribution toward helping the patient achieve a favorable outcome is made mainly through empathic, affirmative, collaborative, and self-congruent engagement with the patient. . . . These consistent process-outcome relations, based on literally hundreds of empirical findings, can be considered *facts* established by forty-plus years of . . . research.

We must set aside the intellectual appeal of theoretical models, the promises of flashy techniques, the charisma of masters, and the marketing acumen of snake oil peddlers. The research indicates that therapy works if clients experience the relationship positively and are active participants. Chapter Three applies this body of information and suggests ways to accommodate clients' perceptions of the alliance and invite their participation in therapy. Monitoring the alliance figures prominently in becoming outcome informed (Chapter Four).

Expectancy, Hope, and Allegiance

Following client and relationship factors come expectancy factors. This class of influences on outcome refers to the portion of improvement deriving from clients' knowledge of being in counseling, the instillation of hope, and the client's perception of the credibility of the therapy's rationale and techniques. These effects are not thought to emerge specifically from a given treatment procedure; they come from the hopeful expectations that accompany the method. Asay and Lambert (1999) put the contribution of expectancy to psychotherapy outcome at 15 percent. Chapter Three suggests ways to offer credible (to the client) solution opportunities that build on client expectations.

A similar idea, but from the therapist's point of view, is the concept of allegiance. Wampold (2001) defines allegiance effects as those attributable to the therapist's belief in the treatment administered. Messer and Wampold (2002) suggest that 70 percent of the effects of a particular approach are accounted for by the therapist's allegiance to the model used. To put this into perspective, consider that only 1 percent of change is due to the impact of any model—and 70 percent of that 1 percent is attributed to the therapist's belief in and enthusiasm for the particular treatment used. In truth, this casts a dim light on any emphasis on technique over and above client, alliance, and expectancy effects.

Model or Technique Factors

Finally, models and techniques make up the last of the four factors and contribute 15 percent to change in therapy (Asay & Lambert, 1999). Model or technique factors are the beliefs and procedures unique to specific treatments; for example, the miracle question in solution-focused therapy, the genogram in Bowen family therapy, desensitization in behavior therapy, transference interpretations in Freudian therapy, and the respective theoretical premises attending these practices. The Wampold meta-analysis (2001) assigns only a 13 percent contribution to the impact of therapy, both general and specific factors combined. Of that 13 percent a mere 8 percent is portioned to the contribution of model effects. Of the total variance of change, only 1 percent can be assigned to specific technique!

How exactly should we view models when so much of the variance is controlled by other factors—85 percent in Asay and Lambert's estimation (1999) (40 percent client factors, 30 percent relationship factors, and 15 percent expectancy factors)—and an incredible 99 percent in Wampold's perspective (2001)? Models provide a structure for conducting therapy and, more important, alternative ways of addressing client concerns when progress is not forthcoming. The different schools of therapy may be at their most helpful when they provide therapists with novel ways of looking at old situations, when they empower counselors to change rather than make up their minds about clients (Miller et al., 1997). With over four hundred therapy models and techniques to choose from, there is little reason for continued allegiance to a particular approach when it is not producing results. No blame need be assigned; therapists and clients can simply go back to the smorgasbord, so to speak, and make another selection.

As Chapter Four will illustrate, viewing models in this way is key to an outcome-informed approach. Models that help the therapist approach the client's goals differently, establish a better match with the client's theory of change, capitalize on chance events, or use environmental supports are likely to be the most beneficial in resolving any impasse.

Evidence-Based Practice: The Ultimate Silver Bullet

Despite the overwhelming support for the dodo bird verdict and all the research endorsing client and alliance factors, the mental health field remains dangerously enamored of flashy techniques and the promise of miracle cures. Clinicians are regularly bombarded by workshop brochures and book announcements touting what's new and different. Of late the call has been for the ultimate, all-powerful silver bullet: the evidence-based treatment. This, you recall, is the empirically bankrupt notion that for a particular problem, there is a specific treatment that is best. The problem here, besides the fact that no one has ever demonstrated the superiority of one approach over another, is that it totally excludes the client from consideration. Its promoters equate the client with the problem and describe the treatment as if it is isolated from the most powerful factors that contribute to change—the client's resources, perceptions, and participation.

Where does this crazy idea come from? As with diagnosis, political and financial implications loom large. The growing ascendancy of evidence-based practice may be best understood as the product of mounting pressures (i.e., legislative bodies defining practice standards, third-party payers adopting empirical guidelines) serving to increase the competition among mental health professions. Remember that since the 1980s the number of mental health practitioners has jumped by some 275 percent. In response the various professional groups have felt an urgent need to document the scientific efficacy of their preferred approaches. Following the trend in medicine toward diagnostic related groups, in the early 1990s, members of American Psychiatric Association decided that they should take the lead in determining the best treatments for the various diagnostic subgroups of mental illness.

Beginning in 1993 with guidelines for major depression and eating disorders, the committee produced guidelines for disorders ranging from bipolar disorder to Alzheimer's disease to nicotine dependence. Practice guidelines cover everything from treatment planning to psychiatric management and treatment selection for each of the disorders. Psychiatry's imprimatur has given an aura of scientific legitimacy to what was primarily an agreement among psychiatrists about their preferred practices, with an emphasis on biological treatment.

Fearing psychiatry's historical hegemony in health care, psychologists jumped on the empirically supported treatment bandwagon. Evidence-based treatments are being promoted as the rallying point, a "common cause" for a clinical profession fighting exclusion (Nathan, 1997, p. 10). Arguing that clients have a right to "proven," not consensus treatments, the American Psychological Association (APA) was quick to follow psychiatry's lead. In 1993 a special task force acting under the auspices of the Division of Clinical Psychology derided psychiatry's approved treatment list as medically biased and unrepresentative of the clinical literature and set forth its conclusions about what constituted scientifically valid treatments (APA, 1993). Instead of clinical consensus and comprehensive guidelines, the task force concentrated its efforts on research demonstrations that a particular treatment has proven to be beneficial for clients in randomized clinical trials (RCTs). Similar to the RCT standards of the Federal Drug Administration, in order to be considered well established, a treatment must demonstrate in only two independent studies that its benefits exceed those of an alternative treatment or a placebo condition.

The idea of having a specific psychological intervention for any given type of problem—the psychological equivalent of a pill for emotional distress—has a certain seductive appeal. But in fact, a closer look reveals that the whole idea of evidence-based practice is critically flawed, especially as any kind of mandate for what should be done in therapy. To start with, consider the RCT. It was designed to compare the effects of a drug (an active compound) to a placebo (a therapeutically inert or inactive substance) for a specific illness. The basic assumption of the RCT is that the active (unique) ingredients of different drugs (or psychotherapies) will produce different effects, superior over placebo, with different disorders.

Quite simply, the active ingredients model or drug metaphor (Stiles & Shapiro, 1989) of the RCT doesn't fit psychotherapy (Wampold et al., 1997). There are no unique or active ingredients to therapy approaches. The common factors rule. For example, in a study of thirty depressed clients, Castonguay, Goldfried, Wiser, Raue, and Hayes (1996) compared the impact of a technique specific to cognitive therapy, the focus on correcting distorted cognitions, with two other so called nonspecific factors: the alliance and the client's emotional involvement with the therapist. Results revealed that although the two common factors were highly related to progress, the technique unique to cognitive therapy—eliminating negative emotions by changing distorted cognitions—was negatively related to successful outcome! Further, component studies, which dismantle approaches to tease out unique ingredients, have similarly found little evidence to support any unique or specific effects of therapy (Jacobson et al., 1996). These studies have shown that it doesn't matter what component you leave out—the approach still works as well as the model containing all of its parts. Perhaps putting this issue to rest, a recent meta-analytic investigation of component studies (Ahn & Wampold, 2001) did not support the notion of unique ingredients in psychotherapy approaches. Bottom line: the evidence that *specific* ingredients account for treatment effectiveness remains weak to nonexistent. Indeed, Wampold (2001) concludes, "Decades of psychotherapy research have failed to find a scintilla of evidence that *any* specific ingredient is necessary for therapeutic change" (p. 204, emphasis added). Consequently, the entire philosophy of the RCT design does not fit the field of psychotherapy.

Second, the criteria used to validate a treatment contain a fatal bias. RCTs require that the treatments being assessed not contain the inevitable improvisations of therapy as practiced in the real world. Instead, the approaches studied are all required to follow a script, a manual, so that the variable presumably being examined—a precisely defined and structured form of treatment—can be strictly controlled. From a clinical perspective, however, manuals fall flat and seem like incontrovertible proof that researchers are card-carrying nerds. Experienced therapists know that the nuances of the work require the unique tailoring of any approach to a particular client and circumstance. Simply put, therapists do not do therapy by the book.

However, the data clearly show that training therapists to deliver manualized care increases adherence to the manual. Notwithstanding, the same research shows no resulting improvement in outcome and the strong possibility of untoward negative consequences (Beutler et al., 2004; Lambert & Ogles, 2004). With regard to the former, researchers Shadish, Matt, Navarro, and Phillips (2000) found non-manualized psychotherapy as effective as manualized in a meta-analysis of ninety studies. As for the latter, Addis, Wade, and Hatgis (1999) showed that manuals negatively impacted the quality of the therapeutic relationship, unnecessarily and inadvertently curtailed the scope of treatment, and decreased likelihood of clinical innovation. In effect, therapists who do therapy by the book develop better relationships with their manuals than with clients and seem to lose the ability to respond creatively.

Although certain kinds of therapy can be scripted—CBT being the most prominent—most cannot. So it should come as no surprise that CBT and other behavioral approaches dominate, amounting to about 80 percent of the royal list of evidence-based treatments. Is this because these treatments are more effective? No, it is really because they are the easiest to manualize and therefore have been the ones chosen to be researched. Consider also that very few approaches ever have the privilege of being researched. So the evidence-based list really is just those approaches that are practiced in settings that support research endeavors and that are able to attain funding. This privilege does not extend to some 250 other approaches around today.

More damning, however, is that demonstrating superiority over placebo or treatment as usual is not really saying that much; psychotherapy has demonstrated its superiority over placebo for nearly fifty years! Therapy is about twice as efficacious as placebo and about four times better than no treatment at all. This research, for all its pomp and circumstance, tells us nothing that we do not already know: therapy works! Further, demonstrating efficacy over placebo is not the same as demonstrating efficacy over other approaches. Recall the dodo bird verdict. There is no differential efficacy among approaches. Why do organizations fund studies that tell us what we already know? Why do evidence-based proponents seem to pretend that efficacy over placebo means that a given treatment is better than other treatments?

When anyone claims differential efficacy for an approach, be suspicious. Recall that the number of studies finding differences are no more than one would expect from chance. Further, closer inspection of studies that claim superiority reveals two major issues that must be considered: allegiance effects and indirect comparisons (Wampold, 2001). Also recall that allegiance effects are those that are attributable to the therapist or researcher's affinity toward the treatment at hand and that Messer and Wampold (2002) suggest that allegiance accounts for up 70 percent of any treatment effects.

For example, though some reviews have found a very small advantage for cognitive-behavioral approaches, later studies found that the differences disappeared completely when researchers took into account the experimenters' allegiance to the methods they were investigating (Lambert & Bergin, 1994). As a point of comparison, consider that in the TDCRP, the principal investigator, Irene Elkin, did not have an affiliation to any of the researched approaches. Further, each of the compared treatments was provided by clinicians who had allegiance to the models they were administering. The TDCRP, therefore, controlled for allegiance effects. Any reported treatment differences must always be tempered by knowledge of the allegiance of the researchers and the therapists in the study.

Consider emotionally focused therapy (EFT), the empirically supported queen of marital therapy, even touted as demonstrating "the best outcomes" and implied to be "the revolution in couple therapy" by one of its developers (Johnson, 2003, p. 363). Calling the dodo bird verdict the "dodo cliché" and saying that it is outdated, Johnson cites but four studies to support her conclusion, notwithstanding the many more that have found no difference (p. 367). Setting aside the overstatement of the revolution (model factors account for just 1 percent of outcome variance) and Johnson's apparent misunderstanding of the meaning of the dodo bird verdict (Johnson explains, "like the

Dodo bird, the idea of some models of intervention being more effective than others is extinct" [p. 367]), let's consider her claim of "best outcomes."

First, all but two EFT studies involve demonstrations of efficacy over placebo or no treatment, and are not comparisons with other treatment approaches to couples. All therapies can make similar claims of best outcomes when compared to no treatment. Two studies investigated differential effects. The first pitted EFT against problem-solving intervention (PS) (Johnson & Greenberg, 1985), a questionable direct comparison to another model of therapy (see below). In this study, EFT showed a significant difference over PS on all but four of thirteen measures at termination. At eight-week follow-up, these meager results became even less remarkable—only two indicated superiority. Setting aside these underwhelming results, consider the claims of "best outcomes" in the context of the allegiance issue. This article acknowledged that the first author had served as a therapist in the study and that the authors developed EFT. Johnson, Hunsley, Greenberg, and Schindler (1999) further recognize that nearly all studies about EFT have been conducted by its developers—suggesting that up to 70 percent of the observed "revolution" is attributable to the researchers' belief in EFT. When allegiance effects are controlled, the dodo bird still rules. Case in point: The other study (Goldman & Greenberg, 1992), conspicuously absent from mention in the "revolution" article, was a head-to-head comparison between EFT and an integrated systemic approach (IST). Not surprisingly, no differences in outcome were found in this study, although at follow-up, IST had an advantage.

Another important issue in evaluating claims of differential efficacy is whether the study really presents a fair contest: Is the comparison offered actually a contrast between two approaches fully intended to be therapeutic? Or is it a case of the experimenters pitting their pet approach against a treatment as usual or a less than ideal opponent? Wampold (2001) calls such unfair matches indirect comparisons. Consider multisystemic therapy (MST), which has impressively shown that it is superior to no treatment or to treatment as usual for reducing juveniles' criminal acts and for other benefits (e.g., Henggeler, Melton, & Smith, 1992). To suggest, however, that it has proven to be differentially better than individual therapy is notable for what is concealed rather than what is exposed.

An inspection of one such comparison involving serious juvenile offenders (Borduin et al., 1995) reveals MST conducted in the home, involving parents and other interacting systems, by therapists regularly supervised by founders of the approach. The study compares MST with therapy of the adolescent only, with little to no outside input from parents or others, conducted in an outpatient clinic by therapists with no special supervision or allegiance. This type of comparison is really a treatment-as-usual contrast rather than a bona fide treatment comparison. If the investigators had compared another home-based approach that controlled for allegiance effects (by including persons with equal conviction conducting the alternative treatment) and involved relevant parties, we suspect that it would fit the dodo bird verdict.

One quick qualifier here: our suggestion that efficacy over placebo or no treatment is not front-page news; and our critical comments on the ability of EFT, CBT, or MST to claim differential efficacy does not diminish the results that these approaches have achieved in ameliorating difficult clinical situations. Rather, we applaud the efforts of the investigators and only suggest caution in interpreting the results as proving the superiority of any approach over any other. Their data do not indicate any such privilege.

Finally, RCT findings are inherently limited because they do not generalize well to the way therapy is conducted in the real world. Unlike these studies, in actual clinical practice, the therapist does not use a manual or ever purely practice a therapy. Therapies are predominantly eclectic; clients are not randomly assigned to treatments; and clients rarely enter therapy for singular *DSM*-defined disorders. Despite all of these pitfalls, empirically supported treatments are privileged in ways the data does not support. Third-party payers and those in control of the various professional groups promulgating the ever expanding list, not unlike the pigs in Orwell's *Animal Farm,* continue to assert that some therapies are more equal than others. Guild and market pressures, not science, motivate this assertion.

DIAGNOSIS PLUS EVIDENCE-BASED PRACTICE DOES NOT EQUAL EFFECTIVENESS. Amy, a twenty-one-year-old student, was diagnosed as having borderline personality disorder (BPD) and was placed in dialectical behavior therapy (DBT), the empirically supported treatment for BPD. DBT has demonstrated its efficacy over placebo or treatment as usual and offers many useful ideas to approach the dangerous behaviors that some clients exhibit. Amy was referred for consultation because she and her therapist considered the therapy to be at an impasse. For training purposes, the consulting interview was conducted on closed-circuit television broadcast to the entire agency.

Amy began the session cautiously and described her biggest concern as trouble in relationships. The outcome measure given at the beginning of the conversation reflected a very high level of distress, particularly on the relational scale, and was indicative of people who are in therapy. When the consulting counselor asked about her distress, Amy reported difficulties with trust and said that she struggled especially when she began to feel close to people. Amy paced the session slowly and left ample space for reflection. Unfolding Amy's concerns about relationships ultimately led the therapist to the question of how Amy thought she might best address this issue and change it.

A moment passed, and Amy said, "I know deep in my heart what I need, and I have known it all along." She was deliberate and contemplative and expressed trepidation about sharing her ideas for fear some would find them inappropriate. The therapist considered the implications of the situation with Amy, the pros and cons of divulging her ideas in front of all the agency counselors. The therapist left plenty of room for Amy to consider the implications of her disclosure, and finally Amy shared her ideas. She simply stated that she needed a relationship with a therapist to help her mature in her approach to relationships. Obviously with the benefit of much prior thought, Amy detailed the precise way this maturation could develop in a trial-and-error, feedback-driven process.

The pace quickened as Amy switched gears and described her current therapy as "too behavioral." Amy felt that her ideas about what needed to happen did not fit the DBT that she was receiving. Further, she shared that she felt reluctant to express her views because they were not acceptable to her DBT therapist. Amy's earlier reticence to report her concerns was now understandable—she was clearly unhappy with her current therapy, and her DBT counselor, who was watching the consultation meeting. The therapist further explored Amy's specific ideas about the kind of relationship that she was seeking from a therapist. The description of a mentor type of relationship gained currency as the dialogue continued. Amy said, "I don't understand the reluctance about giving me this kind of relationship. Isn't therapy really about the relationship anyway—how do the DBT people know that change doesn't happen from the relationship the client has with the therapist or the other group members?"

The therapist closed the conversation by complimenting Amy's many talents and insightfulness and suggesting that she implement what she knew to be right about what would be helpful to her. Amy's process measure scores reflected high degrees of satisfaction including trust and indicated a good match between her ideas and the therapist's. When asked about her experience, she replied:

> This therapy really took my ideas seriously and incorporated my plans in the therapy. I was a part of deciding where the conversation went and what the goals were. It helped me consider what my ideas are about things. I felt respected for what I thought I needed. I found the relationship safe, so I felt free enough to explore my most inner thoughts and ideas. I guess I especially felt that I knew what I was talking about and didn't feel like I was being a rebel to think my own thoughts. This is not what I have felt before in therapy. I always felt like I was difficult or a troublemaker or something. I was looking for a relationship with a therapist that would enable me to be totally honest about my needs. I always felt ashamed to say these things—like it was wrong or inappropriate. The session today helped me explore what I thought I needed instead of therapy already deciding that—it allowed me to have some control of my own therapy.

Again, this is not a story of a therapeutic miracle but rather one of the folly of applying any method, evidence-based or garden-variety model, that doesn't include the client's own sensibilities in the equation of change. This story is not meant as an indictment against DBT for crimes against therapy, nor against the therapist for trying to follow the model, but rather as an appeal for the inclusion of heroic clients in all decisions that affect them. By the way, Amy completed her therapy with a different counselor and is attending graduate school to become a therapist.

A BULLETPROOF VEST FOR SILVER BULLETS. Just as diagnosis fails the test of reliability and validity, evidence-based practice receives a failing grade when its claims are empirically scrutinized.

- Efficacy over placebo is not efficacy over other approaches.
- There are no specific effects to psychotherapy; the RCT doesn't fit.
- Differential efficacy claims must be examined for indirect comparisons and allegiance effects.

- The most important factor of change, the client, is left out of empirically supported treatments.
- Manualized therapy undermines the alliance.

Be wary of the silver bullet. Whatever name it takes or form it comes in, claims of success are overblown. They ignore the most essential ingredients of good therapy and, upon closer inspection, do not hold up to empirical scrutiny. Although we are enthusiastic about empirical inquiry as a valuable path to more successful outcomes, we are equally passionate in rejecting prescribed interventions as a mandate for what should be done.

A DIFFERENT EQUATION

Whoever acquires knowledge and does not practice it resembles him who plows his land and leaves it unsown.

—*Sa'di*, Gulistan

The history of psychotherapy can be characterized as the search for the specific mechanisms or processes that reliably produce change. Few would debate the success of this perspective in medicine, where an organized knowledge base, coupled with improvements in diagnosis and pathology, and the development of treatments containing *specific* therapeutic ingredients, have led to the near extinction of a number of once fatal diseases. Unfortunately, for all the claims and counterclaims, psychotherapy, in spite of numerous years of research and development, can boast of no similar accomplishments. Diagnosis in mental health is empirically bankrupt and evidence-based practice is perpetually receiving overdraft notices from the dodo bird account.

Nevertheless, attempting to fit the round peg of psychotherapy into the square hole of medicine remains attractive for several reasons, including the general acceptance of the medico-scientific view in Western society and the harsh economic realities of our health care system (Miller et al., 2004). Still, the facts are difficult to ignore: psychotherapy does not work in the same way as medicine. As summarized by Wampold (2001) in his thorough review of the outcome literature, "the scientific evidence . . . shows that psychotherapy is incompatible with the medical model and that . . . conceptualizing [it] in this way . . . might well destroy talk therapy" (p. 2).

Therapists have hoped, perhaps, that accommodating the medical model would ensure survival in these tumultuous times of managed care. Complicity, however, merely ensures second-class status for therapists and clients in a climate dominated by the specialized languages of diagnosis and treatment models.

We face a tough situation. By not saying no, we say yes: silence allows business as usual to prevail. The time has come to just say no: no to diagnosis and no to evidence-based treatments. It's time to establish a separate identity, free our adolescent dependence on the medical model, and offer a different equation based in a relational model:

CLIENT RESOURCES AND RESILIENCE + CLIENT THEORIES OF CHANGE + CLIENT FEEDBACK ABOUT THE FIT AND BENEFIT OF SERVICE = CLIENT PERCEPTIONS OF PREFERRED OUTCOMES

We believe that, when offered a choice between the medical and relational model, many will choose the latter. The rest of this book illustrates such an alternative.

CHAPTER THREE

Becoming Client Directed
A Tale of Two Dinosaurs

*We have the answers—we just need someone to help bring
them to the front of our head.*

—Molly, ten-year-old heroic client

The mental health field has tenaciously held on to the
notion of the client as a pathological monster of epic proportions
(e.g., Borderlines). In our workshops, to depict the profession's view
of clients, we try to have a little fun. First, we prepare the audience by
announcing that we are about to show a videotaped case, a particularly troublesome one, seen by the treatment team at our clinic. Then
we show an excerpt from the classic movie *Godzilla.*

As huge guns are raised, tanks hurried into place, and technicians
worriedly look after mysterious instruments, a very young Raymond
Burr looks out over Tokyo Bay giving an eyewitness account of the
horror as it unfolds.

> A prehistoric monster that the Japanese call Godzilla has just stepped
> out of Tokyo Bay. It is as tall as a thirty-story building and it is mak-
> ing its way to Tokyo's main line of defense, a three-hundred-thousand-
> volt barrier, a barrier against Godzilla.

Godzilla reaches the power lines; and the technicians throw the switch,
pouring everything the city has into stopping the monster's progress.

Godzilla thrashes about and makes loud screeching noises that sound like feedback at a heavy metal concert—but to no avail. All it accomplishes is really angering Godzilla to unleash a powerful white ray, setting Tokyo on fire.

We jokingly suggest a new diagnostic category, Godzilla personality disorder, and call the technicians cognitive behaviorists and their electrocution attempt a type of thought-stopping intervention. People laugh and immediately recall the countless number of clinical descriptions that portray clients as larger-than-life, dangerous adversaries who crush therapists between their toes or incinerate them with a deadly white ray. An equally detrimental view of clients, albeit more subtle, is the take on clients as hapless bozos, dim-witted plodders who barely stumble their way from one situation to another.

Another dinosaur story illustrates this. In the summer of 1964, John Ostrom and Grant Meyer, Yale paleontologists, were walking along the slope of an eroded mound in south central Montana. They came across the fossil remains of a creature that Ostrom would later call *Deinonychus* (terrible claw). Although uncovering dinosaurs has become relatively commonplace, the finding of *Deinonychus* shook the very foundation of paleontological thought and fueled the flames of a major revolution in the way dinosaurs were viewed.

Whereas before, dinosaurs were seen as ponderous, cold-blooded, shuffling monsters, *Deinonychus*, by its skeletal anatomy, pointed to the undeniable existence of an agile, aggressive, larger-brained, and perhaps even warm-blooded hunter that was anything but slow, sprawling, and stupid. As a result of the chance encounter with *Deinonychus*, the earlier orthodoxy, solidly in place in paleontology, was doomed, soon to be as extinct as the animals it presumed to explain (Wilford, 1986).

Just as the discovery of *Deinonychus* dramatically changed how dinosaurs were viewed, the crisis of accountability and a renewed interest in what works has highlighted the importance of the client to positive outcome. Much like the meteor that ended the era of the dinosaur, the impact of accountability can stop the reign of dinosaur beliefs that see clients as slow-witted plodders or pathological monsters instead of resourceful, motivated hunters of more satisfying lives.

CASTING THE CLIENT IN HEROIC ROLES

I think I have to do something on my own because I can't keep on depending on my mom all my life.

—*Sean, nine-year-old heroic client*

The dodo bird verdict illustrates that despite the fortunes spent on weekend workshops selling the latest fashion, the competition among the more than 250 therapeutic schools amounts to little more than the competition among aspirin, Advil, and Tylenol. All of them relieve pain and work better than no treatment at all. None stands head and shoulders above the rest. They work equally well because they share one very important but classically ignored ingredient—the client and his or her own regenerative powers (Tallman & Bohart, 1999).

The dodo bird verdict rings true because the client's abilities to change transcend any differences among models. Recall that forty years of outcome data show that clients and their strengths, resources, relational supports—all that is available to them inside and outside of therapy—account for 40 percent or 87 percent (depending on the analysis used) of change (Asay & Lambert, 1999; Wampold, 2001). The methods work equally well because clients use what each method provides to address their problems (Bohart & Tallman, 1999). If this is so and the client is the common denominator of change, then other examples of the equivalence of outcome should occur. And they do: comparisons between professionals and paraprofessionals, more- and less-experienced therapists, self-help treatments and therapy, and computer-assisted and therapist-provided intervention have all yielded no appreciable differences (Duncan & Miller, 2000).

Before you go into your garage, close the door, and start your car, consider what this means. It doesn't mean that the therapist or therapy is useless but rather that what we spend so much time acquiring (silver bullets) may not be worthy of the price we pay. If what we provided in counseling was the real deal, then uniform results across different approaches, training and experience levels of therapists, and self-help would not be the norm. The data point to the inevitable conclusion: the engine of change is the client (Tallman & Bohart, 1999). The implication is that perhaps we should spend our time more wisely gaining experience on ways to employ the client in the process of change.

Incredibly, the founder of common factors, Saul Rosenzweig (1936), spoke to the natural sagacity of the client to take what therapy offers and make the best of it. He argued that therapist formulations of the problem need only have enough relevance to impress the client to begin the work of change. Rosenzweig's comments reflect a basic belief in the client's capacity for change and the enlistment of the client in that endeavor. In the era of Rosenzweig's common factors article, there was far more respect for the potentialities of clients as well as a stated appreciation of the uniqueness of the individual (Duncan, 2002).

Of course, no therapist now would say that he or she views clients as monsters or plodders. They would deny characterizing clients as pathological monsters while simultaneously diagnosing them with equally devastating labels reflecting similar uncomplimentary descriptions. They would bristle at any assessment of their clients as dim-witted plodders while prescribing evidenced-based treatments, reducing the client to a disembodied illness to be intervened upon instead of seeing a contributing, resourceful partner with whom to discuss options. The hyperbolic depiction of clients as monsters or plodders opens up the hidden assumptions of psychotherapy—the heroic therapist riding a white stallion of expert knowledge, brandishing a sword of validated treatments, and rescuing the poor dysfunctional patient plagued by the dragon of mental illness—to examination. It allows us to challenge this story and recast clients as the main characters, the heroes and heroines of the therapeutic stage.

Listening for Heroic Stories

Therapists can begin to cast their clients in the role of the primary agents of change by first listening for and being curious about their competencies—the heroic stories that reflect their part in surmounting obstacles, initiating action, and maintaining positive change. There is no formula here; rather, the key is the attitude the practitioner assumes with regard to the client's inherent abilities and resiliencies. Attending to heroic stories requires a balance between listening empathically to difficulties, with mindfulness toward strengths and resources that you know are there.

Human beings have the beautiful complexity to have polar opposite characteristics simultaneously. The field has traditionally attended to only one side of the continuum. Listening for and being curious about client competencies, resources, and resiliencies does not mean that the therapist ignores the client's pain or assumes a cheerleading attitude. Rather, it requires that the therapist listen to the whole story: the confusion and the clarity, the suffering and the endurance, the pain and the coping, the desperation and the desire.

In essence, listening for heroic stories only suggests that counselors open themselves to the existence of several competing stories about the client's experience. Diagnosis tells but one story; a problem description tells another. Many other stories of survival and courage simultaneously exist. Recall Maria and her real story of a horrific accident and its devastating consequences. But another story, one that not only competed with but transcended the first, was simultaneously present and ready to be told.

Maria Revisited

Maria entered therapy looking for a dream she had lost.

MARIA: Before the accident I was a police officer, a detective.

THERAPIST: Wow, what a responsible job!

MARIA: Yeah, I loved it. You know, I have a degree in law enforcement. I worked on the street for fifteen years. I lived my dream until the accident. A drunk driver, of all things!

THERAPIST: Oh my God.

MARIA: And I was in a coma and they told my family that I wasn't going to live and then they told my family that if I did live, I'd be a vegetable all my life and that there was no hope for me to have a fruitful life.

THERAPIST: Wow.

MARIA: And you know, I miss what I had. When I drive by the police department, there is a part of me that really hurts. I knew when I was a child I was going into law enforcement. I even rode with state troopers when I was in high school! I worked hard all my life to get my dreams.

THERAPIST: Your dream was shattered, not only what you had, but your future as well. . . . How did you work for your dream?

The therapist commented on the loss and also followed up about another part of the story, how Maria accomplished her dream.

MARIA: I went to school for two years, and then I got an associate's degree in law enforcement and criminal justice. Then I worked ten years on the street, and then I became a detective. I was not only the first female in the state to graduate from a major city police academy, I was the youngest in my class as well. I was the first woman to make detective in the state too. I am very proud of my accomplishments.

THERAPIST: Wow!

At least three stories have emerged: the story of a catastrophic accident and Maria's subsequent losses and disabilities; a heroic story of a little girl who knew she wanted to be a police officer, who did everything humanly possible to accomplish her goal and achieve at the highest levels; and a heroic story of survival about a person who came back from the dead to prove everyone wrong, a woman who could not even talk when she awakened from a coma but yet came to the session under her own power with the help of only a cane.

MARIA: I am not trying to make it sound like I am looking down on anybody because anybody who has a disability, it is too bad, but I don't want to be disabled all my life. I'd like to get my dream back. And I guess inside I'm not ready to accept that I'm disabled. And I know there are things I can't do anymore. And it's kind of like forcing it down my throat when I have to say it and when the rehab counselor and the group home therapist and the psychiatrist all tell me I have to accept it, grieve it, and move on to something else.

THERAPIST: You know that part of you that has trouble accepting the disability? I really like that part of you.

MARIA: *[laughs]* You do? Why?

THERAPIST: Well, that's your spirit. That's the fighter in you: that's the person who knew early on that you wanted to be a police officer, that you wanted to break barriers as a woman. That's the part of you that beat the accident and the coma and all the dire predictions of the doctors. That's the part of you that never says die. . . . That's the part that says, "I'm not disabled, and there is so much more of me here that I have to offer the world that there is nothing disabled about."

MARIA: I like the way you put that! That's how I feel.

The therapist reinforced the heroic story, and it rang true for Maria. Her story of heartbreaking loss and diminished abilities to perform police work was real. The therapist, although empathic to the terrible impact of the accident, refused to succumb to that particular story as the only or truest one of Maria's life. Instead, the therapist encouraged and enlisted a story of amazing resilience and courage. Given how potent the client and his or her resources are to a successful outcome, the choice for mental health professionals in these situations seems clear. Clients' heroic stories pave the way for change.

Mental health professionals can also incorporate the heroic aspects of clients' lives by enlisting their resources from the world outside therapy. Whether seeking out a trusted friend or family member, purchasing a book or tape, attending church or a mutual-help group, clients find support outside the therapy relationship. To attend to the client's world outside therapy, the therapist can simply listen for and then be curious about what happens in the client's life that is helpful. Several questions are useful to keep in mind:

- Whom does the client refer to as helpful in his or her day-to-day life?
- What does the client do to get these persons to help him or her?
- What persons, places, or things does the client seek out between sessions for even a small measure of comfort or aid?
- What persons, places, or things has the client sought out in the past that were useful?
- What was different about those times that enabled the client to use those resources?

The counselor may inquire about the helpful aspects of the client's existing social support network; activities that provide relief, even if temporary; and circumstances outside therapy in which the client feels most capable, successful, and composed. Sometimes the therapist may be even more direct by inviting someone from the client's existing social support network (e.g., parent, partner, employer, friend, rabbi) to participate in the therapy or by referring the client to resources in the community (e.g., self-help and spiritual groups, support lines, social clubs). Whatever path the therapist takes, it is important to remember that the purpose is to identify not what clients need but what they already have that they can put to use in reaching their goals.

BECOMING CHANGE FOCUSED: CREATING NEW HEROIC STORIES

If you make one success, you are going to get more successes. That's just how the game works.

—*Sean, nine-year-old heroic client*

Heracleitus is often credited with saying that nothing is permanent but change. Unlike diagnoses—static characterizations connoting a measure of constancy and even permanence in clients' presenting complaints—the magnitude, severity, and frequency of problems are in flux, constantly changing. With or without prompting, clients can describe these changes—the ebb and flow of the problem's presence and ascendancy in their daily affairs. These reported changes and seemingly unrelated events that often occur serendipitously can provide powerful opportunities for telling new heroic stories.

From this standpoint change itself is a potent client factor—affecting the lives of clients before, during, and after therapy—that can be harnessed for the cocreation of possibilities and perhaps new identities. Supporting this conclusion is the phenomenon of pretreatment change. Many (e.g., Lawson, 1994; Weiner-Davis, de Shazer, & Gingerich, 1987) have found that 60 percent or more of clients coming to their first session report improvement in the presenting problem since making the appointment. Simply scheduling an appointment may help set the wheel of change in motion and present the possibility for an emergent story of competence and mastery.

Consequently, we suggest that therapists view clients through a change-focused lens. Shining a spotlight on change, as solution-focused therapy has taught us, illuminates existing client resources and allows their enlistment. Perhaps most importantly, showcasing client change of any kind opens the possibility of new heroic stories by encouraging the client to make "before and after" distinctions. Clients reflect upon their experiences and distinguish between the way they were and the way they are now—essentially creating a newfound identity of wisdom and competence gained from the school of hard knocks of their lives.

Listening for a Change

To develop a change-focus, a therapist can listen for and validate change for the better, whenever and for whatever reason it occurs. A change-focus also requires that the therapist believe, like Heracleitus, in the certainty of change and create a context in which to welcome, explore, and develop new or different perspectives, behaviors, and experiences into new heroic narratives. Of special interest is what the client has done or is doing to bring about or take advantage of change and how the client makes sense of it all.

Inquiry into change can proceed along two lines. First, the therapist can ask the client about pretreatment change.

• Many people notice that, between the time they called for the appointment and the actual first session, things already seem different. What have you noticed about your situation (Weiner-Davis et al., 1987)?

Or therapists can listen for opportunities to highlight changes that clients mention. Follow up on key words or phases (e.g., *except, until recently, first time*) to elicit further articulation. When clients report changes, the practitioner can ask questions to elaborate the change and the client's contribution to it. In effect, this helps to link the positive change to the client's own behavior, thus highlighting it as an instance of self-healing and perhaps the beginning of an important new chapter.

• What was happening at those times? [Obtain a detailed description.] What do you think you were doing to help that along? What would you need to do (or what would need to happen) for you to experience more of that? How do you account for the change at this point in your life?
• As you continue to do these good things for yourself (or take advantage of what is helping), what difference will that make to you tomorrow? How will your day go better? What are these changes saying about you?

Similarly, should the client return for additional visits, the counselor can direct attention to changes taking place between sessions. For example, therapists can heed and then amplify any references the client makes during the session to between-session improvement or events not directly related to the client's stated concerns. Also, in the opening moments of the session, the therapist can directly ask the client about what, if any, changes have occurred since their last visit. The simplest question comes in this form, "What is different?" or "What is better?" Such inquiry, when used judiciously and with sensitivity to the client's acceptance, focuses both on change and the client's contribution in bringing it about. In this way the clinician may assist the client in attributing any change to his or her own efforts. The client's experience of change figures very prominently in the approach to outcome management we will discuss in Chapter Four.

Expanding Change into Heroic Stories

Whether change begins before or during therapy, whether it results from the client's own actions or by happenstance, a crucial step in enhancing the effects of change is helping clients see any gains as a consequence of their own efforts—and as part of an emerging heroic story of a new identity. Naturally, a cardinal consideration is perception—specifically, the clients' perception of the relationship between their own efforts and the occurrence of change and its meaning in the context of the story of their lives. At the least, it is important that clients come to view the change as resulting from something they did and can repeat in the future.

Therapists can support change in several ways. As we illustrated, the counselor can express curiosity about the client's role in any changes that occur. Additionally, the therapist can ask questions or make direct statements that presuppose client involvement in the resulting change (Berg & Miller, 1992; Walter & Peller, 1992).

• Wait a second. You did what? Tell me more about that. How did you know to do what you did? That was thoughtful. What is it about you that helped you to do what you did?

As part of a last meeting, therapists may also summarize the changes that occurred and invite clients to review their own role in the change. Even if clients resolutely attribute change to luck, fate, the therapist's acumen, or a medication, the practitioner should still ask them to consider in detail (1) how they adopted the change in their lives, (2) what they did to use the changes to their benefit, (3) what they will do in the future to ensure their gains remain in place, and (4) how the changes reflect new chapters in their lives.

Callslip Request   2/23/2014 3:29:09 PM

Request date:2/21/2014 11:02 PM
Request ID: 44430
Call Number:616 8914 D9112 2004
Item Barcode:

3 4 7 1 1 0 0 2 2 2 8 3 5 3

Author: Duncan, Barry L.
Title: Heroic client : a revolutionary way to imp
Enumeration:c.1Year:
Patron Name:Jennifer Anne Costello
Patron Barcode:

2 3 3 1 1 9 6 0 0 9 4 7 8

Patron comment:

Request number:

Route to:
4 4 4 3 0
I-Share Library:

Library Pick Up Location:

Joan

Joan, a twenty-eight-year-old woman recovering from a cocaine addiction, was scheduled for a consult because her group counselor perceived an impasse, and both Joan and her counselor were looking for new directions.

THERAPIST: What would be most useful for us to talk about today?

JOAN: Well, I think that the biggest thing that is going on in my life is that I have a gentleman who is interested in me.

THERAPIST: OK, great.

JOAN: It has been a very long time, and what happened was, the first time that we hung out together, he was like very, very forward and obviously very horny. So before I saw him the next time, I did a lot of thinking. And it was the first time in my life, as far as a relationship with a man, that I was honest about my needs. I mean he wanted to set a date when we were going to make love.

THERAPIST: Wow.

JOAN: I know, and I was totally turned off by that. I could have just used the phone to say, "I don't need this." But I wanted to challenge myself and face him. So we went out for a cup of coffee, and when the time was right, I came right out and was totally real, totally honest, which was new for me, and I had good results. I said to him, "If this is not good for you, not something that you want, then you know, let's just end it right here." And he completely turned around, and he was like, "It's fine." And "You are right, it should be spontaneous. We should be in love." You know, it was like, wow, honesty and being real works!

In the opening moments of the conversation, despite the fact that both the referring counselor and the client perceived an impasse (more on that later), Joan mentions a "new" and "first-time" experience. The change-focused therapist follows up with curiosity about the meaning of this important milestone in the client's life.

THERAPIST: Absolutely. So I am really curious about how you were able to do that at this point in time? And how is it that you were able to challenge yourself to overcome the fear of standing up to this situation and being honest so that you could see a possibility of something good working out?

JOAN: You mean, like, what was my thought process?

THERAPIST: Yeah, yeah. Because that seems like a real breakthrough.

JOAN: Definitely. You are right about that. A big part of it was the safety issue. I think the biggest thing was to protect myself.

THERAPIST: OK, so somehow you have been able to put yourself first and protect yourself in trying to be honest with someone and making sure that you are safe.

JOAN: Yeah, and that was the second time in my life that I have done this. The first time was about a month ago, and that also had positive results when I was honest.

THERAPIST: Wow. And the incident about a month ago makes me think that you are on a swell here of making some pretty major life changes for yourself.

JOAN: Definitely. It's huge.

The therapist now moves to co-delineate all the factors that have contributed to this important event and explore what they mean.

THERAPIST: Gosh, so how do you account for that at this point in your life? That you are pulling some very important things together for yourself and are able to start implementing them in your closest relationships?

JOAN: OK, hmm. Having support is really important. And for the first time in my life I have not only support from my parents and my sisters but also being here at the clinic and doing the group.

THERAPIST: You have had this breakthrough experience; you have some support from your family and the clinic here and have noticed the benefits of the group. And I'm just wondering what else accounts for your being at this juncture in your life where you are starting to implement what you have learned.

JOAN: Another thing is that my whole life I was very spontaneous; and there was no regimen, no schedule. And now I am on a schedule. I do my work, same hours every week. And I attend group three times a week. It's just having that stability. I just feel so, you know, safe. I think the last thing to answer this question is challenging myself. You know, to push the envelope.

THERAPIST: Uh huh.

Here is where it really gets exciting. Joan has described how "huge" the changes are and how several different things have come into play to support these changes. Now she is starting to tell a new story about Joan. Notice the "before and after" implications and the past tense of her statements—what constitutes her identity then and how she describes her identity now.

JOAN: At this point in my life, if I challenge myself and it doesn't work, you know, I have learned not to beat myself up.

THERAPIST: Oh wow.

JOAN: And not maintain a victim mentality. Which I did all my life, you know. It's just unproductive.

THERAPIST: And this is what today is about, challenging yourself, pushing yourself?

JOAN: Yes, yeah.

THERAPIST: That's incredible. And that is what it's about, being honest with your male friend?

JOAN: Yes, that was also challenging. As I said, it would have been very easy for me to pick up the phone and do it. But I said, "No, I want that eye contact, I want that face to face," you know?

THERAPIST: Where it would have been easy to just call him and say, "No, I don't want to get together again," without ever seeing if the relationship can go to the next level.

JOAN: That's true. I didn't think of that. That's a very good point. It makes me feel good because what you are saying is that I am ready to have a healthy relationship. Right?

THERAPIST: Exactly.

JOAN: That makes me feel good.

THERAPIST: It definitely means that you have created the possibility for a healthy relationship to happen. Because, you know, if you can't tell someone that there is something pretty wrong with the way they are approaching it, that means that you have to give in and maybe even lose your integrity. And they are going to take over, and you are going to start pleasing them to make the relationship work, and then you are screwed.

JOAN: You are so on! That's exactly how all my relationships were; I lost myself.

THERAPIST: Hmm.

JOAN: I lost myself and I tell you, I had made a pact with myself that I would never let that happen again. And if it meant that I had to be alone, without a relationship in my life, I have no problem with that.

THERAPIST: That's a pretty incredible thing to say. Some people, rather than be alone, would continue to give themselves up until there is nothing left of them. But you are so beyond that, to make the statement that you'd rather be alone.

JOAN: Yes.

THERAPIST: And second, [that] you [will] actually take the next step and be honest is pretty amazing.

JOAN: This is just like the beginning. As I said, this was quite recently, over the last one or two months that I had the two real honest experiences. And at the same time, I got my puppy. So it has to have something to do with this. You know what I am saying? Because getting the puppy was a huge step. You have this big responsibility. You have this little life to take care of, and then in return you get the unconditional love.

THERAPIST: Uh huh.

JOAN: God, I mean, it's such a huge step to get out of that victim mentality—which stifles you. I mean even the way that I deal with my own father. I no longer am reacting to him. Because my whole life all I did was react. My mood and the way I acted was a direct reflection of how the other person was acting towards me. I had no individuality whatsoever.

THERAPIST: Now you are thinking about how you want to be rather than reacting how they are. This is an amazing change you have made. A part that interests me is that this revolves, some of it, around the decision to get a puppy. Somehow this was part of this breakthrough experience or you are putting into life these changes, this new you, by having another creature to take care of.

JOAN: Yes, and I hadn't realized that until you asked me that question. I didn't even realize that that was the time that I started making the breakthroughs of honesty and being real.

The discussion culminated in a heroic story about Joan's new way of approaching her life. The puppy came to symbolize her new identity and represented a concrete marker of the before and after of Joan's life. It is amazing to witness how clients get on a roll as they reflect about their lives and construct new stories of competence and courage as they make sense of their experiences. Joan had obviously gained much from her work in the groups she attended. So why did she and her counselor perceive an impasse? Joan had previously attempted to discuss her interest in dating, but it had been discouraged because of program rules about postponing relationships until clients had been clean and sober for two years. Joan therefore had not felt comfortable discussing her new relationship and the gains she was making there.

CLIENTS AS CRITICS OF THE THERAPY PERFORMANCE

The therapists asked me questions about different subjects and I am like thinking, I don't really want to answer these questions because shouldn't I be telling you what I think about this?

—Molly, ten-year-old heroic client

Just as clients have traditionally been miscast as villains or dimwits, clients' perspectives regarding therapy and the therapist frequently wind up on the cutting room floor. This is curious given that client perceptions of relationship factors account for 30 percent of successful outcome (Asay & Lambert, 1999) and their views of the alliance account for as much as 54 percent of therapeutic gains (Wampold, 2001). Recall also how the alliance, early on, is a robust predictor of eventual outcome. The alliance data suggest that therapy works if clients experience the relationship positively, perceive therapy to be relevant to their concerns and goals, and are active participants. The practitioner should take the client, like a *New York Times* film critic, very seriously if any desire exists for box office success.

Influencing the client's perceptions of the alliance represents the most direct impact we can have on change. Bordin (1979) defines the alliance as having three interacting elements: (1) the development of a relationship bond between the therapist and client, (2) agreement on the goals of therapy, and (3) agreement on the tasks of therapy.

Cementing the Relational Bond

As with listening for heroic stories, therapist attitude is also critical to developing a relational bond. Part and parcel of this attitude is the belief that the alliance is the master to be served. To implement this attitude, we have found it useful to think of each meeting as a first date (without the romantic overtones), in which we consciously put our best foot forward, actively woo the client's favor, and entice his or her participation. Recall that clients' active engagement in the process, the quality of their participation, is the single best indication of the likelihood of success. Because the relationship is formed early, paying close attention to the client's initial perceptions and reactions only makes sense.

From this attitude about the alliance, the therapist is positioned to fit the client's view of a good relationship. This requires monitoring the client's response to the process itself and quickly calibrating therapy to the client's expectations. We pay particular attention to what excites the client: When does he lean forward? When does she raise her voice? What sets the client's eyes sparkling? What topics and ways of relating raise activity and engagement?

Recall the Bachelor study (1995) and how clients vary widely in their experience of what constitutes a good relationship. Verifying with the client his or her expectations and perceptions and monitoring the helpfulness of particular therapist responses can assist the counselor in recalibrating to the client's individual needs. Conveying to clients that the practitioner values and will actually act on their perspectives, including dissatisfactions, sends a powerful message. Therapists need to be particularly alert to cues that signal problems, because clients are often reluctant to communicate negative feelings and their dissatisfaction (Hill, Nutt-Williams, Heaton, Thompson, & Rhodes, 1996). Alliance monitoring is a crucial component of outcome management. Chapter Four provides a systematic method of acquiring client ideas about the alliance.

Fitting the many different relational expectations requires a high measure of flexibility on the therapist's part, as well as willingness to change one's relational stance to fit with the client's perceptions of what is most helpful. Some clients, for instance, will prefer a formal or professional manner over a casual or warmer one. Others might prefer more self-disclosure from the therapist, greater directiveness, a focus on their symptoms or an emphasis on the possible meanings beneath them, a faster or perhaps a more laid-back pace for therapeutic work (Bachelor & Horvath, 1999). The one-approach-fits-all strategy is guaranteed to undermine alliance formation.

In addition to continual monitoring and flexibility, a useful way of thinking of therapist relational responses is the idea of *validation*—a process in which the therapist respects the client's struggle as important, perhaps representing a critical juncture in the client's life, and accepts, believes, and considers the client's thoughts, feelings, and behaviors as completely understandable given trying circumstances (Duncan, Solovey, & Rusk, 1992). Validation reflects a genuine acceptance of the client at face value and includes an empathic search for justification of the client's experience. The therapist legitimizes the client's frame of reference and thereby replaces the invalidation that may be a part of it.

In summary, the therapist serves the alliance by

- Being likable, friendly, and responsive (like on a first date).
- Carefully monitoring the client's reaction to comments, explanations, interpretations, questions, and suggestions.
- Being flexible: doing whatever it takes to engage the client. You are many things to many people (friend, partner, parent, child, sibling). Use your complexity to fit differing clients.
- Validating the client. Legitimizing the client's concerns and highlighting the importance of the client's struggle.

Sam

Sam, a fifty-one-year-old man recovering from a heroin addiction, was scheduled for a consult because he and his counselor perceived things to be stuck. Sam's lack of participation in either Narcotics Anonymous (NA) or other support groups fueled this perception. We pick up here after Sam has shared several troubling aspects of his life.

THERAPIST: Well, this gives me an idea of how much crap you have to deal with on a daily basis. God, you have all these catch 22's going on. Work versus disability, AIDS and taking the medicine versus feeling OK, the epilepsy, working with your brother and him not really knowing whether to trust you. Plus on top of all that, your friend leaves and starts using again. You are not really sure what to do at this point. But you decide, even with all this shit, that you are not going to use. I was wondering how the hell you did that.

SAM: It's a battle. But even though I did not use yet, I got this barrier. Bob [Sam's counselor] said a few times, which I know, a bad part of me is that I am lazy.

THERAPIST: OK, tell me about that barrier.

The therapist attempts to enlist the client's reflections about his miraculous ability to stay clean in the face of such obstacles. Sam responds with his perception, and his counselor's, that he is lazy. Not exactly a validating explanation of his "barrier." So the search is on for a more validating explanation.

SAM: Well, I want everything thrown in my lap. Like the job thing. If somebody came to me and said, "Hey listen, I have got this nice little gig for you" and did the work for me—and it's just a mile or two from the house and just a few days a week. I want it to be easy.

THERAPIST: No wonder, Sam. . . . You are like Napoleon fighting these battles at all these different fronts. . . . You are not just trying to find a job, you are fighting AIDS here and addiction there, and you got epilepsy for Christ's sake! That's a lot of fronts to be fighting at the same time.

SAM: Absolutely. And it's definitely wearing, very wearing. I lost my old lady to AIDS in '95. She died in my arms, and that was really traumatic. It took me years to bounce back from that.

THERAPIST: Wow, you have been through a hell of a lot!

SAM: Yes. But I guess I am lazy. I will admit it. I don't really want to put a lot of work in my recovery. Maybe I don't give myself enough credit sometimes. But when I say lazy, like I know Bob says it a lot, "Why don't you go to a meeting?" I do not like twelve-step meetings. I really dislike them. When I go to a meeting, I feel like using!

THERAPIST: Sounds like a good decision not to go.

SAM: But I heard of another support group that started a few weeks ago at this place uptown that is a support group for HIV-positive people. So I am really thinking about doing that.

THERAPIST: OK.

SAM: But that's what I mean with the lazy thing. I know that there is something there that I can do, a stepping-stone in a right path for me, but why do I refuse to do it?

THERAPIST: What's your hunch about that?

SAM: I really honestly don't know. Except for the lazy thing . . .

THERAPIST: OK. Any ideas about what it would take to help you take that step toward the AIDS support group?

SAM: If it was later in the day. *[laughs]*

THERAPIST: So it's a pragmatic thing.

SAM: Well, that's pretty silly. It's two o'clock in the afternoon. That shouldn't be a reason really. It is like a bullshit reason.

THERAPIST: You don't think it's a very good one.

SAM: Right. If I want it bad enough, you should be able to do it. . . . I think I have something with letting people really in close. I am a very friendly person. I have got a good heart. I wanna be friends with people, but the other part of this, I like keeping them away too.

The therapist accepts Sam's statements about not liking NA groups at face value and validates Sam's decision not to go. Later, Sam identifies a reason, other than being lazy, for not attending the HIV group.

THERAPIST: Hmm. Oh God, no wonder. You've lost someone very close to you.

SAM: Yeah . . . maybe that has a lot more to do with it.

THERAPIST: There is a lot to be said about why you would never want to get close to anyone, especially given how you lost her and the context of that group.

SAM: Right . . . right.

THERAPIST: So it's a risk to go to that AIDS meeting because you could meet somebody that would die.

SAM: . . . Right . . . right. Absolutely with that . . . yeah.

The search for a reason other than laziness paid off. Sam did not want to revisit the situation he experienced when his partner died. Replacing the invalidation that is often embedded in client stories sometimes frees clients to do what they need to do for themselves.

THERAPIST: So there is something there that would give you some support and friendship, but there is a risk that goes along with that, and you know that risk only too well!

SAM: Right.

THERAPIST: So I can understand your bind with not wanting to get there.

SAM: Right. Well, that is something that I wanna do. I want to make a commitment to myself to at least make one meeting.

THERAPIST: OK.

SAM: And do it and just see what happens. And I know a person that goes to it. So at least I know somebody that's gonna be there.

THERAPIST: It sounds like you are ready to make that commitment to do that.

SAM: Yes. Matter of fact, tomorrow would be a good day to start.

And he did.

Accepting the Client's Goals

The second aspect of the alliance is the agreement on the goals of therapy. When we talk to clients, we spend little time developing diagnoses or theorizing about possible etiology of the presenting complaint and even less on what therapeutic approach or technique will be most useful. Rather, the process is composed of careful listening and alliance monitoring, combined with questions aimed at defining and redefining the client's goals. We depend on the client's input, participation, and involvement to determine the goals for therapy.

When we ask clients what they want out of therapy, what they want to be different, we give credibility to their beliefs and values regarding the problem and its solution. We are saying to them that their opinion is important and therapy is to serve them. As simple an act as this is, it invites clients to see themselves as collaborators in making their lives better.

Counselors can accommodate clients' goals by listening and then amplifying the stories and experiences that clients offer about their problems, including their thoughts, feelings, and ideas about where they want to go and the best way to get there. The therapist can also directly inquire about the client's goals. For instance, the therapist might ask:

- What is your goal for our work together?
- What did you hope, wish, or think would be different because of coming here?
- What did you want to change about your life, problem, and so on?
- What would have to be minimally different in your life for you to consider our work together a success?
- What will be the first sign to you that you have taken a solid step on the road to improvement even though you might not yet be out of the woods?

Once again, counselor attitude is paramount to the process of eliciting and respecting the client's goals. Regardless of how they sound, we accept client's goals at face value because those are the desires that will excite and motivate the client to initiate action on his or her own behalf. If we are serving the alliance master, we know that agreement with the client about the goals of therapy is essential to positive outcome. It begins the process of change, wherever the client may ultimately travel.

Sometimes clients' goals do not fit our own sensibilities about what they need. This may be particularly true if clients carry certain diagnoses or problem scenarios. It is in precisely such circumstances, those in which people look "psychotic" or most destitute or desperate, that we must take the most caution regarding our own perspective about client goals.

Consider Sarah, a twenty-four-year-old woman who lived in a supervised residence and was considered "mentally ill." She spent much of her time watching TV and eating snack foods. Sarah repeatedly expressed her desire to be a BenGal, a cheerleader for the Cincinnati Bengals (a professional football team). But her therapist just couldn't accept this goal. After all, it was just not possible. So no one listened or even knew why Sarah had such an interesting goal. And the work with Sarah floundered. She rarely spoke and minimally answered questions. The counselor was genuinely worried and truly wanted Sarah to get out in the world more and out of sitting in front of the TV with a bag of chips in her hand. He brought his concerns to his team, and they recommended two things: that he find out where the desire to be a cheerleader came from and then find a way to accept the client's goal and recognize the motivation and energy it represented.

When the counselor asked Sarah about her goal, Sarah told the story of growing up watching the Bengals with her dad, who delighted in Sarah's learning and practicing the cheers. Sarah sparkled when she talked of her father, who had passed away several years previously, and the counselor noted that it was the most he had ever heard her speak. The therapist took this experience to heart and often asked Sarah questions about her father, to which she invariably was delighted to respond. In addition, the counselor decided to slow down efforts to get Sarah to socialize or exercise, and he instead leaned more toward Sarah's interest in cheerleading. Sarah regularly watched cheerleading contests on ESPN, so her counselor decided to just sit with her and watch. The therapist learned that Sarah knew a lot about cheerleading and really enjoyed showing her considerable expertise. These vibrant conversations came to dominate the interactions between Sarah and her counselor. After a while, Sarah decided on her own to organize a cheerleading squad for the community basketball team sponsored by the agency that managed the supervised residence. Sarah maintains her involvement in cheerleading for the team; she now spends less time sitting in front of the TV and is actively involved in the community.

Tailoring the Tasks of Therapy

The final aspect of the alliance is the agreement on the tasks of therapy. Tasks include specific techniques or therapeutic points of view, topics of conversation, interview procedures, frequency of meeting, and so on. Another demonstration of our respect for the client's capabilities and our conscious efforts to enlist participation occurs when we ask the client to help set the tasks of therapy.

In a working alliance, the client perceives the tasks, what is actually taking place, as germane and effective. In a well-functioning alliance, counselors and clients jointly work to construct interventions that are in accordance with clients' preferred outcomes. Traditionally, the therapeutic search has been for interventions reflecting objective truths that promote change by validating the therapist's favored theory. The search, when fostering a strong alliance, is for ideas and actions that promote change by validating the client's view of what is helpful.

Gaston (1990) provides a little different spin. She reiterates the major alliance themes but also emphasizes that the congruence between the client's and the therapist's beliefs about how people change in therapy is essential for a strong alliance. This aspect, matching the client's theory of change, is discussed now.

THE CLIENT'S THEORY OF CHANGE

The therapist told me what to do, but I didn't want to do it because they weren't my ideas and they didn't seem . . . right.

—Molly, ten-year-old heroic client

Because all approaches are equivalent with respect to outcome and because technique pales in comparison to client and relationship factors, an evolving story casts the client as not only the star of the therapeutic show but also the director of the change process (Duncan et al., 1992). We now consider our clients' worldview, their map of the territory, as the determining theory for therapy (Duncan et al., 1997), directing both the destination desired and the routes of restoration.

The notion that client perceptions of problem formation and resolution—what we call the client's theory of change—have important implications for therapy has a rich although somewhat ignored theoretical heritage. Although many have noted the clinical wisdom in attending to the client's own formulations about change (see Chapter Five), few have systematically attempted to draw client ideas about change into the process.

Similarly, little research has studied the intentional use of clients' preferences in the selection of treatment approaches. However, studies in which the treatment offered was later found to have been congruent with client preferences point to increased client engagement and better treatment outcomes. For example, a post hoc analysis of the data from the Treatment of Depression Collaborative Research Project (TDCRP, the large-scale study of treatments for depression) found that congruence between a person's beliefs about the causes of his or her depression and the treatment approach offered resulted in stronger therapeutic alliances, increased duration of treatment, and therefore improved outcomes (Elkin et al., 1999). Additional empirical support for matching the client's theory of change is provided in findings from the attribution, expectancy, and acceptability literatures (see Hubble et al., 1999b, for a review).

Rather than the therapist reformulating the client's complaint into his or her own orientation, we are suggesting the exact opposite: that counselors elevate the client's perceptions above theory and allow the client's view of change to direct therapeutic choices. Such a process all but guarantees the security of a strong alliance. The alliance and its relationship to the client's theory can be understood as a three-legged stool (Figure 3.1). Set against a backdrop of client strengths and resources, each leg of the stool stands for one of the core ingredients of the alliance. One of the legs represents the counselor and client's agreement about the goals, meaning, or purpose of the counseling; another symbolizes the client's view of the relationship and the therapist's role; and the final leg signifies the agreement about the means or methods used. If one leg is missing or wobbly, you know the result—the alliance and any hope of a positive outcome will fall flat. The client's theory of change is the metaphorical seat of our

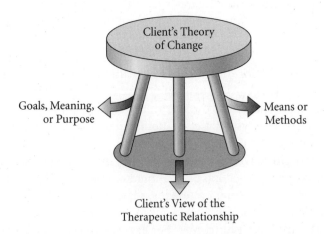

Figure 3.1. The Therapeutic Alliance.

alliance stool. It allows the client to sit comfortably in therapy secured by a good relational fit.

Learning and Honoring the Client's Theory

The client has a uniquely personal theory waiting for discovery, a framework for change to be unfolded and used for a successful outcome. We can best explore the client's theory by viewing ourselves as aliens from another planet. We seek a pristine understanding of a close encounter with the client's unique interpretations and cultural experiences. To learn clients' theories, we must adopt their views on their terms, with a very strong bias in their favor.

We begin by listening closely to the client's language. We often take notes so that we can record the exact words that clients choose to describe problems, desires, and solutions. Taking notes unobtrusively conveys the therapist's interest in, as well as the importance of, the client's input. We show clients our notes or make copies if they desire. We explain that the purpose of the notes is to record what they say so that we don't miss their descriptions of their experiences and what they want from therapy.

Using clients' language privileges their idiosyncratic understandings and conveys the importance of their ideas and participation; it represents one more way for therapists to keep clients center stage. Finally, speaking in and working with the client's language provides the container for learning the client's theory.

After making direct inquiries about the client's goals, we ask questions regarding his or her ideas about change. What the client wants and how those goals can be accomplished may be the most important pieces of information that the therapist can obtain. We believe that clients not only have all that is necessary to resolve problems but may have a very good idea about how to do it. Questions that elicit the client's hunches and educated guesses encourage participation, emphasize the client's input, and provide direct access to the client's theory of change. Ask the client

- What ideas do you have about what needs to happen for improvement to occur?
- Many times people have a pretty good hunch not only about what is causing a problem but also about what will resolve it. Do you have a theory of how change is going to happen here?

Listen for or inquire about the client's usual method of or experience with change:

- How does change usually happen in your life?
- What do you and others do to initiate change?

In addition, discussing prior solutions provides an excellent way for learning the client's theory of change and preferred way of working. Exploring the client's earlier solutions enables the therapist to hear the client's frank evaluation of previous attempts and their fit with what the client believes to be helpful.

- What have you tried to help the problem or situation so far? Did it help? How did it help? Why didn't it help?

Finally, finding out what your role is in the change process is integral to implementing the client's theory. Some clients want a sounding board; some want a confidant; some want to brainstorm and solve problems; some want advice; and some want an expert to tell them what to do. Explore the client's preferences about your role by asking

- How do you see me fitting into what you would like to see happen?
- How can I be of most help to you now?
- What role do you see me playing in your endeavor to change this situation?
- Let me make sure I am getting this right. Are you looking for suggestions from me about that situation?
- In what ways do you see me and this process as helpful to attaining your goals?

Honoring the client's theory occurs when a given therapeutic procedure fits or complements the client's preexisting beliefs about his or her problems and the change process. We simply listen and then amplify the stories, experiences, and interpretations that clients offer about their problems, as well as their thoughts, feelings, and ideas about how we might best address those problems. As the client's theory evolves, we implement the client's identified solutions or seek an approach that both fits the client's theory and provides possibilities for change.

Given the frequent hyping of the method of the month, there's a temptation to turn an idea like the client's theory of change into one more invariant therapeutic prescription: ask what the client would like to do (or prescribe a ritual, finger waving, etc.), and watch the miracles roll out the office door! This is not what we're saying. All solutions will not blossom from the first question about the client's theory. The client's theory of change is an emergent reality that unfolds from a conversation structured by the therapist's curiosity about the client's ideas, attitudes, and speculations about change.

We are also not saying that we never offer ideas or suggestions or that we do not contribute to the construction of the client's theory of change. Exploration for and discovery of the client's theory is a coevolutionary process, a crisscrossing of ideas that generates a seamless connection of socially constructed meanings. The degree and intensity of our input vary and are driven by the client's expectations of our role. Some clients want a lot from us in terms of generating ideas, whereas others prefer to keep us in a sounding-board role. Chapter Five further explores the client's theory of change and provides guidelines for the selection of methods and ideas that match the client's views of change.

Mike

Mike, a thirty-one-year-old man diagnosed with schizophrenia and struggling with alcohol dependence, was scheduled for a consult because his counselor perceived an impasse regarding Mike's drinking.

THERAPIST: Was there something that you felt like you would like to talk with me about today?

MIKE: I don't know. I have a therapist already, Marty. She does it well.

THERAPIST: Oh, great. How long have you been seeing Marty?

MIKE: Off and on now, about four years.

THERAPIST: OK. And you talk with her about things?

MIKE: Lately, it's been my sobriety that we've been talking about. Because I've been drinking and then I see her and it doesn't seem to go anywhere. I don't know. It's like, there's no point in seeing her if I'm going to keep drinking.

THERAPIST: Uh huh.

MIKE: I've been doing pretty good for the past month.

THERAPIST: Wow. How is that happening? What's your idea about that?

MIKE: If I were to sit here and talk to you about how I should stop drinking and in the meantime I'm popping open beers . . . I mean, it's not going to look good for you being my therapist.

THERAPIST: It wouldn't look like we were being too effective.

MIKE: Right, right.

THERAPIST: Right, right. And so somehow in the last month, you say, you're making Marty look better?

The therapist picks up on Mike's idea of how he was able to change and inquires further about this emerging reality or theory of change. Note that the counselor asks no specific questions about the theory of change. The therapist simply explores and expands the client's ideas as they come forth.

MIKE: I guess so because I care about her.

THERAPIST: Yeah, you do.

MIKE: I really do. I've really grown to care about her.

THERAPIST: Yeah. And then that caring about her, that somehow has contributed to your being sober. Am I understanding this?

MIKE: Yeah, yeah. Sometimes I wonder what's worse, the drinking or the aftermath of it. It starts to hurt people, other people, the next day. If I go to my mother and say, "Ma, I'm having severe . . . anxiety." . . . But you see what I'm doing? I'm throwing it on my mother.

THERAPIST: Uh huh.

MIKE: She has to deal with the aftereffects. That's one of those people who gets affected by the drinking even though she doesn't know about it. She gets affected by it because she sees me in pain, and I don't think she should have to see me in pain.

THERAPIST: It seems like your sobriety is about doing for others, keeping other people in your heart and in your mind.

The therapist makes a stab at articulating Mike's theory of change or his theory of sobriety. Mike responds with another instance or example of doing for others, a very good indication that the therapist is on the right track.

MIKE: Yeah, like my roommate drinks when I drink, and I don't like that because I know he won't sleep that night.

THERAPIST: See, I'm really getting this now.

MIKE: I like, I really like the pope.

This statement throws the therapist for a bit of a loop, because it seems to come out of nowhere. But the therapist trusts that it will make sense if Mike is allowed the space and time to connect the dots. And it does.

THERAPIST: Pope Paul?

MIKE: Pope John Paul, and I find him to be a very humble person.

THERAPIST: Yeah.

MIKE: So I watch him as often as I can. 'Cause I learn a lot from him.

THERAPIST: Yeah, incredible example.

MIKE: But to put yourself aside for somebody else. I mean, like, somebody shoots him, and he goes and visits him in jail.

THERAPIST: Right.

MIKE: The guy is going away for life, but the pope went to forgive him.

THERAPIST: That's a tough example to follow.

MIKE: That wouldn't be hard for me.

THERAPIST: That's what I imagine. That's the way you're saying you are about your sobriety then. That to boast that you were doing it for yourself, that would be boasting.

MIKE: Right, and that to me is not me.

THERAPIST: That's not you.

MIKE: No.

The therapist can now partially understand some of the impasse perceived with this client. The twelve-step model preaches that sobriety must be done for the individual, not for others. This of course was tantamount to sacrilege from Mike's point of view.

MIKE: Another thing is that I wake up the next morning from a drunk, like, I can't pray the rosary when I'm drunk. So the spiritual part of me is, like, tossed out the door.

THERAPIST: And the spiritual piece is a big important piece.

MIKE: Yes, the most important part. I think this is going to help me with Marty because these are things that I never talk about with her. She doesn't like know about my religious beliefs. How deep they go. And here you're like a perfect stranger, and I'm talking about it.

Sometimes our training just plain gets in the way of enlisting the client's theories about change (see Duncan et al., 1997). Everyone always told Mike that he needed to stay sober for himself—he couldn't do it for anybody else. Unfortunately, such a perspective, sound as it may seem, couldn't have been further from Mike's religious convictions. Counselors are often reluctant to discuss religious beliefs with persons, like Mike, who are diagnosed "schizophrenic" for fear of where the discussion might go. These prescriptive ideas often do not leave space for the client's theories to emerge and evolve into plans of action. We encouraged Mike to discuss his views of staying sober, and he unfolded a different map of the road to recovery. His profound faith in God and sincere conviction of humility and selflessness, rather than being an obstacle, provided a viable path to continued sobriety.

Sometimes it is helpful to fill in the three-legged stool metaphor to understand the client's theory. Figure 3.2 provides a look at Mike's perspective put into the framework of the alliance and theory of change.

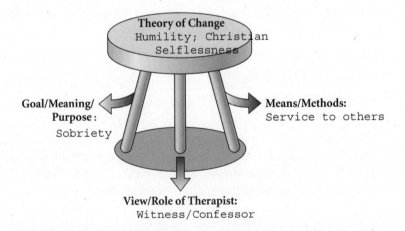

Figure 3.2. The Therapeutic Alliance: Mike.

EVOLUTION AND THE DANGERS
OF APPLYING THE COMMON FACTORS

It is a lot better when you ask the person what they want to do . . . because you just don't get any joy out of it when someone tells you what to do.

—*Molly, ten-year-old heroic client*

In each of the client examples presented in this chapter, we demonstrated the application of the common factors; the therapist recruited client heroism, proactively served the alliance master, and followed the client's sensibilities about change. But a caveat is in order. Just as our thinking evolved from an allegiance to a preferred model to a common factors perspective, we are now thinking about the application of the common factors in a different way. As we have discussed, the data indicated that the client and therapeutic alliance accounted for the majority of the variance in treatment outcome. Such data made a strong empirical case for putting the client in the driver's seat of therapy. Successful treatment, we argued, was a matter of tapping into client resources and ensuring a positive experience of the alliance. To these two elements, a third aspect was added: namely, the client's theory of change (Duncan et al., 1997; Duncan & Miller, 2000; Duncan et al., 1992). Adopting the *client's* frame of reference as the defining theory for the therapy fit with several major findings from the extant, process-outcome literature. What better way to enlist clients' partnership than by accommodating their preexisting beliefs about the problem and the change process?

Yes, at first blush, tapping into client resources, ensuring the client's positive experience of the alliance, and accommodating therapy to the client's theory of change capitalizes on the two largest contributors to success. At the same time, there is a danger—no matter how abstractly the ideas might be presented, whether defined as principles rather than mandates, closer examination made clear that any concrete application across clients merely leads to the creation of another model for how to do therapy. On this point, the research is clear; whether client-directed or not, models ultimately matter little in terms of outcome.

There is also a danger that such efforts to define principles based on the common factors, albeit unintentionally, has subtly but surely continued to privilege the therapist's role and perspective. As had been true throughout much of the history of psychotherapy, the therapist was still "in charge"—in this case, finding client strengths, determining the status of the alliance, understanding the nature of the client's theory, and choosing which, if any methods, might be congruent with that theory. To remedy the mere creation of yet another model and the continued privilege of the therapist's point of view, and to give clients the voice in treatment that the research literature said they deserved, we began to informally monitor the alliance and outcome of our services with clients. When our research proved informal monitoring to be unreliable, we began using formal measures to track our work with clients and embarked on a course of research to see if it made any difference.

We have learned that a client-directed approach can only be implemented one client at a time based on that unique individual's perceptions of the progress and fit of therapy—the client's experience of benefit must direct therapeutic choices. We have learned that to be client directed is to be outcome informed. Chapter Four describes this turn in our thinking and demonstrates a remarkably easy way to improve effectiveness and legitimize our services to third-party payers. Becoming outcome informed assigns clients the key roles in determining the way mental health services are both delivered and funded—taking client-directed practice a giant step forward.

Becoming Outcome Informed
Practice-Based Evidence

with Lynn Johnson, Jeb Brown, and Morten Anker

> *The proof of the pudding is in the eating.*
>
> —*Cervantes,* Don Quixote

Throughout much of the 1800s and the century that followed, the railroad industry was the most successful business in America. Various companies raced to lay track from city to city and across the continent, speeding up the pace of life and making a mountain of money in the process. By the 1960s, however, this once great stalwart of American commerce was in serious decline—in truth, dying. When asked about the cause, business executives usually answered that the need was being filled in other ways (i.e., cars, trucks, airplanes, and new and expanding technologies such as the telephone). It was hard to argue with such logic. Where transportation was concerned, consumers were seeking faster, easier, more individualized alternatives.

For Harvard business professor Theodore Levitt, the conventionally held wisdom made no sense at all and, in fact, begged the question. The industry, Levitt (1975) argued, was not in trouble "because the need was filled by others . . . but because it was *not* filled by the railroads themselves" (p. 19). Why did the industry not diversify when it had the chance? Because, as it turns out, railroad executives had come to believe they were in the *train* rather than *transportation* business. Consequently, trucking and airfreight industries flourished while the old iron horse rusted away on the back lots of abandoned railroad yards.

In what has become one of the most cited articles in the business literature, Levitt (1975) shows how various industries, from the railroads to Hollywood, suffered dramatic reversals in fortune when they became "product-oriented instead of customer-oriented" (p. 19). Movie moguls, for instance, were caught totally off guard by the television industry because they wrongly thought themselves in the movie rather than entertainment business. And so famed director and studio executive Darryl F. Zanuck boldly asserted, "Television won't be able to hold onto any market it captures after the first six months. People will soon get tired of staring at a plywood box every night" (Lee, 2000). Such extraordinary lack of foresight eventually forced the closure of once powerful studios and bankrupted numerous high rollers in the trade.

Applying these ideas to the field of psychotherapy suggests that the decades-long debate between this or that model of therapy misses the point in a major way. Put bluntly, it has proceeded as though the field were in the therapy business rather than the business of change. "The illusion," according to Levitt, is "that continued growth is a matter of continued product innovation and improvement" (p. 27). For their part, however, consumers (and payers) care little about how change comes about—they simply want it. As such, the field's exclusive focus on the means of producing change (i.e., models, techniques, therapeutic process) has been and continues to be on the wrong track. Like their counterparts in the railroad and movie business, therapists are in danger of losing their customer base.

In this regard, the data indicate that consumers are already abandoning psychotherapy as a means to personal fulfillment and psychological health. Recall that mental health care benefits dropped by a startling 54 percent between 1988 and 1998—the last decade for which data is available. During that same period, visits to outpatient therapists dropped by as much as 30 percent. While it might be tempting to attribute such problems to restrictions imposed by managed care, other studies suggest something more unsettling. Last year, Americans spent $13.7 billion *out of pocket* on alternative health care—a figure that does not include memberships in health clubs, purchases of vitamins and supplements, or visits to a masseuse. Clearly, the flagging fortunes of psychotherapy are not caused by a decline in consumers' desire for meaningful change. On the contrary, as the American Psychological Association focus groups indicated in Chapter One, the field is perceived as not fulfilling that need.

According to Levitt (1975), in business, an industry that thrives *starts* with the customer's needs and works *backward*, "first concerning itself with the ... delivery of customer satisfactions. Then it moves back further to creating the things by which these satisfactions are in part achieved" (p. 27). Less time and fewer resources are spent identifying, codifying, and controlling the means of production and more effort is expended in staying in touch with customer desires. Doing otherwise, Levitt warns, risks "defining an industry, or a product, or a cluster of know-how so narrowly as to guarantee its premature senescence" (p. 20).

From this perspective, the important question is not what constitutes effective therapy practice—eclectic or empirically supported, integrated or diversified—but whether consumers experience the changes they desire *by whatever means possible.* Instead of assuming that the right process leads to favorable results, the field needs to use outcome to construct and guide therapeutic process as well as inspire innovation.

FROM PROCESS TO OUTCOME IN THERAPY

For a field as intent on identifying and codifying the methods of treatment as therapy is, abandoning process in favor of outcome may seem radical indeed. Nonetheless, an entire tradition of using outcome to inform process exists. Outcome research indicates that *the general trajectory of change in successful therapy is highly predictable,* with most change occurring earlier rather than later in the treatment process (Brown, Dreis, & Nace, 1999; Hansen & Lambert, 2003; Haas, Hill, Lambert, & Morrell, 2002; Howard, Moras, Brill, Martinovich, & Lutz, 1996; Whipple et al., 2003). In their now classic article on the dose-effect relationship, Howard, Kopte, Krause, and Orlinsky (1986) found that between 60 and 65 percent of people experienced significant symptomatic relief within one to seven visits—figures that increased to 70–75 percent after six months, and 85 percent at one year. These same findings further showed, "a course of diminishing returns with more and more effort required to achieve just noticeable differences in patient improvement" as time in treatment lengthened (Howard et al., 1986, p. 160; see Figure 4.1).

More recently, researchers have been using early improvement—specifically, the *client's* subjective experience of meaningful change in the first few visits—to predict whether a given pairing of client and therapist or treatment system will result in a successful outcome (Haas et al., 2002; Lambert et al., 2001). To illustrate, Howard, Lueger, Maling, and Martinovich (1993) not only confirmed that most change in treatment took place earlier than later, but also found that an absence of early improvement in the *client's* subjective sense of well-being significantly decreased the chances of achieving symptomatic relief and healthier life functioning by the end of treatment.

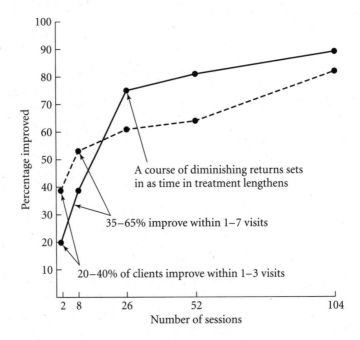

Figure 4.1. Relation of Number of Sessions of Psychotherapy and Percentage of Clients Improved.

Note: The solid line shows objective ratings at termination; the broken line shows subjective ratings during therapy.

Source: From "The Dose-Effect Relationship in Psychotherapy," by K. I. Howard, S. M. Kopte, M. S. Krause, and D. E. Orlinsky, 1986, *American Psychologist, 41*(2), 159–164. Reprinted with permission.

Similarly, in a study of more than two thousand therapists and thousands of clients, researchers Brown et al. (1999) found that therapeutic relationships in which no improvement occurred by the third visit did not on average result in improvement over the entire course of treatment. This study further showed that clients who worsened by the third visit were twice as likely to drop out than those reporting progress. Importantly, variables such as diagnosis, severity, family support, and type of therapy were "*not* . . . as important [in predicting eventual outcome] as knowing whether or not the treatment being provided [was] actually working" (p. 404, emphasis added).

In the mid-nineties, a number of researchers began using data generated *during* treatment to improve the quality and outcome of care. In 1996, Howard et al. demonstrated how measures of client progress could be used to "determine the appropriateness of the current treatment . . . [determine] the need for further treatment . . . [and] prompt a clinical consultation for patients who [were] not progressing at expected rates" (p. 1063). That same year, Lambert and Brown (1996) made a similar argument using a shorter, and hence more feasible, outcome tool. Finally, Johnson and Shaha (1996) published a quasi-experimental, clinical case study combining feedback regarding progress *and* the strength of the therapeutic alliance. Other researchers had already documented that *clients'* early ratings of the alliance, like progress, were "significant predictors of final treatment outcome" (Bachelor & Horvath, 1999, p. 139). Building on this and their own earlier work (Johnson, 1995), Johnson and Shaha (1996, 1997) were the first to document the impact of outcome and process tools on the quality and outcome of psychotherapy as well as to show how such data could foster a cooperative, accountable relationship with payers.

The conclusion to be drawn from the foregoing research is clear: feedback from clients is essential and even improves success. As for method, the diverse number of approaches encompassed in such data clearly hints that the particular brand of therapy employed is of less importance. Therapists do not need to know ahead of time what approach to use for a given diagnosis as much as whether the current relationship is a good fit and providing benefit, and, if not, need to be able to adjust and accommodate early enough to maximize the chances of success.

TRACKING OUTCOME

So teach us to number our days, that we may apply our hearts unto wisdom.

Psalms 90:12

The concern for outcome in mental health is well founded. In a study of over six thousand clients in six different outpatient settings, on average only a paltry 35 percent of clients improved or recovered (Hansen, Lambert, & Forman, 2002). Although therapy can be very helpful, that it can also be of no benefit at all comes as no great surprise. Further, we all know that no one is effective with everyone; unfortunately, until now, little has been done to find who is not benefiting so that something different could occur.

Presently, a variety of approaches exist for evaluating the outcome of psychotherapy. Most such efforts draw on well-established measures designed mainly for research purposes, both clinician- and client-rated, as well as on observer ratings, physiological indices, and environmental information (Lambert, Ogles, & Masters, 1992). Although these multidimensional assessments of outcome are valid and reliable, their methodological complexity, length of administration, and cost often render them infeasible for many service providers and settings. In truth, the average clinician in today's practice environment is overloaded with paperwork and other activities not related to service (e.g., phone calls, team meetings, treatment plans, progress notes, etc.). Clearly, this reality must be considered when becoming outcome informed. Brown et al. (1999), for example, found that the majority of clinicians did not consider practical any measure or combination of measures that took more than five minutes to complete, score, and interpret. As a result, a strong argument can be made for adopting measures that are brief in addition to being reliable and valid. It is also important to note that many of the measures presently used to assess outcome of therapy were not designed to measure change. On the contrary, most were specifically developed to assess stable personality traits or enduring patterns of problematic behavior.

The Outcome Questionnaire 45.2 (OQ) (Lambert et al., 1996) is one example of an outcome measure specifically designed to be sensitive to the changes that research suggests are likely in successful therapy. The OQ assesses three dimensions of client functioning: (1) personal or symptomatic distress (measuring depression, anxiety, alcohol and drug use, etc.), (2) interpersonal involvement (measuring how well the client is getting along in intimate relationships), and (3) social role (measuring satisfaction with work and relationships outside of the home). Two studies have now shown that the OQ is sensitive to change in those undergoing treatment while being stable in nontreated populations (Kadera, Lambert, & Andrews, 1996; Vermeersch, Lambert, & Burlingame, 2000). Such results mean that any differences in scores between administrations can be confidently attributed to the treatment given rather than to measurement error or general improvement (Lambert & Hill, 1994).

The OQ is the gold standard of outcome assessment for outpatient practice. It has ample normative data, is indisputably reliable and valid, is applicable to a broad range of clients and presenting complaints, and is relatively cheap (costing the same as a photocopy). Further, software is also available for scoring and interpretation, and at least one vendor offers a computerized version administered over the telephone.

The first two authors were familiar with the OQ, having used it in their own practices as well as in research and consultation with numerous mental health agencies and a number of third-party payers. In virtually all instances, clinicians and clients complained about the length of time needed to complete the measure (up to fifteen minutes), in addition to the size of the print and the content and relevance of the questions. In spite of the availability of computerized and telephonic versions as well as the possibility of intermittent rather than consistent use of the scale from session to session, problems with administration persisted. In busy clinics, for example, a single client showing up late could wreak havoc with the schedule. Use of the instrument in emerging telephonic and Internet-based services was deemed impossible for similar reasons. In addition, clients and counselors alike complained that the measure did not seem to fit the concerns that clients brought to therapy. It just did not have "face validity" to many who tried to use it. Therapists essentially revolted. It became apparent that in spite of the quality of the measure, the benefits of outcome management would not occur if therapists didn't use it.

The Outcome Rating Scale

Because of these experiences, and in an attempt to make an instrument that would be user friendly to both clients and therapists and would encourage the collaborative discussion of outcome with clients,

Miller and Duncan (2000a) developed the Outcome Rating Scale (ORS) as an ultrabrief, feasible alternative to the OQ. They adapted the specific items on the ORS from the three areas of client functioning assessed by the OQ: individual, relational, and social. Changes in these three areas are widely considered to be valid indicators of successful treatment outcome (Lambert et al., 1996). The ORS simply translated these three areas and an overall rating into a visual analog format of four 10-centimeter lines, with instructions to place a hash mark on each line with low estimates to the left and high to the right (see Appendix IV). The four lines add to a total score of 40. The score is simply the summation of the marks made by the client measured to the nearest centimeter on each of the four lines. A score of 25, the clinical cutoff, differentiates those who are experiencing enough distress to be in a therapy relationship from those who are not. Those scoring above 25 typically reflect scores of persons not in therapy.

Research has demonstrated the reliability and validity of ultrabrief visual analog scales in several areas including assessment and management of pain (cf., Ger, Ho, Sun, Wang, & Cleeland, 1999); perceived quality of care (cf., Arneill & Devlin, 2002); psychoeducation (cf., Dannon, Iancu, & Grunhaus, 2002); and even the assessment of change in response to medical treatments (cf., Grunhaus, Dolberg, Polak, & Dannon, 2002). In addition to their brevity and ease of administration and scoring, such scales frequently enjoy face validity with clients, something typically missing from longer and more technical measures that seem distant from the client's experience.

The ORS is brief, simple to score and interpret, and easy to administer; in fact, it takes less than a minute to administer and score. Clients can begin prior to the start of the actual session and without help from the therapist. The client and therapist can then spend the beginning of the visit jointly considering the results rather than wasting valuable time administering the instrument. Because of the ORS's simplicity, feedback from the measure is immediately available for use *at the time the service is delivered.* Any delay necessarily limits the usefulness of the results. Measurement systems that provide feedback regarding progress at the *next* scheduled session may be too late—it is virtually impossible to predict whether a client will return.

The ORS also rates at a second-grade reading level, making it feasible for most adults who seek therapy. For clients the scale is less distant from their day-to-day or lived experience so they can immediately translate it into the specifics of their circumstances. As for therapists,

Miller, Duncan, Brown, Sparks, and Claud (in press) reported that clinicians found the measure far easier to use and integrate into the workload of everyday practice than they did the OQ.

Finally, in a time when the average therapist has realized a drop in income, few will be interested in increasing their basic operating expenses. Measurement is a big industry in mental health, with the cost of instruments ranging anywhere from a few dollars to literally thousands. Some measures may be purchased outright; others require paying a fee to the developer every time the scale is used. As is true of most things, the most expensive will not necessarily be the best. Indeed, many well-established measures are available free in the public domain. The ORS is free for individual use and may be downloaded from http://www.talkingcure.com.

The Session Rating Scale: Monitoring Fit

Even though it adds more precious time to the outcome management process, we believe it is important to also partner with the client to monitor the fit of the service with the client's expectations and sensibilities about the relationship and change. The addition of an ongoing assessment of the alliance enables individual clinicians to identify and correct areas of weakness in the delivery of services before these weaknesses exert a negative effect on outcome.

Recall that clients' ratings of the therapeutic alliance were more predictive of improvement in the landmark Treatment of Depression Collaborative Research Project than were type of treatment received or severity of the presenting problem (Blatt, Zuroff, Quinlan, & Pilkonis, 1996; Krupnick et al., 1996). Also remember that researchers found a largely similar result in the Project MATCH study on the treatment of people with alcohol problems (Connors et al., 1997). Finally, recall research discussed in Chapter Three, showing that clients' ratings of the therapeutic relationship have a much higher correlation with outcome than do therapists' ratings (Bachelor & Horvath, 1999).

Recognizing that the therapeutic alliance was paramount, Lynn Johnson created the Session Rating Scale in the early 1990s to help track his own progress with clients (see Johnson, 1995). Scott Miller and Barry Duncan later implemented this first "working" alliance measure in a variety of different mental health settings. Despite the fact that the measure was only ten items, in virtually all instances, complaints regarding the length and the time needed to complete the Session Rating Scale were quick to surface among clinicians and clients (mainly clinicians). Similar difficulties were experienced implementing the twelve-item Working Alliance Inventory (WAI) (Horvath & Greenberg, 1989), making the nineteen-item Helping Alliance Questionnaire II (HAQ) (Luborsky et al., 1996) infeasible as well (Duncan et al., in press). Consequently, the Session Rating Scale version 3.0 (hereafter just SRS) was developed (Johnson, Miller, & Duncan, 2000) to be a briefer alternative, especially compared to longer research-based alliance measures, to address the complaints of clinicians and to encourage routine conversation with clients about the alliance.

Also a visual analogue scale, the SRS contains four items. First, a relationship scale rates the session on a continuum from "I did not feel heard, understood, and respected" to "I felt heard, understood, and respected" (one leg of the alliance stool). Second is a goals and topics scale that rates the session on a continuum from "We did not work on or talk about what I wanted to work on or talk about" to "We worked on or talked about what I wanted to work on or talk about" (another leg of the stool). Third is an approach or method scale (not only one leg of the alliance but also an indication of a match with the client's theory of change) requiring the client to rate the session on a continuum from "The therapist's approach is not a good fit for me" to "The therapist's approach is a good fit for me." Finally, the fourth scale looks at how the client perceives the session in total along the continuum: "There was something missing in the session today" to "Overall, today's session was right for me."

The first three SRS items were adapted from Bordin's (1979) classic definition of the alliance, with a focus on the client's theory of change suggested by Gaston (1990). The fourth item reflects guidance received from a factor analysis of the major alliance scales in use (i.e., the HAQ, the WAI, and the California Psychotherapy Alliance Scales [Gaston, 1990]). Hatcher and Barends (1996) revealed that in addition to the general factor most measured by all alliance scales (i.e., strength of the alliance), two other factors were predictive: *confident collaboration* and *the expression of negative feelings*. Confident collaboration speaks to the level of confidence that the client has that therapy and the therapist will be helpful. Although overlapping with question three on the SRS (the fit of the therapist's approach), the fourth scale of the SRS directly addresses this factor, and measures the client's confidence in the session.

The other factor predictive beyond the general strength of the alliance is the client's freedom to voice negative feelings and reactions to the therapist. This factor suggests that clients who express even low levels of disagreement with their therapists report better progress (Hatcher & Barends, 1996). The entire SRS is based on encouraging clients to identify alliance problems, to elicit client disagreements about the therapeutic process so that the clinician may change the process to better fit client expectations.

The SRS simply translated these theoretical ideas into four visual analog scales, with instructions to place a hash mark on a line with negative responses depicted on the left and positive responses indicated on the right. Research had long identified these factors as important, but until Johnson's pioneering work, no clinical measure proactively provided alliance feedback to the therapist in real time so that problems could be addressed.

In addition to assessing factors that research has linked to positive outcomes, the SRS is highly feasible. Like the ORS, the instrument takes less than a minute to administer and score. Furthermore, the content of the items makes sense to both clients and therapists, giving the scale good face validity. The SRS is scored similarly to the ORS, by adding the total of the client's marks on the 10-centimeter lines.

Using the ORS and SRS in concert represents the only feasible measurement system available that tracks both outcome *and* process, thereby taking advantage of the two known predictors of outcome. This outcome management process is also the only one that partners with clients to jointly address the effectiveness, fit, and accountability of services. The therapist uses the measures in collaboration with clients to amplify their voices, their say-so, during the helping process, finally inviting clients into the inner circle of therapy. For that reason, these client-based measures represent a radical departure from mental health business as usual, having the capability of changing how services are delivered, administered, and funded.

Reliability, Validity, and Feasibility of the ORS and SRS

To be considered reliable, any differences between two administrations of the same instrument must be attributable to changes in the variable being measured (McCall, 1980). A thermometer, for example, that gives different readings under similar circumstances is not a trustworthy or *reliable* measure of the temperature. Similarly, scores that vary in spite of little or no difference in the treatment or client are not reliable measures of therapeutic process or clinical outcome. In turn, any decisions based on such measures (e.g., whether therapy is effective or not or whether the service contains the qualities of effective work, etc.) would not be trustworthy.

There are a variety of ways for documenting the reliability of assessment tools. In general, these include reports of the correlation or degree of correspondence between repeated administrations of the same instrument, alternate forms of the instrument, or the individual items on the scale (Anastasi, 1982). For example, in one study of the ORS, a statistical estimate of the degree of correlation between the four items on the scale (known as coefficient alpha) ranged between .87 and .96, comparing favorably to the .93 reported for the OQ (Miller, Duncan, Brown, Sparks, & Claud, in press). Similarly, available research indicates high estimates of reliability for the SRS (.88) (Duncan et al., in press).

The validity of the ORS is established in several ways. The first way is by assessing concurrent validity, or the degree to which it correlates with established instruments that measure approximately the same thing, the OQ for example. The overall correlation between the ORS and OQ total scores is .59, a moderate indication of concurrent validity. Though the ORS is modeled on the OQ, it is not reasonable to expect very high coefficients of correlation between the two measures given the much shorter nature of the ORS. Nonetheless, the correlation is respectable and provides evidence that the ORS is an ultrabrief alternative for assessing global subjective distress similar to that measured by the full-scale score on the OQ.

Similarly, the overall correlation between the SRS and another longer (nineteen items) and more established alliance scale, the HAQ (Luborsky et al., 1996), is .48; again, this is a moderate indication of concurrent validity (Duncan et al., in press). While one can never reduce items by that much (from the forty-five-item OQ to the four-item ORS and from the nineteen-item HAQ to the four-item SRS) and not lose some of the richness of the original, the ORS and SRS more than accomplished our main goal—to give reliable and valid measures that mental health professionals could use in real settings on a client-by-client basis. These simple measures allow everyone to know, and to react to, the client's view of whether the services are helping the client and fitting client expectations.

Another way to assess validity is to determine if the ORS is sensitive to change, as it purports to be. This would constitute construct validity. The ORS, if valid, would reflect change following psychotherapy but would remain stable in an untreated or nonclinical population (Lambert & Bergin, 1994). Therefore, we would expect that ORS scores in clinical samples would increase while those in the nonclinical samples would vary only minimally. And indeed this was the case in our recent study: the ORS was sensitive to change in those receiving psychotherapy and relatively stable for those not receiving therapy (Miller, Duncan, Brown, Sparks, & Claud, in press).

Comparing scores for clinical and nonclinical groups can also be used to provide evidence of construct validity. Were the ORS able to accurately discriminate between the two samples, initial scores would be expected to be significantly lower (showing more distress) for the clinical group. This indeed was the case. Furthermore, in the two clinical samples used in the ORS study (Miller, Duncan, Brown, Sparks, & Claud, in press), the average score at intake was similar (19), indicating that the ORS provides a stable measure of the average level of distress that people experience at therapy entrance. Further, a Norwegian sample of over four hundred persons entering therapy for relationship difficulties noted a similar average intake score, suggesting a cross-cultural parallel of the level of distress for which people typically seek services (Anker & Duncan, 2003).

Regarding the SRS, one way to establish construct validity is by examining the correlation between the SRS and outcome. Research has established a robust relationship between early ratings of the alliance and treatment outcome. If the SRS demonstrated a relationship to outcome similar to other established alliance measures, it would be an indication of construct validity. Duncan et al. (in press) randomly selected one hundred clients at a community mental health center and took the client's ratings on the SRS in the second session and correlated those scores with outcome as measured by the ORS. The analysis revealed a correlation of .29, indicating that the SRS functions in much the same way as other alliance measures.

Finally, let's look at feasibility, an equally important consideration in any outcome-monitoring endeavor. Feasibility of an outcome instrument involves the likelihood that the instrument will in fact be used; feasibility is the degree to which an instrument can be explained, completed, and interpreted quickly and easily. If outcome measures do not meet the time demands of actual clinical practice, staff and clients alike may meet them with resistance. In addition, measures that are difficult to score or appear irrelevant to clients and therapists are less likely to be used. The ORS study (Miller, Duncan, Brown, Sparks, & Claud, in press) examined utilization rates over time in two clinical sites with similar clients and mandates to assess the feasibility of the ORS as compared to the OQ. The overall utilization rate after one year was 25 percent for the OQ and 89 percent for the ORS. Similarly, the SRS study (Duncan et al., in press) examined compliance rates among therapists at similar agencies; one agency implemented the SRS and the other used the twelve-item WAI. After one year, the SRS enjoyed a 96 percent utilization rate while the WAI was used only 29 percent of the time. Gains in feasibility offset losses in reliability and validity when switching to shorter measures such as the ORS and SRS.

Measures that are easy to integrate into treatment and have face validity encourage a partnership between the client and therapist for monitoring the effectiveness of services. Accountability becomes a joint endeavor, integral to alliance building, rather than simply more paperwork. Obviously, no matter how reliable and valid a measure is, if it is not used, the benefits of outcome management will not be realized.

The ORS and SRS in Action

The SRS and ORS have been employed in a number of clinical settings with positive effect. As noted, given the brief, clinician- and client-friendly nature of the scales, the number of complaints regarding the use of the tools has plummeted and compliance rates have soared. Providing feedback to therapists regarding clients' experience of the alliance and progress in treatment via the SRS and ORS has also been shown to result in significant improvements in both client retention and outcome. For example, Miller et al. (in press) found that clients of therapists who opted out of completing the SRS were twice as likely to drop out of treatment and three to four times more likely to have a negative or null outcome. In the same study, the average effect size of services at the agency where both measures were employed shifted from .5 to .8—a 60 percent increase. A detailed analysis of the twelve thousand cases included in the sample showed that this improvement was due to a combination of decreasing negative outcomes, increasing positive outcomes, and an overall positive shift in the outcome for therapists working at the clinic.

As incredible as the results may appear at first glance, they are entirely consistent with findings from other researchers. For example, in a meta-analysis of three studies, Lambert et al. (2003) reported that those therapeutic relationships at risk for a negative or null outcome which received formal feedback were, at the conclusion of therapy, better off than 65 percent of those without the benefit of information regarding treatment progress (Average ES $= .39$, $p < .05$). In another study, Whipple et al. (2003) found that clients whose therapists had access to outcome *and* alliance information were less likely to deteriorate, more likely to stay longer, and *twice as likely* to achieve a clinically significant change.

Notably, the results of our own research as well as that of Lambert and colleagues were obtained without any attempt to organize, systematize, or otherwise control treatment process. Neither were the therapists in these studies trained in any new therapeutic modalities, treatment techniques, or diagnostic procedures. Rather the individual clinicians were completely free to engage their individual clients in the manner they saw fit. Availability of formal client feedback provided the only constant in an otherwise diverse and chaotic treatment environment.

Client feedback on the ORS about the success or failure of the first few visits can provide valuable information about the match between client, therapist, and approach. In particular, such feedback informs key decisions about how to tailor therapy to the specific needs and characteristics of individual clients and when to terminate or refer to another therapist or venue of service when the client is not receiving benefit. Regarding the alliance, because research indicates that clients frequently drop out of treatment *before* discussing problems in the alliance, the SRS provides the opportunity to open discussion and remedy whatever problems exist.

Importantly, the twin findings that (1) change happens earlier rather than later in successful therapy; and (2) there is a course of diminishing returns as time in therapy lengthens should *not* be construed as an indictment of therapies that extend beyond a handful of sessions. On the contrary, as Figure 4.1 shows, the data provide a compelling case for continuing *as long as progress is being made and the client is interested.* In other words, while the amount of change decreases over time, clients nonetheless do benefit from continued contact. At the same time, however, the findings make clear that therapies in which little or no change (or a worsening of symptoms) occurs *early* in the process are at significant risk for a null or even negative outcome (Brown et al., 1999).

Another area where the outcome-informed approach can exert influence on therapeutic process is in the scheduling and duration of treatment. Clients may be scheduled on a more regular basis in the beginning of therapy when the slope of change is steep and then with tapering contact as the pace of change lessens. Other outcome data strongly suggest that every effort be made to minimize the amount of time between scheduling and the first appointment. Howard et al. (1986) and others (Lawson, 1994; Weiner-Davis, de Shazer, & Gingerich, 1987) have documented the significant percentage of clients that improve prior to the formal initiation of treatment (15, 60, and 66 percent, respectively). The longer the interim, the greater the likelihood that the expected outcome will have reached a point of diminishing returns thereby decreasing client motivation for attending treatment. Since available evidence indicates that therapy increases both the magnitude and durability of such pretreatment change, client dropout while waiting for services—in spite of any measured improvement in functioning—can only be viewed as a missed opportunity (Lambert & Ogles, 2004).

Outcome feedback can also inform decisions regarding treatment intensity (e.g., outpatient versus inpatient, treatment versus education or supportive care). For example, Brown et al. (1999) and Miller et al. (in press) found that as many as one-third of clients entering therapy started with a score on the outcome tool that exceeded the clinical cutoff. Such clients, it turns out, are at significant risk for worsening rather than improving over the course of treatment. Encouraging therapists to adopt a strengths-based or problem-solving approach in lieu of depth-oriented or other intensive treatment strategies can serve to maximize engagement while minimizing the risk of client deterioration. Similarly, when a mandated or involuntary client scores above the clinical cutoff, the client's view of the referral source's rating of him or her on the ORS can be used to guide decisions regarding scheduling and intensity of treatment. In such cases, the client and therapist would be working together to resolve the problem that the referent has with the client.

The benefits described here, when taken in combination with the field's obvious failure to discover and systematize therapeutic process in a manner that reliably improves success, have led us to conclude that the best hope for the field will be found in outcome.

PARTNERING WITH CLIENTS: THE NUTS AND BOLTS

. . . frothy eloquence neither convinces nor satisfies me . . . you've got to show me.

—*Willard Duncan Vandiver,*
Speech at a Naval Banquet in Philadelphia

Partnering with clients to monitor outcome and fit actually starts before clients begin formal therapy, for both therapists and clients. Counselors have to be on board with two things: first, they have to think that privileging the client's perceptions, ideas, and experiences is a good thing. If the mental health professional does not value the client's perspective first and foremost and believe that the client should direct the therapy and be an active participant in the decisions that affect them, then the proposed outcome process will have no impact. Second, the therapist must want to be accountable to the client most of all but also to the system that pays for the services. Part and parcel of this idea is that services are precious commodities and should be used wisely to ensure that all who want services will have access to them. Continuing to see clients in the absence of benefit is a tremendous waste of resources.

Clients also need to be on board. This means informing the client about the nature of the partnership when scheduling the first appointment and creating a feedback culture in which the therapist considers the client's voice essential and proactively invites client input. For example, in a client-directed, outcome-informed practice, the counselor could say:

> Let me tell you how we like to work. As therapists, we are dedicated to helping our clients achieve the outcome they desire. We also believe that you have a right to know sooner rather than later whether or not we are likely to be helpful to you. For these reasons we have found it important to monitor our progress from session to session using two very short paper-and-pencil forms. Your ongoing feedback will tell us if we are on track, need to change something about our approach, or need to refer you elsewhere to help you get what you want. Is that something you think you can help me with?

As the statement indicates, results from the measurement process are continuously fed back into therapy (Duncan, Sparks, & Miller, 2000;

Miller & Duncan, 2000b). In a typical outpatient setting, the therapist would give the client the ORS *prior* to each session and the SRS toward the end. With regard to the ORS, it is useful to ask clients to start their appointment five minutes *prior* to meeting with the therapist; they may simply find the ORS at a reception desk or on a clipboard for them to complete. Many clients will complete the ORS (some will even plot their scores on provided graphs) and walk into the therapist's office already discussing the implications. Using a scale that is simple enough for clients (and therapists) to score and interpret not only speeds the process but also increases client engagement in the evaluation of the services they receive. Anything that increases participation in therapy is likely to have a beneficial impact on outcome.

All scoring and interpretation of the measures are done together *with* clients. This not only represents a radical departure from the traditional use of assessment instruments but also gives clients a new way to look at and comment on their experience of both progress and the therapy itself. Assessment, rather than an expert-driven evaluation of the client, becomes a pivotal part of the therapeutic relationship and change itself (Duncan et al., 2000).

Administering the measures at each meeting is important for two reasons. First, as noted earlier, it is difficult if not impossible to anticipate when clients will stop coming for therapy. If the plan is to assess at the beginning and the end or at various intervals (e.g., first, third, fifth session; cf., Brown et al., 1999), there is a substantial risk that a large number of clients will terminate prior to being given the final measures. As a result, no outcome information will be available for a sizable group of clients—a fact that could seriously hamper any later attempts to make sense of the overall results.

STEP 1: INTRODUCING THE ORS IN THE FIRST MEETING. Recall that establishing a feedback culture in which the client's voice is privileged has already begun in the first contact with the client. In the first meeting, that culture is continued. It is important to avoid technical jargon and instead explain the purpose of the measures and their rationale in a natural, commonsense way. The overwhelming majority of clients think monitoring whether therapy is working makes sense. The idea here is to make the monitoring part of a relaxed and ordinary way of having conversations and working with clients. The specific words are not important. The therapist's interest in the client's desired outcome speaks volumes about the therapist's commitment to the individual and the quality of service he or she receives (Duncan & Sparks, 2002).

Remember our phone conversation? During the course of our work together, I will be giving you two very short forms asking you how you think things are going and whether you think things are on track. We believe that to make the most of our time together and get the best outcome, it is important to make sure we are on the same page with one another about how you are doing, how we are doing, and where we are going. We will be using your answers to keep us on track. Will that be OK with you?

Here is that form our intake person mentioned to you. Let me just take a moment to provide you with a little more information about it. The ORS is an outcome measure that allows me to track where you're at, how you're doing, how things are changing, or if they are not. It allows us to determine whether I am being helpful. I use this because I want to ensure that I am providing you with the best services possible. It only takes a minute to fill out, and most clients find it to be very helpful. Would you like to give it a try? Great!

STEP 2: INCORPORATING THE ORS IN THE FIRST MEETING. The ORS pinpoints where the client is and allows a comparison point for later sessions. It involves the client in a collaborative effort to observe progress in a number of life domains. Incorporating the ORS entails simply bringing the client's initial and subsequent results into the conversation for discussion, clarification, and problem solving.

From your ORS it looks like you're experiencing some real problems. [Or] From your score, it looks like you're feeling OK. What brings you here today? [Or] Your total score is 15—wow, that's pretty low. A score of 24 or lower indicates people who are in enough distress to seek help. Things must be pretty tough for you. What's going on?

The way this ORS works is that marks toward the left (or scores under 24) indicate that things are hard for you now or you are hurting enough to bring you to therapy. Your score on the individual scale indicates that you are really having a hard time. Would you like to tell me about it? [Or if all the marks are to the right] Generally when most people make their marks so far to the right (or when people score above 25), it is an indication that things are going well for them. It would be really helpful for me to get an understanding of what it is that brought you to therapy now.

Clients often start the conversation by making a comment on their lowest mark on the ORS. Because the ORS has immediate face validity, clients regularly remark about their score on the different scales in relation to the reason they are seeking therapy. In other situations the therapist must initiate the connection between the client's descriptions of the reasons for therapy and the client's scores on the ORS. The ORS makes no sense as either an outcome tool or therapy helper unless the therapist connects it to the described experience of the client's life. It is not an X ray of the client's experience. This is a critical point because both the therapist and the client must know what the mark on the line represents to the client and what will need to happen so that the client will both realize a change *and* indicate that change on the ORS. The line on the ORS is irrelevant until and unless the client bestows meaning on it. Connecting the ORS to the client's experience is also quite easy to do and takes less than a minute to integrate into the conversation.

At some point in the meeting, the therapist needs only to pick up on the client's comments and connect them to the ORS:

> Oh, OK, it sounds like dealing with the loss of your brother (or relationship with your husband, daughter's drinking, or anxiety attacks, etc.), is an important part of what we are doing here. Does the distress from that situation account for your mark here on the individual (or other) scale on the ORS? OK, so what do you think will need to happen for that mark to move toward the right?

The ORS, by design, is a general outcome instrument and provides no specific content to direct the client's or therapist's impressions. The ORS offers only a bare skeleton to which clients must add the flesh and blood of their experiences, into which they breathe life with their ideas and perceptions. They imbue the ORS with meaning that provides a rich source of understanding of the clients' idiosyncratic experiences of their world. At the moment in which the client connects the mark on the ORS with the situation that is distressing, the ORS becomes a meaningful measure of the client's progress.

STEP 3: INTRODUCING THE SRS. The SRS, like the ORS, is best presented in a relaxed way that is seamlessly integrated into the therapist's typical way of working. The use of the SRS continues the culture of client privilege and feedback, and it further amplifies or at least opens space for the client's voice about the alliance. The SRS can be given during a break in the session (usually around forty to forty-five minutes into the meeting) or at the very end of the meeting, leaving enough time for discussing the client's responses.

During the session, we will take a short break in which I will give you the other form on which you give your opinion of our work together and say whether I am meeting your expectations. It's kind of like taking the temperature of our relationship today. Are we too hot or too cold? This information helps me stay on track. The ultimate purpose of using these forms is to make every possible effort to make coming to therapy a beneficial experience for you. Would that be OK with you?

Before we wrap up tonight, I would like to ask you to fill out that other short form. This one deals directly with how I am doing. It is very important to me that I am meeting your needs. A lot of research has shown that how well we work together directly relates to how well things go. If you could take a moment to fill it out, I will discuss it with you before you leave.

STEP 4: INCORPORATING THE SRS. The SRS is incorporated at the end of the session during the final message or summary process. Because the SRS is easy to score and interpret, the therapist can do a quick visual check and integrate it into the conversation. If the SRS looks good (score above 36), the therapist need only comment on that fact and invite any other comments or suggestions. If the client has marked any scales lower than 9 centimeters, this is a good indication that the counselor should follow up. Clients tend to score all alliance measures highly, so the therapist should address any suggestion of a problem. Anything less than a total score of 37 might signal a concern, and therefore it is prudent to invite the client to comment. Sometimes clients say that not enough time has passed for them to know or that the score is the best they can give. All answers are OK and extend the open invitation to the client to continue the feedback process. Thanking the client for this feedback and soliciting continued honesty keeps the avenues of communication open. The therapist's appreciation of any negative feedback is a powerful alliance builder. In fact, alliances that start off negatively but result in therapist flexibility to client input tend to be very predictive of a positive outcome. The SRS allows the opportunity to fix any alliance problems that are developing and shows clients that the counselor does more than give lip service to honoring the client's perspectives.

> Let me just take a second here to look at this SRS—it's kind of like a thermometer that takes the temperature of our meeting here today. Wow, great, it looks good, looks like we are on the same page, that we are talking about what you think is important and you believe today's meeting was right for you.
> Let me quickly look at this other form here that lets me know how you think we are doing. OK, seems like I am missing the boat here. Thanks very much for your honesty and giving me a chance to address what I can do differently. Was there something else I should have asked you about or should have done to make this meeting work better for you? What was missing here?

Graceful acceptance of any problems and a willingness to be flexible and nondefensive speak reams to the client and usually turn things around. Recall that clients rarely bring up problems and have traditionally let therapists know that the alliance is shaky by either not returning for sessions or by not participating in therapy. The SRS provides a way to talk about and address alliance difficulties, thereby keeping clients engaged in therapy.

STEP 5: CHECKING FOR CHANGE IN SUBSEQUENT MEETINGS. With the feedback culture set in the first session, the business of being outcome informed can begin, with the client's view of progress and fit really influencing what happens in therapy. Each subsequent session compares the current session's ORS with the previous one and looks for any changes. The counselor discusses with the client whether there is an improvement (a move to the right on any scale or an increase in score), a slide (a move to the left or a decrease in score), or no change of any kind. The scores are used to engage the client in a discussion about progress, and more important, what should be done differently if there isn't any.

> Wow, your marks on the personal well-being and overall lines really moved—about 4 centimeters to the right each! Your total increased by 8 points to 29 points. That's quite a jump! What happened? How did you pull that off? . . . This kind of change is called a reliable change

and may mean that it's time for us to reevaluate. Where do you think we should go from here?

If a change has occurred, the therapist should implement all the ways to validate the progress and encourage the client to take responsibility for a new chapter in his or her life (see Chapter Three). If no change has occurred, the scores also invite a discussion, perhaps an even more important one.

OK, so things haven't changed since the last time we talked. How do you make sense of that? Should we be doing something different here, or should we continue on course steady as we go? If we are going to stay on the same track, how long should we go before getting worried? When will we know when to say "when"?

Again, the idea is to involve the client in the process of monitoring progress and the decision about what to do next. The ORS/SRS feedback process is repeated in all sessions, but later sessions gain increasing significance and warrant additional action. The precise number of encounters that trigger extra attention or increased discussion are totally dependent on the specific setting in which the service is conducted.

We call these later session interactions with clients either checkpoint conversations or last-chance discussions depending on the urgency reflected by the data from a particular agency or practice. For example, in typical outpatient settings, checkpoint conversations are usually conducted by the third session and last-chance discussions are initiated in the sixth meeting. This is simply saying that by the third session, clients who receive benefit from the services of a given agency are showing that benefit on the ORS, and if change is not noted by session six, then the client is at a significant risk for a null or negative outcome, based on the trajectories of change for the average client in that particular setting. Different settings will have different checkpoints and last-chance numbers. In one large employee assistance program, for example, clients who have not shown some benefit by the second session are at risk, because for that setting the average client who benefits from services reflects a change by the second session. In that setting, the last-chance session is the third session.

Other settings—residential, inpatient, or ones that have longer-term relationships with clients—will have other checkpoint and last-chance numbers. In these settings, instead of the number of sessions, the checkpoint and last-chance indicators will likely be units of time. The important point is for each specific setting to choose two points during the course of therapy, case management, or residential treatment at which to evaluate whether a client needs a change of venue based on the desired outcome expected by the service and the trajectory of typical successful clients in the agency. We will discuss later a simple method of determining the checkpoint and last-chance sessions for your practice or agency.

Here are simple rules of thumb for checkpoint conversations and last-chance discussions. Remember that the main idea is to invite clients into a meaningful exchange about the options that exist to help them meet their goals. If significant change has not occurred by the checkpoint conversation session, the therapist responds by going through the SRS item by item. Alliance problems are a significant contributor to a lack of progress. Sometimes it is useful to say something such as "It doesn't seem like we are getting anywhere. Let me go over the items on this SRS to make sure you are getting exactly what you are looking for from me and our time together." Going through the SRS and eliciting client responses in detail can help the therapist and client get a better sense of what may or may not be working.

Next, a lack of progress at this stage is a clear indication that the therapist needs to try something different, because the client has not reported change in a fashion that is usual for the therapist or the setting. This can take as many forms as there are clients. The therapist involves the client in brainstorming options: bringing in different people, a team, a cotherapist, a different approach; referring to another counselor, religious adviser, or self-help group—whatever seems to be of value to the client. Any ideas that surface are then implemented, and progress is continually monitored via the ORS and the client's outcome preferences.

If the therapist and client have brainstormed and implemented different possibilities and the client has still experienced no change, it is time for the last-chance discussion. As the name implies, there is some urgency for something different because the average successful client at a given practice has already achieved change by this point, and the current client is at significant risk for a negative conclusion of therapy. Remember that the purpose of the comparison between this client and the average client who has a successful outcome is to encourage an open exchange and enable new options for addressing the client's goals. A metaphor we like is that of the therapist and client driving into a vast desert and running on empty, when a sign appears on the road that says "last chance for gas." The metaphor depicts the necessity of stopping and discussing the implications of continuing a therapy without the client reaching a desired change.

This is the time when a referral should be considered and frankly discussed. If the therapist has created a feedback culture from the beginning, then this conversation will not be a surprise to the client. Client response to an open discussion about lack of progress is varied. Some terminate prior to identifying an alternative; others ask for or accept a referral to another therapist or setting. Rarely do clients want to continue in a relationship in which they are not benefiting. If the client chooses, the therapist may continue in a supportive fashion until other arrangements can be made. Rarely, however, is there justification for continuing to work with clients who have not achieved change in a period typical for the majority of cases seen by a particular therapist or agency. Rarely, though, is not never.

It is particularly important to consider a referral because by keeping clients in ineffective therapy, therapists may actually become obstacles to clients making the changes they desire. Research shows that there is no correlation between a therapy with poor outcome and the likelihood of success in the next therapy. Becoming outcome informed helps therapists get out of the way and not be impediments to the client's efforts to change.

Therapists cannot be effective with everyone, and other relational fits may work out better for the client. Although some clients may want to continue therapy with the same provider in the absence of change, far more do not want to continue ineffective therapy when given a graceful way to exit. The ORS allows therapists to ask themselves the hard questions when clients are not, by their own ratings, seeing benefit from services, thereby bringing the client into the loop about such decisions. Outcome management does not help therapists with the clients they are already effective with; rather, it helps with those who are not benefiting by enabling an open discussion of other options and, in the absence of change, the ability to honorably end therapy and move the client on to a more productive relationship.

Children, adolescents, couples, and families offer additional challenges and opportunities to the outcome management process. Children have typically been excluded, and most systems ask only parents or significant others to evaluate the child's well-being. We think this is a mistake, so in addition to having parents rate the child on the ORS, we have also developed experimental measures (see Appendix IV) that allow children to comment on their progress as well as give their opinion about the therapy itself. Although the children's forms have not yet been validated (a study is in progress), at the very least, the measures serve to engage children and convey the importance of their perspective as well.

With adolescents, couples, and families, the measures encourage conversations about similarities and differences of individual ratings; and they allow therapists to attend to each person's perspective of both change and the alliance. The ORS and SRS provide a common ground on which to make comparisons and draw distinctions, allowing each individual to be part of the discussion of what needs to happen next.

Couples frequently come in with very different ratings on their ORSs. When the therapist inquires about this, a lively discussion generally ensues about who in the couple is more interested in having things change, where each feels the problem lies, and what each believes needs to happen for the relationship to improve—their respective theories of change. Clarifying these points, with the help of the ORS, enables counselors to search for common themes and goals. It is not unusual for a couple's ORS scores to reflect a familiar scenario—one person's perception of improvement, as scored on the ORS, is met with a worsening of the other partner's score (using a graph with different-colored lines for each person helps illustrate this kind of pattern). This can open up a productive conversation about the costs and benefits of change to both, and whether and how they want to proceed.

The same process can graphically illustrate not only the different levels of distress and change but also the varied perceptions of multiple family members. The SRS gives therapists a chance to see which, if any, family members are feeling the least connected to the process. The therapist then has accurate knowledge of where to focus more attention. Using the ORS and SRS with couples and families is an invaluable way to keep track of many change trajectories and many agendas—all it takes is a willingness on the therapist's part to become adept at quick and seamless data gathering for sometimes as many as five or six people in session and the ability to make that information meaningful by using it as a springboard for conversation. The reward is the same, whether for a couple, a family, or an individual: reliable feedback about whether things are changing and about the strength of the alliance, so counseling can better fit client preferences for the best outcome.

Making the Numbers Count

Figuring out the current or potential benefit of a particular service for a specific client can be challenging. Some general guidance may be taken from the literature reviewed earlier in this chapter. Recall that this data indicates the following: (1) the majority of clients (60 to 65 percent) experience symptomatic relief within one to seven visits; (2) clients reporting little or no change early, on average, show no improvement over the entire course of therapy; and, finally, (3) clients who deteriorate early on are at significant risk for dropping out or having a negative or null outcome.

Not all clients or therapists are alike, however. Using the same broad guidelines to evaluate the therapy at an employee assistance program *and* a local community mental health center would make little sense, for example, because the clients in the two settings likely differ in ways that would affect the nature, duration, and outcome of treatment. The same would be true for agencies or individual therapists who limit their practice to particular presenting complaints (substance abuse) or client groups (e.g., children). To develop valid guidelines for such instances, the group or solo practitioner would need to determine how change happens for clients *in their particular practice* at specific points in time.

Methods for estimating how change takes place in a particular practice run the gamut from simple, crude, and inexpensive to sophisticated, precise, and costly. With regard to the latter, several available services use proprietary measures and databases for tracking and predicting client response. A large agency or organization serving a highly diverse clientele might find the precision of such programs more appropriate to its needs. However, not all therapists or agencies have the means to engage such services. Moreover, research has not established the efficacy of such systems *over and above* simpler alternatives.

In this section, one simple and one highly sophisticated method for determining how change happens for clients in a particular context or setting will be illustrated.

Change by Session Curve

A relatively simple method for tracking the occurrence of change is based on the pioneering work of psychologist Ken Howard. Briefly, Howard et al. (1996, p. 1060) found, "a lawful linear relationship between . . . the number of sessions and the . . . probability of improvement." The outcome literature frequently refers to this finding as the *dose-effect* relationship. By creating a change-by-session curve (CBSC) that shows the relationship between the number of sessions (dose) and outcome (effect), clinicians can determine the probability of success for a specific client by a given session at any particular time in treatment.

The process begins with collecting outcome data on a representative sample of clients. Simply set a specific time period (e.g., one year) during which to gather results from all clients. Generally speaking, the larger the number, the more accurate the data will be in representing the clients that a given agency or therapist typically serves.

The next step is separating successful from unsuccessful cases, noting in particular the session at which each client met or exceeded the change in outcome scores indicative of "reliable change." For the ORS a difference of 5 points or more is evidence that the change exhibited by an individual in therapy is reliable or clinically significant (Duncan & Sparks, 2002). In other words, the measured changes are greater than any chance variation in the instrument or normal maturation of the client (Lambert & Hill, 1994).

The final step is charting the results for the successful clients on a graph with the number of sessions increasing along the bottom (x-axis) and the percentage of successful clients along the side (y-axis). Figure 4.2 gives an example of a CBSC of data collected at the Family Counseling Office in Vestfold, Norway (Anker & Duncan, 2003).

The total number of clients in this study was 422, involving thirteen therapists. Seventy-four clients were seen individually, while the rest were seen in couples therapy. Just looking at the individuals, a simple comparison of the number of successful to unsuccessful clients revealed that approximately 57 percent (42) of the 74 individual clients who began treatment at this clinic experienced clinically significant or reliable change prior to termination. Visual inspection of the graph also shows that the majority of these successful clients began change by the third session, and the overwhelming majority achieved a reliable change by the sixth meeting. So for clients in this sample, the checkpoint conversation should likely occur in the third session and

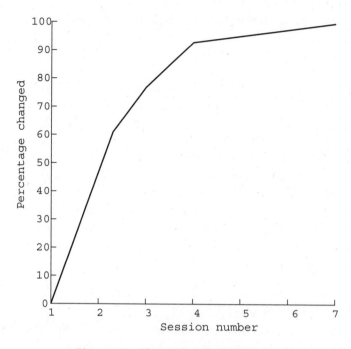

Figure 4.2. Change-by-Session Curve.
Source: From "Using the Outcome Rating Scale with Couples," by M. Anker and
B. Duncan, 2003. Used with permission.

the last-chance discussion by the sixth meeting. All of the clients in this small sample who achieved a reliable change had done so by the seventh session. This graph of the CBSC confirms Howard et al.'s (1996) observation that change in treatment is related to the number of sessions—but only up to a certain point. Beyond a certain number of sessions (five in this sample), "more and more efforts are need to produce . . . just noticeable differences" (p. 1060). The obvious advantage to this approach is that the client and therapist can quickly determine whether therapy is progressing in a manner typical for successful cases *without* having to make any statistical calculations.

Before we move on, we must note that therapists should not use the CBSC to make decisions about when *to terminate successful* psychotherapy. On the contrary the CBSC merely tells the therapist when to expect change in a given practice or agency. As noted earlier in the chapter, the research literature makes a strong empirical case for continuing to meet with clients as long as they are making measurable progress and are interested in continuing (see the Epilogue for an example of this).

Neither should the concept of reliable change discussed earlier be confused with that of recovery. Although researchers debate the particulars, most agree that recovery means a person's scores on the outcome measure are not only indicative of reliable change but also more similar to the scores of people not in treatment (Lambert & Hill, 1994). In other words, the client is no longer distinguishable from peers (Ogles, Lambert, & Masters, 1996).

Recall that the dividing line between a clinical and nonclinical population is derived statistically and is known as the clinical cutoff. As noted, on the ORS, the number is 25. For clients to be considered recovered, therefore, scores over the course of therapy would have to change 5 or more points (the reliable change index) *and* climb above a total score of 25 (Duncan & Sparks, 2002).

Simple Linear Regression (SLR)

The word *simple* occurring in the same sentence as *linear regression* may strike some as oxymoronic. And truthfully, the average clinician working in a solo practice can skip this section entirely without missing a great deal. In such instances, the CBSC will be sufficient for generating a dialogue with clients about the value of treatment. However, for those practitioners, administrators, and payers who require greater precision or need to compare the effectiveness of one clinician or treatment site to another, the CBSC method will quickly prove seriously deficient.

A significant limitation of the CBSC is the curve's reliance on the reliable change index (RCI) to identify and separate successful and unsuccessful cases. As noted earlier, a change in scores that exceeds the RCI can be considered greater than any variation in scores due to chance or the mere passage of time. In other words, and importantly, the change may be attributed to treatment. The problem is that the RCI is an average, arrived at by aggregating clients of varying levels of severity. As a result, it is likely to underestimate the amount of change necessary to be considered reliable for some (i.e., those in the severe range) while overestimating the amount for others (i.e., those in the mild range).

In real-world settings, it is not uncommon for a significant percentage of people seeking treatment to score in the mild range on outcome measures like the ORS. Indeed, in one large system of care that is using the measure, over 30 percent of clients began treatment with scores in the mild range or above the clinical cutoff (i.e., the nonclinical range). In the Norwegian sample (Anker & Duncan, 2003), 24 percent of the total clients scored above the cutoff. A therapist seeing many clients with relatively mild distress is likely to show a relatively small percentage of persons improving, according to the RCI. Indeed, a CBSC generated for such a therapist might well show as many clients getting worse as improving, with a great many remaining unchanged. To compare that therapist's results to those of another whose clients scored mostly in the more-severe range at the outset of treatment would not be only unfair but also inaccurate.

The simplest method for dealing with this problem is to disaggregate the data and compare clients with similar levels of severity. For example, ORS scores at intake could be assigned to one of four differing levels of severity (i.e., quartiles) determined by the typical range at a specific agency. The average change score could then be calculated for each of the four levels. The final step would be calculating the difference between the average and actual outcome for a given individual to determine if the outcome was better or worse than the average client in that severity range.

A more precise method is to use a simple linear regression model to predict the score at the end of therapy (or at any intermediate point) based on the score at intake. Although it is beyond our discussion here, briefly, it is possible to use the slope and an intercept to calculate a regression formula for all clients in a given sample. Once completed, the formula can be used to calculate the expected outcome for any new client based on the intake score. In addition, analyzing the difference between the predicted change and the measured change over time and across clients can be used to compare therapists and treatment settings.

Ignorance Is Not Bliss: The SRS in Action

Linda, a forty-two-year-old software company executive and mother of two, presented with complaints of depression. In the first meeting, she explained that her depression resulted from problems she was having at work. In particular, once friendly coworkers had recently turned on her, accusing her of having sex with a senior executive to gain a

promotion. Linda's initial score on the ORS was 11, which only reinforced her story of being profoundly distressed.

At the conclusion of the session, Linda completed the SRS and
made an appointment for the following week. Believing that the session had gone quite well, however, the therapist neglected to look at
the instrument prior to Linda's leaving the office. Later that day, the
therapist did look at the SRS and learned that Linda had been *dissat-
isfied* with the session. Specifically, her answers indicated that she had
expected something very different and had made a mark far to the left
on both the "approach or method" and "overall" lines.

As a result of the feedback, the therapist immediately phoned and
offered to meet Linda the following day during the lunch hour. During the conversation, Linda confirmed her dissatisfaction with the first
meeting and admitted feeling uncertain about whether she would
return for the second. Specifically, Linda had wanted the therapist to
give her more concrete suggestions for dealing with her situation—
something that the therapist had not done during the initial hour.

The phone call, she said, made all the difference. Showing up on
time for the scheduled appointment, she worked with the therapist
on specific strategies for addressing the problems at work. Linda's
scores on the SRS she took at the end of that session, totaling 38, indicated that she was much more satisfied with the visit. Over the course
of four additional meetings, her scores on the ORS gradually inclined,
reaching a recovered level of 27 by the last session.

Practice-Based Evidence: Doing What Works, Challenging What Doesn't

Barbara presented for therapy with complaints of depression, lapses
in memory, difficulty with concentration, mood swings, and low self-
esteem. Barbara's initial score of 13 on the ORS showed her to be
significantly distressed. She told the therapist that she had been vic-
timized sexually by a family member from the age of thirteen to
sixteen and expressed a strong desire to bring her "mood swings under
control" and "learn to cope better" with her history of abuse.

Using a combination of competency-oriented and cognitive-
behavioral methods, the therapist highlighted times when Barbara
coped unusually well with her memories and symptoms. Barbara's
score on the SRS at the end of the visit indicated a high degree of fit
(a total of 39). The therapist asked her "do more of what had worked"

for her previously as a homework assignment between visits. The following week Barbara returned, looking and sounding better. Her scores on the ORS confirmed the changes that continued through the third visit, with her score increasing to 18.

In spite of the positive results, Barbara expressed a strong desire to "change directions" in therapy. In particular, she wanted to remember more about the abuse she had suffered. After exploring the pros and cons of this, she and the therapist agreed to try recovering some memories. The effect was immediate and dramatic. Barbara's scores on the ORS at the fourth visit indicated that she was in even greater distress than she had been at her first: the score plummeted to a 9. Together, Barbara and the therapist discussed the appropriateness of continuing to recover memories. Eventually, Barbara decided to return to what had been working for her in the first three sessions. Her scores quickly reversed direction and improved over the next two visits, back up to a 19.

At session six, Barbara once again expressed a desire to recover memories about her abuse. After some discussion, the therapist took the client's direction and began exploring the memories with Barbara. When her ORS score again dropped the following week, however, both agreed to stop pursuing the memories and work instead on coping strategies. By the eighth and final visit, Barbara had had improved significantly and her ORS score reached 22. A routine telephone contact a year later found her living comfortably without any further complaints.

In this situation, the use of ORS promoted an open discussion of the costs and benefits of different methods and allowed the client to make an informed choice. The process was simple, strengthened the therapeutic relationship, and improved the overall process. Importantly, the example says nothing about the *absolute* value of competency-oriented, cognitive-behavioral, or recovered memory treatment approaches. Rather, it shows what worked for this client seen at a given point in time by a single therapist using one type of treatment modality versus another. Outcome data can also be useful, however, in the absence of change.

Bringing Results to Light: When Change Isn't Happening

Steven, a man in his thirties, presented for therapy with complaints of chronic depression. The son of a well-known and respected minister, Steven was a gentle and deeply spiritual person who had been in counseling a number of times with both secular and religious counselors. On at least two occasions, his relationships with therapists had lasted for several years. Although Steven believed that each of these experiences had been helpful, his continuing struggle with what he called "the darkness" left him feeling that some "underlying issue" remained unresolved from his childhood. He expressed a strong desire to "get to the root" of the matter in the present treatment. The therapist agreed and, over the course of the next few sessions, worked with Steven in a psychodynamic framework exploring various experiences from his childhood and attempting to make connections to his current problem.

Steven's ratings on the SRS scale given at the end of each visit could not have been higher. In other words, according to his answers, the therapy he was receiving matched what he determined to be the right approach for him. His scores on the ORS told a different story, however. From week to week, the measure showed that he was not only *not* improving, he was slowly getting worse. In particular, as the therapy progressed, he intimated that his lowered scores showed that he was becoming more withdrawn in his interpersonal and social relationships.

When the therapist discussed these results with Steven at the outset of each session, Steven agreed but was genuinely at a loss to explain the decline. The therapist could not explain them either. Knowing there was no empirical support for the old therapy adage that "some clients have to get worse before they get better," the therapist began actively exploring different options by the end of the fourth visit. Steven and the therapist explored several possibilities in a checkpoint conversation but settled on a team consult. Steven chose a reflecting team format (Anderson, 1987) out of three different team structures in hopes of generating possibilities (Duncan & Sparks, 2002).

In what amounted to a free-for-all of unedited speculations and suggestions, a range of alternatives was considered including: changing nothing, taking medication, attending a support group, and shifting approaches. Steven expressed the most interest in an idea bandied about near the start of the process: that his recurring struggle with "the darkness" might not be due to some yet-to-be-discovered underlying issue but rather from having learned to downplay his abilities so as not to outshine his well-known and respected parents. In the four sessions that followed, the focus shifted. Rather than rooting around in the past for something that might explain his recurring problem, Steven and the therapist worked to bring his positive characteristics to light. They actively explored the strengths and character traits he possessed that could be of use when he was tempted to give in to the depression.

The material that emerged in the visits had a distinctly religious quality. In one particularly dramatic moment, for example, Steven quoted passages from the Bible, noting that although benevolently motivated, he had spent much of his childhood "hiding his light under a bushel basket" (Matthew 5:14–17). Now that he was aware of this tendency, he vowed instead to "let his light shine before others," warding off future depressions by cloaking himself in "the armor of God." The results were dramatic. His score on the ORS reversed and began improving, ultimately leveling off above the clinical cutoff.

With Steven, the presence of the ORS data helped circumvent a negative outcome by pushing the therapist to explore alternatives early in the process. When contacted again a year after the therapy ended, Steven reported that although tempted, he had managed to avoid becoming depressed again. Another administration of the ORS corroborated his report. Of course, opening a dialogue about a lack of progress does not always result in finding a helpful alternative. Where in the past such situations would have been viewed as failures, a lack of results actually gives therapists a crucial opportunity to stop being an impediment to the client and his or her change process. Simply put, there is no reason to take it personally.

Neither does the failure of any given therapeutic relationship say anything about the client or his or her potential for change in general. For most of the history of the field, therapists have been trained to attribute a lack of progress either to the client (mainly) or the therapy offered. Common sense suggests that it is simply not possible for therapists to form successful working relationships with every person they encounter. However, client-directed, outcome-informed clinical work can be considered successful both when clients achieve change and when, in the absence of change, the therapist works with the client to get out of the way.

Failing Successfully: An Honorable Conclusion

Consider Robyn, a thirty-five-year-old self-described "agoraphobic" whose partner brought her to therapy because Robyn was too frightened to come alone. Once an outgoing and energetic person making steady progress up the career ladder, Robyn had grown progressively more anxious and fearful over the last several years. "I've always been a nervous kind of person," she indicated during her first visit, "now I can hardly get out of my house." She added that she had been to see a couple of therapists and tried several medications. "It's not like these things *haven't* helped," she further said, "it's just that it never goes away, completely. Last year, I spent a couple of days in the hospital."

In a handful of sessions, the therapist worked with Robyn alone and, on a couple of occasions, with her partner present, to develop and implement a plan for dealing with her anxiety. Although her fear was palpable during the visits, Robyn nonetheless gave the therapy the highest ratings on the SRS. Unfortunately, however, her scores on the ORS evinced little evidence of improvement. In this particular setting, 50 percent of clients experienced reliable change by the fourth visit. After four sessions, the CBSC began to flatten out. Obviously, the therapy with Robyn was at risk for a negative or null outcome.

The ORS data led the therapist and Robyn to review her responses to the SRS at the end of the fourth visit (recall the checkpoint conversation). As the example of software company executive Linda demonstrated, such reviews are not only helpful in ensuring that the therapy contains the elements necessary for a successful outcome but also for uncovering problems in the relationship that the therapist may have missed or the client left unreported. This time, however, the checkpoint conversation revealed nothing new. Indeed, Robyn indicated that her high marks matched her experience of the visits. Knowing that more of the same would lead to more of the same results, the therapist and Robyn agreed to organize a participatory team (like a reflecting team but one in which the client joins in the free-for-all) for a short brainstorming session. When the ideas that emerged in that meeting had not resulted in any measurable change by the eighth visit, however, the therapist knew it was time to get out of Robyn's way. It was time for the last-chance discussion. After all, the slope of the CBSC after session six for this particular therapist was completely flat. Translation? There was precious little chance that this relationship would result in success.

In the discussions that followed, Robyn indicated a desire for more intensive treatment. She mentioned having read about an out-of-state residential treatment center that specialized in her particular problem. When her insurance company refused to cover the cost of the treatment, Robyn and her partner put their only car up for sale to cover the expense. After being released from the program some six weeks later, Robyn called to report about the progress she had made and described her aftercare plans. She also asked for an opportunity to complete the

ORS once again! Needless to say, her scores had significantly improved. In effect, the therapist had managed to fail successfully.

OUTCOME AND THE FUTURE: IMAGINE . . .

Here, indeed, is just our problem. We must bridge this gap of poetry from science.

—*John Dewey,*
"Wandering Between Two Worlds"

Health care policy has undergone tremendous change over the last two decades. Among the differences, research and commentary have documented an increasing emphasis on outcome. The shift toward outcome is so significant that Brown et al. (1999) argued, "In the emerging environment, the *outcome* of the service *rather than the service itself* is the product that providers have to market and sell. Those unable to systematically evaluate the outcome of treatment will have nothing to sell to purchasers of health care services" (p. 393).

In this chapter we have called for a shift from process to outcome, from evidence-based practice to practice-based evidence. Support for this perspective dates back eighteen years, beginning with the pioneering work of Howard et al. (1986) and extending forward to Lambert et al. (2003), Johnson and Shaha (1996), and our own studies (Miller et al., in press). The approach we advocate is simple and straightforward, and could potentially unify the field around the common goal of change. Unlike the process-oriented efforts the field has employed thus far, outcome management results in significant improvements in effectiveness of psychotherapy services.

It is true that studies to date are somewhat limited. As Lambert et al. (2003) point out, however, "those advocating the use of empirically supported psychotherapies do so on the basis of much smaller treatment effects" (p. 296). Regardless, the evidence raises serious questions about professional specialization, training and certification, reimbursement for clinical services, research, and above all, the public welfare. Of course, standards are important—if for no other reason than to protect consumers. Given current licensing and training standards, however, it is theoretically possible for therapists to obtain a license to practice and work their entire careers without ever helping a single person. Who would know?

Adopting an outcome-informed approach would go a long way toward correcting this problem, at the same time offering the first "real-time" protection to consumers and payers. After all, training, certification, and standards of care would involve ongoing and systematic evaluation of outcome—the primary concern of those seeking and paying for treatment. Instead of empirically supported thera*pies,* consumers would have access to empirically validated thera*pists.* Rather than evidence-based practice, therapists would tailor their work to the individual client via practice-based evidence. Liberated from the traditional focus on process, therapists would be better able to achieve what they always claimed to have been in the business of doing—assisting change. More important, clients would finally gain the voice in treatment that the literature has long suggested they deserve.

This would indeed be revolutionary because psychotherapy has operated outside the purview of the very people it intends to serve, resulting in unaccountable practices bordering on oppression. Imagine clients in charge of every aspect of therapy and receiving services based on their theory of change, using their feedback to guide all decisions. Imagine no more diagnostic workups, treatment plans, intake forms; no personal or confidential information divulged or electronically submitted for payment purposes; or any other form or practice that has no relevance to outcome. Imagine instead simply submitting contentless outcome data that triggers payment automatically for unlimited meetings as long as clients are benefiting. You may say that we are dreamers, but we are not the only ones. In fact, all of these things are already happening. One managed care company is experimenting with such a payment system, while another global EAP company is setting up a provider network based on outcome alone. Further, therapists and agencies worldwide are implementing heroic client ideas and practices and are becoming heroic agencies (Duncan & Sparks, 2002).

Imagine for the first time in history that mental health professionals will have proof of the effectiveness and value of day-to-day clinical work and will no longer need to rely on the medical model for legitimacy. Imagine no longer gaining acceptance by adopting the questionable language and practices of the medical profession (e.g., the *DSM,* prescriptive treatments) only to secure the permanent second-class status to which therapy has been relegated since the time of Freud. Imagine establishing an identity separate from the field of medicine. It is easy if you try.

CHAPTER FIVE

The Client's Theory of Change

Integrating Approaches One Client at a Time

with Susanne Coleman, Lisa Kelledy, and Steven Kopp

> *Then they said, "Come and let us build ourselves a city, and . . . let us make a name for ourselves." The Lord said, " . . . Come, let us go down, and confuse their language there, so that they will not understand one another's speech." . . . Therefore it was called Babel, because there the Lord confused the language of all the earth.*
>
> —*Genesis 11:1, 4–5, 7–9*

An historical review of psychotherapy, or just plain experience with clients, leads to the disappointing recognition that all models are limited. One size does not fit all. The field's response has been the creation of rival schools, each designed to address the inadequacies of the others. Thus, therapists have not suffered a dearth of models from which to choose. They now have more choices than Baskin-Robbins and Howard Johnson combined.

The upside, of course, is that under certain circumstances a given flavor may really hit the spot. The lure of increasing the efficiency of therapy through the selective application of disparate models has fueled interest in eclectic strategies for practice. Indeed, eclecticism is the predominant theoretical orientation of English-speaking therapists (Norcross, 1997). That therapists of all stripes prefer to identify themselves as eclectic indicates an acknowledgment of the inadequacies of any one school and the value of combining many in efforts to help clients.

Although the eclectic movement is laudable in its diversion from the "dogma eat dogma" (Saltzman & Norcross, 1990, p. xv) world of warring factions of therapy, it suffers the same problems that have all but reduced psychotherapy to medical diagnoses and the prescription of empirically supported treatments—the key figure, the client, has been left out of the loop, and the search for the magical processes that produce change has blinded us to the far more critical variable of the outcome of our services. Consequently, any integrative or eclectic effort must occur at the individual client level. That can only happen by tailoring the combination or blend of approaches with client ideas via direct client feedback about the outcome of therapy, *one client at a time*.

With that caveat in mind, this chapter takes our discussion regarding the client's theory of change further. We suggest that honoring the client's theory of change not only influences successful outcome but also provides a way to integrate the myriad approaches available today. Client examples illustrate how recruiting the client's unique perceptions enables creative solutions from a broad base of different ideas and methods.

THE CLIENT'S THEORY: A RICH TRADITION

It is the familiar that usually eludes in life. What is before our nose is what we see last.

William Barrett, unknown

As early as 1955, psychiatrist Paul Hoch stated, "There are some patients who would like to submit to a psychotherapeutic procedure whose theoretical foundations are in agreement with their own ideas about psychic functioning" (p. 322). At about the same time, psychologist George Kelly (1955, p. 228) posited that each individual has a "personal construct theory," a scientific theory "worth taking into account" in the process of therapy. Kelly saw treatment as formulating hypotheses on this theory, planning field trials, and evaluating outcomes, allowing the client to actively test the theory.

Later, Torrey (1972) asserted that sharing similar beliefs with clients about both the causes and treatment of mental disorders is a prerequisite to successful psychotherapy. Wile (1977) also believed that clients enter therapy with their own theories about problems—how they developed and how they are to be solved. Wile stated that "many of the classic disputes which arise between clients and therapists can be attributed to differences in their theories of [etiology and] cure" (p. 437). Similarly, Brickman et al. (1982, p. 375) hypothesized that "many of the problems characterizing relationships between help givers and help recipients arise from the fact that the two parties are applying models that are out of phase with one another."

Erickson (1980) railed against imposing therapists' theories on clients. He instead advocated what he called *utilization:* "exploring a patient's individuality to ascertain what life learnings, experiences, and mental skills are available to deal with the problem . . . [and] then utilizing these uniquely personal internal responses to achieve therapeutic goals" (Erickson & Rossi, 1979, p. 1). Building on Erickson's tradition, the Mental Research Institute (MRI) (Watzlawick, Weakland, & Fisch, 1974) developed the concept of *position,* the client's beliefs that specifically influence the presenting problem and the client's participation in therapy (Fisch, Weakland, & Segal, 1982). The MRI recommended rapid assessment of the client's position so that the therapist could tailor all intervention accordingly. Similarly, Frank and Frank (1991, p. xv) suggested that "ideally therapists should select for each patient the therapy that accords, or can be brought to accord, with the patient's personal characteristics and view of the problem."

Held (1991) separates therapist and client beliefs into two categories. Formal theory consists of the explanatory schemes that the therapist addresses across cases to solve problems. Informal theory involves clients' specific notions about the causes of their particular complaints. Held suggests that the therapist may select strategies from any model based on congruence with the client's informal theory. Duncan et al. (1992) clinically demonstrate such a selection process in their client-directed approach.

Duncan and Moynihan (1994) asserted that using the client's theory of change facilitates a favorable relationship, increases client participation, and therefore enhances positive outcome. Duncan et al. (1997) view the client's theory of change as holding the keys to success regardless of the model the therapist uses, and especially with "impossible" cases. Similarly, Frank (1995, p. 91) concludes: "I'm inclined to entertain the notion that the relative efficacy of most psychotherapeutic methods depends almost exclusively on how successfully the therapist is able to make the methods fit the patient's expectations."

Scholars representing a wide variety of clinical orientations tend to agree that the client's perceptions about problem etiology and resolution are likely to affect the process and outcome of therapy.

Conversation, Content, and Change

We prefer calling what we do with clients conversing, or conversation rather than interviewing (Goolishian & Anderson, 1987). Interviewing implies something done to clients rather than with them, and it connotes an expert gathering information for evaluative purposes (e.g., diagnostic or mental status interview, matching characteristics). Conversation, on the other hand, enlists clients in the discovery of possibility, defining therapy as an intimately interpersonal event committed to the client's goals. One way of looking at the conversation is to examine the content of the topics discussed.

Recall that Held (1991) defines the content of the conversation on either formal or informal theoretical levels. Formal theory consists of either general notions regarding the cause of problems (e.g., symptoms result from faulty thinking) or specific explanations (e.g., overgeneralization), which must be addressed to solve problems. The therapist recasts clients' complaints into these preconceived contents, compelling therapy down well-trodden paths cut from the formal theory. If the therapist sees a client's complaint of anxiety, for example, as caused by faulty thinking, then therapy will examine and correct the faulty thinking. The formal theory of the therapist enjoys a privileged position over the client's views, and it structures problem definition as well as outcome criteria.

Informal theory, on the other hand, involves the specific notions that clients hold about the causes of their particular situations. As discussed in Chapter Three, we also include the client's specific views about how change can occur. Rather than recasting the client's personal views into the therapist's formal theory, we calibrate applicable theories to the client's beliefs. Each client, therefore, presents the therapist with a new theory to discover and a different solution path to follow.

Therapist allegiance to any particular theoretical content involves a trade-off that enables and restricts options. Theoretical loyalty provides clear direction but is inherently limiting; theoretical anarchy enables flexibility but also inserts uncertainty. Although all therapists have preferences, there are no fixed and correct ideas or methods that run across the situations that clients bring to therapy and therefore no inherently right ways to conduct therapy. As mind-boggling as it sounds and as frightening as it feels, such a view opens unlimited possibilities for change. The only caveat is that any selected idea must produce benefit.

It is this indeterminacy that gives therapy its texture and infuses it with the excitement of discovery. Given this indeterminacy, a purpose of the conversation is to make explicit the client's perspectives specifically related to change. Spotlighting the client's ideas requires a focused effort to follow the client's lead regarding the conversation's content.

Therapy begins by inviting clients to tell their stories: "What brings you here today?" In the course of telling their stories, clients express their philosophies of life—their reasons for living or not wanting to. Clients reveal the heroes, heroines, villains, and plot lines as they share the comedies, tragedies, and triumphs of their lives. This adventure story sets the content parameters of the therapist's questions. The therapist converses in the client's language because the words the client uses represent an edited commentary of the client's view of life; clients are novelists who carefully choose words to convey their story in a specific light.

The therapist's questions stay within the client's content frame and add to it over time. The counselor imposes minimal content in these questions and allows maximum space for the client to find new connections, distinctions, and meanings. The questions are designed not to influence particular meanings or other theory-based realities but rather to invite the client's reactions to and descriptions of the concerns that initiated therapy. A candid exchange evolves, resulting in a collaborative formulation of what the therapist and client will address, criteria for successful resolution, and a plan for how therapy will proceed.

The counselor respects the client's judgment regarding experiences relevant for discussion and revision. As an active participant, the therapist draws on possibly relevant ideas to interject into the conversation. This input grows into meaningful dialogue or fades away depending upon the client's response. Studious attention to client reactions to therapist-generated content provides guidance to what the client finds important. Client enthusiasm about particular ideas informs the choice of what comes next in the conversation. Therapists' moment-to-moment experiences of what enlivens clients and brightens their participation mediates the next step and so on.

When introducing ideas to the conversation, we keep three things in mind. First, although we all have our favorites, we discard them like yesterday's news if the ideas don't enlist clients' strengths or rally their energies to address their concerns. Second, any idea must explicitly accept what the client wants and provide an option that addresses the client's desires. If an idea does not pass that test, then we discard it as quickly as we would sour milk. Finally, the client must heartily agree to the therapist's ideas. If the client does not enthusiastically endorse the idea, the therapist abandons it as if it were a blind date with a "born to lose" tattoo. Reliance on a warm reception not only continues the client's intimate involvement, it immerses the client in a collaborative pool of possibilities from which the client can emerge as owner of the ideas.

The therapist liberally sprinkles checking-out questions, questions verifying that therapy is on the right track and addressing key issues, in the conversational recipe to ensure that clients find dialogue delicious and to whet their appetites for change. The Outcome Rating Scale (ORS) and Session Rating Scale (SRS) helpfully contribute to the conversation. The client combines aspects of his or her experience with other views that arise from therapeutic dialogue. Therapy, then, uniquely intertwines ideas, forming a theory of change pertaining to the client's specific circumstance.

Clients are in essence in charge of the content and their lives; whereas therapists are in charge of unfolding that content, evolving a theory of change, and channeling it toward the client's goals. The client is also in charge of whether or not any emergent idea or action step proves beneficial.

Selecting Content

Recall that honoring the client's theory requires that selected methods or ideas fit or complement clients' beliefs about the change process. We implement the client's identified solutions or seek an approach that both fits the client's theory and provides possibilities for change. The correct or corrective nature of selected content is not important; what is important is the relationship between the content and the client's theory of change that provides change potential. The therapist can respond to the client from a number of content sources: (1) specific problems; (2) specific approaches; and most likely, (3) solely from the client's descriptions and experiences. Specific problems are made up of generic response patterns and particular areas of concern. Generic response patterns (e.g., the grief process, rape trauma, posttraumatic stress, etc.) describe typical phases of response to developmental transitions or incidental crises. Likewise, content derived from a particular area of concern (e.g., anxiety, AIDS, etc.) may provide an organizing framework for introducing ideas to the conversation.

With some complaints researchers have suggested particular approaches (e.g., cognitive-behavioral therapy for depression), thereby providing options to discuss with clients. Similarly, should the client's views appear congruent with a particular theoretical framework, the therapist may use that approach to provide input and direction. As we have emphasized, though, regardless of how well research, tradition, or clinical literature supports the selected content (technique or approach), client acceptance is the critical variable. Selected content is virtually worthless if clients do not view it as applicable or helpful to their particular circumstances. It also is of no value if it does not result in client benefit.

Content, then, is only the vehicle through which the conversation flows and possibilities arise. Evidence-based treatments and specific approaches are merely lenses to try on that may or may not fit the client's frame and prescription requirements. In this way, the therapist neither deifies nor demonizes methods and models but keeps them as useful adjuncts that offer metaphorical accounts of how people can change.

The work of Milton Erickson exemplifies the third and most prevalent source of content: the client. Unencumbered by the prevailing orthodoxy of his time, Erickson drew upon the creativity of his clients. Consider the following: Erickson saw Kim, a teacher troubled by nude young men hovering just above her head. She requested that Erickson not take her young men away but rather stop their interference with her everyday life. He suggested that Kim leave the nude young men in a closet in his office, where they would be secure and not interfere with her teaching. She checked on the young men at first but gradually stopped. Much later, Kim moved to another city and worried about what she called her psychotic episodes. Erickson suggested that she put her psychotic episodes in a manila envelope and mail them to him.

Occasionally, she would send Erickson a psychotic episode and meanwhile continued a productive life (Erickson, 1980).

Erickson saw another client, Bob, who wanted to correct his irresponsible and reckless driving. When Erickson asked what he could do to be helpful, Bob answered that Erickson could do nothing, that Bob would have to do it his own way. Erickson asked how soon he wished to make the changes, and Bob said that by the next month he should be driving properly. Bob repeated the statement that he would have to quit in his own way in various ways over two sessions. Two weeks later, Bob reported jubilantly that he had handled things in his own way: he had driven so recklessly that, at one point, he had to abandon his car just before it hurtled down a mountainside. Since that incident, he stated, he had been driving safely and within legal speed limits.

Because Erickson had an unwavering belief in clients' self-healing capabilities, he intensely focused on clients' views of their concerns, their goals for therapy, and their ideas about change. Erickson understood the importance of not attempting to eliminate Kim's nude men or confronting Bob's desire to "do it [his] own way." Erickson did not become mired in his own fears (e.g., that he might be reinforcing Kim's delusions) or a priori treatment preferences (e.g., that he needed to do something with Bob). Instead, he offered input based solely on the content that the client provided and inserted no outside theoretical content.

Therapists at our workshops often ask us about clients who present theories of change that we don't agree with or have ideas or behaviors that we find objectionable. Each case below represents such an instance; each is provocative and tested our resolve to honor the client's theory of change.

PRIVILEGING THE CLIENT'S VOICE WHEN IT AIN'T SUCH A PRIVILEGE

People are generally better persuaded by the reasons which they have themselves discovered than by those which have come into the minds of others.

—*Blaise Pascal,* Pensées

Examples illustrating the three areas of content follow. The first client challenged our antimedical-model stance and taught us that the customer is always right. This client exemplifies how discussing a specific problem created solution possibilities. The second client demonstrates the selection of a specific approach and the value in following a client idea to its logical conclusion. This client frightened us with her pathological view of herself, as well as her theory of how change needed to happen. Finally, the third and fourth cases illustrate the selection of content that arises solely from the client. In the third the client began with a theory of change that included chemical castration. In the fourth a woman described her husband's drinking binges and her concerns about their toddler, left in his care.

Specific Problem Area: "Genetic Depression"

Perhaps no approach has influenced a nonpathological view of clients more than the MRI (Watzlawick et al., 1974) and the problem-solving therapy of Jay Haley (Haley, 1976). About three decades ago, the MRI proposed a model that normalized problems in living and did not require the encumbrances of an illness-based view (Duncan et al., 2003). Similarly, Haley viewed problems in their developmental and relational context and satirically challenged the prevailing conventions of pathology and long-term therapy (Haley, 1980). Today's competency-oriented therapies owe a debt of gratitude rarely expressed to these pioneers of positive perspectives of clients.

Although the MRI and Haley wrote the first notes of an antipathology melody, the so-called postmodern therapies have composed an entire symphony. Swimming upstream against the dominant discourses of diagnosis and pathology, narrative and solution-focused approaches put the client's voice center stage, highlight client capabilities, and challenge oppressive discourses in clients' lives (e.g., Eron & Lund, 1996; Madigan & Epston, 1995; Walter & Peller, 2000; White & Epston, 1990). We, of course, have similarly abandoned a reliance on the killer *D*s (diagnosis, disorders, dysfunction, disease, disabilities, and deficit) and have stepped down from the throne of the exalted expert. Instead, we invite and formalize client input and feedback, enlist client resources, and value collaboration. Privileging the client's voice is central to not only our approach but our values as well.

That's all fine and dandy until you are faced with clients who, in spite of therapists' best efforts to highlight strengths, adhere to a pathological view of themselves and even seem cast adrift without it. How do you avoid taking an expert stance when clients plead for advice and downplay their own abilities and expertise? How do you draw on the client's theory of change when it is so contrary to your core values that it sounds like screeching feedback from a microphone?

Fortunately, clients help us grapple with these struggles. They are the best teachers of therapy. The next client taught us the value of following the client's theory of change even when it was contrary to our own views. Moreover, she taught us that honoring the client's perspective opens up possibilities beyond gaining compliance—actually enabling solutions we could not even imagine before the fact.

Pat, a thirty-seven-year-old homemaker, was referred by the principal of her daughter's school (Murphy & Duncan, 1997). Pat had apparently ruffled feathers with her ardent concerns about what she considered her daughter Ann's depression. The school did not share her concerns. Ann was a well-behaved nine-year-old child, according to her teacher; the school psychologist, however, believed Pat to be a "certifiable nut."

Pat was an interesting character, beautifully complex and full of polar extremes. She broadcast her words in a boisterous Phyllis Diller manner, periodically pausing to take a drag from a cigarette that dangled at the end of a smoke-reducing holder. Ann had the look of a potential rascal but slumped in the chair and didn't look up as her mother opened the session.

SESSION ONE, EXCERPT ONE

PAT: Ann is so depressed. She gets very upset when kids at school tease her. She complains about being bored and mopes around when she can't find a friend. . . . I'm depressed and have been seeing a psychiatrist for ten years, and I understand that I have a chemical imbalance and will need to take antidepressants for the rest of my life. I also take antipsychotics because I had a break after Ann was born—tried to kill myself and the whole nine yards! I've been depressed all my life, and my mother is also depressed and takes antidepressants. My doctor told me it was genetic, and I'm sure that Ann is just like my mother and me and probably needs to be on medication. I was hoping that she was going to be OK chemically, but the genetics were just too strong.

A more problematic script could not have been written for the therapist. Pat's words were like the flash of the proverbial middle finger, a loud voice yelling, "Privilege this!" Pat not only wrapped herself in a cloak of psychiatric terminology and medications but, worse, wanted the therapist to pass these along like some cherished heirloom to her daughter. Sometimes privileging the client's voice ain't such a privilege.

Yet the therapist knew that he must court Pat's favorable view and woo her participation if anything positive was going to happen. Actually, the courtship of Pat began in the waiting room. Wielding an oversized soft drink and smoking paraphernalia, Pat had no sooner introduced herself than she asserted that she would like to smoke. The therapist agreed. As silly as it sounds, it helped things start off on the right foot.

The therapist didn't have any trouble liking Pat, which she instantly knew. Sometimes the art of this work is valuing and forming alliances with those whom others find difficult. For some, perhaps, the problem would have been Pat—and her view of genetic depression. Challenging her would have only meant joining the conga line of failure. Ann's teacher, school psychologist, and principal had attempted to persuade Pat that nothing was wrong. Pat had unfortunately perceived these efforts as belittling the seriousness of Ann's problems and as subtle indictments of her parenting. The therapist, although unsure of where it would lead, was careful not to enter a needless clash of ideologies.

Privately, Ann insisted that she was not depressed. Her only problem was that boys occasionally teased her at school—something that, she indicated, happened to all the girls in her class. All she wanted was for her mom to stop asking whether she was depressed.

SESSION ONE, EXCERPT TWO

PAT: I try to comfort Ann, and I do everything humanly possible to make her happy— I keep a very close watch on the depression. . . . I guess my fear is that these early signs will worsen and doom her to the depression and heartache that Mom and I have had to endure.

THERAPIST: Sounds like you have done a lot to try and prevent dooming her to your mother's and your bouts with depression. Given what you've told me about Ann's genetic depression, I was wondering what you were hoping to get here. Why are you seeing me instead of someone who could give you medication?

PAT: You are the expert. I want you to confirm the depression and tell me what I can do to help her. I can get the medication from my doctor.

Pat said this with intensity, and the therapist took it very seriously. The task was now to work within her genetic depression perspective and discover possibilities for different actions or conclusions. This required a selection of content that matched Pat's perspective, creating space for an evolving theory of change. This task began in the second session, by conveying right off the bat an acceptance of Pat's genetic depression theory.

SESSION TWO, EXCERPT ONE

THERAPIST: We have come to the conclusion that you are absolutely correct in your estimation of Ann's problem. Given her family history of depression in both her mother and her grandmother, it seems very likely that she is genetically predisposed to depression.

PAT: I knew it. So you see it too.

Finding a way to validate what may seem initially bizarre opens the conversation to possibility—to new directions. The therapist offered input specifically derived from a genetic perspective of depression, a content area derived from a specific problem. Relying on a popular theory of genetics and depression (the diathesis-stress paradigm), the therapist proposed, in as didactic and expert a fashion as he could muster, that given the familial predisposition to depression, environmental factors were critical.

SESSION TWO, EXCERPT TWO

THERAPIST: Because she is genetically predisposed to depression, what happens in the environment is particularly important. While the predisposition to depression is always there, the depression may or may not be expressed, depending on what happens in her environment and how she learns to cope. You can help Ann with her depression by helping her with the environmental aspects.

PAT: What are the environmental aspects? You mean like the things we do for her self-esteem and how our family relates to one another?

Pat was now an active participant. At that moment, collaboration began. Before, the therapist had collaborated with Pat's expectation of his role as an expert and with her view of Ann's depression. That stance laid the groundwork for real collaboration regarding the environmental contributions to the depression. They explored and evaluated several options in an open and lively exchange.

Pat reported that she was a "stroker" and often rewarded Ann in an attempt to build her self-esteem. She concluded that she could not do much more here. Pat also extolled the virtues of her marriage and did not see any connection there to Ann's problems.

Later, in a discussion of parental contributions, the therapist suggested that sometimes parents inadvertently discount a child's negative feelings because of a belief that kids should always be happy.

SESSION TWO, EXCERPT THREE

THERAPIST: Because we love them so much, we don't want them to experience any pain whatsoever, and therefore, we unknowingly minimize their concerns rather than helping them deal with them.

PAT: That's exactly what I do! I'm always upbeat with her . . . always telling her how smart and pretty she is and how school is fun. And that's all wrong. I guess I sort of discount her feelings, and it's not helping. Is that what you are getting at? I need to allow her to be and support her feelings, even if it's negative. . . .

THERAPIST: Exactly, except you are not doing anything wrong. You are doing what any parent would do faced with a depressed kid. You are trying to help her. What I am suggesting is that you "lean to" her depression, allowing it to be, encourage its expression, and perhaps even exaggerate it as a way to help her work through her feelings and learn to cope with them.

PAT: When you say "exaggeration," I'm thinking that when she criticizes herself, how about if I exaggerate them to the point of ridiculousness? Like if she says she's ugly, I'll say, "Yeah, you're so ugly I've had to replace three broken mirrors because you looked at them," instead of trying to convince her how pretty she is.

The idea of exaggeration especially struck a chord with Pat, and consequently, was emphasized in the ensuing conversation. She responded in a way that demonstrated the fit of the ideas; she immediately began discussing applications and proposed her own example. The therapist observed Pat's reaction and would not have pursued any cool or lukewarm responses. The therapist looks for full-blown positive responses in which clients react with applications specific to their lives or connect the idea to something similar in their experience.

Suggestions derived from the client's theory are inherently validating. Each time Pat encouraged and exaggerated her daughter's complaints, she did so in service of helping Ann with her genetic depression. Medication remained an option if environmental efforts failed.

Pat's husband, Chris, attended the next session. Chris was a nice guy, but he had a patronizing attitude toward Pat that rubbed the therapist the wrong way. Chris emphasized Pat's illness (psychotic depression) and was condescending most of the time. But it didn't bother Pat. In fact, she seemed in total awe of her husband. Once again, the therapist swallowed his lofty ideas and followed the clients' lead.

Pat returned for two more meetings. In session four she reported that Ann was smiling more and complaining less, the negotiated signs of improvement. Pat laughed as she described how Ann had giggled in response to her exaggerations. Pat altered the proposed ideas to fit her sense of humor, her strengths. Although she leaned toward Ann's complaints, Pat's exaggerations of Ann's conundrums were funny instead of the serious fare the therapist had originally suggested. They became Pat's inventions, not the therapist's interventions, a result of her imagination and experimentation.

In the final session, Pat insightfully recounted that although it was difficult for her, she was not attempting to rescue Ann from her depression. Instead, she felt very good about helping Ann cope with her sadness and disappointments. Pat concluded that perhaps her daughter was only "mildly" predisposed to depression and medication was not needed, although she would continue to monitor Ann's depressive tendencies. Admittedly, this was music to the therapist's ears.

Adopting Pat's theory of change had opened the door to other options—other means for accomplishing the same end. It seemed, in retrospect, that Pat's theory of change only required for someone to take her fears of genetic depression seriously. Pat instilled in us the value of following the client—it ultimately takes us where we want to go in a way that we can feel good about once we get there.

Specific Approach: The Courage to Heal—the Client's Way

Without allegiance to any particular model, the therapist may select content from any approach as long as it is consistent with the client's perspective. We are opportunists who sift for seeds within the client's realm of experience in order to nurture them to grow possibilities for revising what clients find distressing. But what if we fear these seeds will grow into the people-gobbling plant in *The Little Shop of Horrors?* What if the client selects a method that not only is not the therapist's preferred choice but also makes the therapist downright squeamish? This was exactly the situation with the next client.

Stacey, a very bright marketing representative for a computer software company in her early thirties, was very uncomfortable with the idea of therapy ("You don't air your dirty laundry to strangers"). She looked lost in oversized clothes and sheepishly shared that she wanted some answers because she knew there was something very wrong. "I think I am seriously dysfunctional," she said. She described having "episodes" that often forced her to become a person she did not like. In these episodes she felt panicky and volatile, fearful of impending doom, depressed, sometimes crying for hours. She reported that the episodes capped off a night laden with nightmares. Stacey intimated that she was perhaps horribly damaged from something in her past. She needed therapy to help her figure this out. Stacey also reported having "terribly addictive relationships with men" in which she often assumed a "victim" role.

Stacey was seen in a setting using a team approach. Her initial score on the ORS was 8, which put her in the very distressed range.

About forty minutes into the session, the therapist took a break with the team and scored the SRS. A score of 25 dramatically indicated that Stacey felt that the therapist didn't understand her and that she was uncertain whether the therapist was following her ideas for therapy. This was indeed a rocky beginning but not surprising. The team was uneasy and feared fanning the flames of Stacey's pathological view of herself, as well as her desire for an archeological dig in her past.

To this point the therapist's preferences were to reflect Stacey's resources and emphasize her expertise at resolving her dilemma. As Chapter Three asserts, this is a good place to start. The problem, though, was that Stacey did not see things this way. Stacey met early attempts to highlight her competencies and magnify her coping mechanisms with frustration and a redirection to her festering pathology.

Further, although Stacey was very clear about what she wanted, the therapist resisted in subtle ways. Stacey sought the calm hand of an expert on the wheel to guide her through her perilous journey of discovery. The therapist, instead, seemed uncomfortable with a leadership role and reticent to address Stacey's perceived psychic damage.

Getting clients to admit to either their competence or their equal status in therapy is rarely productive. The client's view takes priority over our own preferences, even about these cherished ideas. This does not mean that the therapist can never challenge clients but rather that such challenges must be evaluated in light of the client's reaction. Did the challenge engage or alienate participation, and did it promote movement toward the client's goals? Although difficult at times, it is possible to accommodate a client's negative views of him- or herself and the authority status the client attributes to therapists while retaining a faith in the client to lead in a productive direction. This is the essence of honoring the client's theory of change—to follow the client's preferences, trusting that they will evolve into change possibilities.

The therapist reentered the session and discussed the SRS with Stacey, demonstrating a genuine desire to get on track. Stacey reiterated her purpose for being in therapy, and the two avoided an alliance rupture. The session acquired a more collaborative purpose as the therapist went with Stacey's content focus.

SESSION ONE

THERAPIST: So you say that these episodes arise after a night of bad dreams?

STACEY: Yes. I can't seem to remember the dreams, though. All I know is that I wake up sweating profusely and extremely scared. I try to remember the dreams, but for some reason, I can't. Then the next day is horrible. I can't sleep; I have uncontrollable anger; and I scream and cry at everything. Basically, I can't function the next day.

THERAPIST: So that there is a definite connection between the dreams and how you feel the next day, these episodes. But you can't remember the nightmares?

STACEY: Exactly. I have no recollection at all. It bothers me that I can't remember what occurred during them. These nightmares are the key to what's wrong with me. I know it's sick, and I know it's about my past, but I have to find out.

THERAPIST: So you feel pretty strongly that understanding these dreams will help you resolve what's going on now?

STACEY: Yes.

THERAPIST: Can you remember anything about them?

STACEY: I seem to always be a child.

Stacey believed that her dreams held the key that would open the doors of her childhood and the experiences that troubled her. Following her vision of change to its logical conclusion was what the team decided to do, but not without trepidation. At the end of the first session, the therapist asked Stacey to think of her earliest memories as a child and monitor her nightmares, writing down as much as she could remember. The team's task was to investigate possible ways to interpret dreams. The session ended on a hopeful note, far different than the feeling at the break. The SRS helped significantly in this process.

SESSION TWO

THERAPIST: Your ORS score is lower—things look worse. Does this make sense to you?

STACEY: Yes, it's been a rough week. The nightmares are becoming more vivid and are occurring more often. It seems as though there is a particular man that keeps frightening me. I can't see who it is. I am only about five years old in the nightmares. . . . How am I to interpret this? What do they mean, and please don't ask me what they mean, because that's why I am consulting you. And why are the nightmares increasing?

The team had done its homework and was ready for this question.

THERAPIST: First, there are several ways to interpret dreams. A strictly Freudian interpretation would examine the dreams for their symbolic content in light of their wish-fulfillment meanings. Another more currently popular viewpoint is that dreams access the unconscious more directly—dreams may be less symbolic and more apparent than once believed. Additionally, since you are the ultimate author of the dream, we can look at each aspect of the dream as representing a part of you being expressed. And we feel compelled to bring this up, there are some that believe, with good reason, that dreams and their connection to memory can be dangerous, that memories can actually be created in the therapy rather than representing something that actually happened. And finally, things are picking up now because you have opened Pandora's box. As you confront these situations and embrace these feelings, more will likely occur to you.

STACEY: OK, that makes sense. I'm not worried about the false memory stuff—I saw that on *Oprah*—I'll know when something rings true. I am not one to imagine things or just come up with a convenient scapegoat. I guess I think that dreams are more like a movie of my life straight out of childhood. I know that our discussion last week has helped me remember more of my dreams and my childhood. The other night, I was trying to remember incidences from my childhood. What I did remember happened was when I was in kindergarten. I remembered my teacher telling us to draw a picture of our family. So I did. However, the picture I drew made my teacher call my mother. I drew my mother, my father, and myself. But I drew them all with no clothes on. My teacher became alarmed because my parent's anatomies were drawn with precision. I didn't think it was a bad thing, but I can remember being embarrassed because of my mother's embarrassment. I had forgotten totally about that. I think it is significant, but I don't know why.

THERAPIST: We agree that you are on to something—that your internal wisdom is guiding you to the answer you are looking for.

STACEY: Yeah, I was reading a book a while back, I think it was *Courage to Heal*, and it said something about reliving the memories or reexperiencing them with a therapist to sort them out.

Stacey's nightmares and recollections of her early life provided the framework for therapy. Content was selected to match her ideas about dreams. We trusted her to find what she needed from our discussions and to provide us direction. She did exactly that. The client's last comment indicated her view of how to proceed. It also raised the heebie-jeebie factor because the team now knew she was on the quest for a perpetrator. The therapist closed the session by agreeing that there was more to learn from the picture incident and asked Stacey to redraw the picture and see what memories she could call up.

SESSION THREE

STACEY: I've been thinking a lot about our session last week, and I redrew the picture like you asked me to. I had a hard time doing it. I mean, I remembered exactly what the picture looked like, but the embarrassment all came back. I think the embarrassment came from knowing that I should not know the male genitalia so explicitly.

THERAPIST: What sort of thoughts and feelings did you have while you recreated the picture?

STACEY: I felt disgusted. I felt as if I had been violated in some way. I can't help but think now that I may have been sexually abused at that age. Do you think it's possible?

THERAPIST: Yes, it's possible.

STACEY: I need to figure out what is going on. I can't live my life like this! I seem to pick real jerks or ruin all my relationships, and I have to know why. With the nightmares, my episodes, and the possibility that I may have been sexually abused, I feel like I could go insane! But I know there is a connection between all this stuff.

THERAPIST: That is a lot to deal with. So are you saying that if we can make a connection between the nightmares and the sexual abuse, that things in your present situation may change?

STACEY: Yes! I really do think so. I need to understand why this is happening to me. If I could connect those things together, then it will all make sense and I can start dealing with it.

THERAPIST: What would be the first step in starting this connection?

STACEY: I feel like I need to know who the man is in my nightmares. He feels as if he is familiar, and that really bothers me.

Stacey's theory of change has emerged. She could solve her difficulties with the episodes and her negative relationships if she could name the perpetrator, giving a face to the intimidating figure in her dreams. She and her therapist did not yet explore how this knowledge could help her current situation, but the therapist considered it important and worthy of follow-up in the next session. The session concluded with a discussion of men who could have abused her. The therapist asked her to think further of these men and to identify ways her life would be different if she discovered who it was.

SESSION FOUR

THERAPIST: Wow, the ORS score really went up, to a 15. What do you make of that?

STACEY: I'm scared to death, but these dreams are bringing me closer to the truth. During the past week, I have given it a lot of thought about when I was sexually abused and the possible perpetrator. Last session, we discussed different people and the feelings

I felt about them. . . . I had another nightmare. But this time I saw who it was. I am afraid to even talk about it but know that I need to. I guess I'm hoping that you can help me understand this dream. Well, in the dream, I am a young girl. I am with my parents in a restaurant. My father takes me and walks away from the table. All of a sudden, he starts to urinate on the wall! I told him to stop doing that, but he told me to be quiet. He then told me not to tell my mother. I remember struggling with if I should tell her or not. Somehow, I ended up back at the table with her, and I told her that Dad urinated on the wall. She told me that I must be mistaken, that my father wouldn't do such a thing. I woke up at that point. I woke up hating my mother for not believing me.

THERAPIST: Your dreams went from not having any familiar faces to now this one. Wow. What did you think after you woke up from that dream? What types of feelings did it leave you with?

STACEY: It left me feeling disgusted, just like when I drew that picture. Do you think that there is a reason for me dreaming this, for me dreaming that my father would do something so wrong?

THERAPIST: Your dreams have been strong indicators so far. What significance does your father urinating have to you?

STACEY: He is doing something he shouldn't be. He is using his private parts for a dirty act and then telling me not to tell my mother.

THERAPIST: Does that have any relevance to the other things we have been talking about in therapy?

STACEY: Are you asking me if I think my father sexually abused me? Yes, I do. The minute I woke up from the dream, I knew I had my answer. I guess I just didn't want it to be true. I wanted there to be some logical explanation, but the only explanation is that he did something to me that changed my life. But there's more. As I was thinking about that I had my answer, I remembered something else. I remember my father watching TV in his underwear, but it was ripped out, and he was hanging all out and maybe was even erect. I told my mother and she yelled at me and told me to go to my room. I felt so bad [crying], I didn't know what I had done so bad. That's just what she did in that dream— it was me who did something wrong. Maybe I told her other things and she didn't believe me. Or it may be that I am preparing myself for her not to believe me this time.

THERAPIST: *[sometime later]* How do you think knowing it was your dad will change things for you?

STACEY: I'm not exactly sure, but I know I already feel different. I just don't feel as intimidated by my father as much now. I'll never confront him, but he won't scare me anymore.

It was a grueling session but a powerful one. Stacey spent the next couple of sessions preparing for an upcoming holiday visit with her family. Her ORS scores continued to increase (to a 23), and the SRS reflected that the therapeutic relationship was on track. The nightmares had all but stopped. Stacey identified that knowing it was her dad who abused her would allow her to deal with him better. She wasn't sure yet how it would help her in her relationships. With her self-confidence growing, Stacey returned home for the first time since rediscovering the abuse.

SESSION SEVEN

THERAPIST: Hey, I can't believe this. Your ORS score is over the cutoff for people in therapy versus people who are not in therapy. What does this mean?

STACEY: It means I'm kicking butt and taking names. No more "missy victim" here. The trip home was great. It was uncomfortable and all, but under no circumstances did I take any shit from my dad, and I didn't let my mother smooth it over. He started on my job, then my part-time school stuff, and finally on whether or not I am ever going to marry anyone. I nailed him to the wall—not in any hissy fit or anything—I just dismissed him like he has no control over me at all. I was great. . . . But that's not all. When I got back, I dumped the guy I was with. He was telling me how I should dress and even what I should do in therapy. I believe I am going without a man for while. It's going to take me a while to sort all this out, but I don't feel so desperate about it anymore.

Perhaps for many therapists, this would have not been a challenging case. After all, Stacey was a sensational young woman bound and determined to find the truth about her troubled past. Yet for competency-oriented therapists who cut their teeth on horror stories of competent clients changed into damaged goods that can only cope with their deficits with interminable therapy, this case took on epic proportions. But in the end, the heroic client prevailed.

No Outside Content: I'm a Pedophile

With Pat, we didn't like the conclusion of a nine-year-old being genetically depressed. With Stacey, we weren't crazy about dream analysis as a method for addressing panic, depression, and relationship problems. In the client case that follows, we didn't like the diagnosis or one of the client's proposed solutions. For ten years Bill, a twenty-six-year-old chemical engineer, had become increasingly distressed by thoughts of having sex with young boys. Bill was very quiet and obviously very embarrassed but at the same time very determined to do the right thing. Bill's initial ORS score was 10.

SESSION ONE, EXCERPT ONE

BILL: I am physically attracted to children, but I haven't acted on my thoughts. I'm a pedophile. I've done lots of reading about pedophiles. You can wean yourself out of your behavior if you're young and willing to do it. But just in case, I'm looking into chemical castration. But I know if I got help from an expert, my chances might improve. You know, a normal person's mind doesn't function like that, dreaming about children. It's programmed into my mind.

Bill starts the session out with a bomb! He is a self-proclaimed pedophile and is considering chemical castration as an option. His sincerity is touching, and the team greatly respects his courage in addressing such a difficult topic. Bill's perspective on things is pretty much there for the asking. The team's job is to take that theory to its logical conclusion, connecting and channeling it to change possibilities. Bill even has a hypothesis about how his problem likely started when he was molested by a neighborhood boy when he was eight years old. He shared his beliefs about his problem (he is a pedophile), the way change will happen (wean himself out of it), and the role of the therapist (expert). Although the therapist did not believe Bill to be a pedophile, she did not challenge his view. We do not have to agree with clients' theories to work within them. At some point, however, if following the client's theory is not yielding any fruit, then the therapist's disagreement may be relevant for discussion.

SESSION ONE, EXCERPT TWO

THERAPIST: Since you have given it much thought and research and you have your own diagnosis, have you given thought to how you would accomplish your goals, how you would wean yourself out of it?

BILL: Yes. It will take time. I need you to give me homework assignments to help me figure all this out. All I want is to meet a woman who is very special to me. Someone who cares about me, someone I feel comfortable and safe with. But first, I need to focus on the thoughts.

The client's theory of change is crystallizing. He will wean himself off his thoughts of children by meeting someone who will care about him. His cure of pedophilia is by way of a relationship with an adult. The team instantly thought, like the old song, "we got to get you a woman!" But Bill said three other things that were critical. The first was that it would take time; the second was that he wanted homework assignments; and the third was that he needed to focus on the thoughts first. Therefore, he was assigned the task of focusing on his thoughts and learning from them.

SESSION TWO

BILL: The more I focused on the thoughts, the more it became apparent to me that there is something missing from my life. My obsession with these thoughts needs to be replaced with something healthy. I need someone to share my life with me besides my family, a relationship. But I really don't know where to start.

THERAPIST: So do you think that if you find a relationship, the thoughts of children will go away?

BILL: Yes, I do. Yes, I am convinced.

THERAPIST: And you would like input from us about how to go about doing that?

BILL: Yeah, I have never even dated anyone, let alone been in a relationship.

Bill's theory of change had unfolded. Finding a relationship was his chosen method of eliminating the thoughts. The therapist reinforced the connection between the removal of the thoughts and finding a relationship to ensure the therapy was on the right track. In addition, the therapist asked a checking-out question to see if Bill wanted ideas about finding a relationship. The therapist assigned another task that gave credibility to Bill's beliefs regarding the problem and its solution, as well as honoring his request for homework. Building on Bill's existing research skills and his success with self-learning, he was asked to observe relationships to identify the type of one that he would like to have.

SESSION THREE

THERAPIST: Wow! Your ORS score has increased above the cutoff—that's great, I think. What do you think?

BILL: I am feeling much better about things, so I think it is right. But that doesn't mean I have to stop coming does it?

THERAPIST: No, not at all.

BILL: I looked into relationships, talked to people, and found some interesting books. I also observed people in relationships and noted what I liked and what I didn't like. I wanted to tell you that if the situation presented itself, I wouldn't do anything with a child. Dreams are dreams, and actions are actions. There's a difference. There has been positive change. I thought I was a pedophile. Now I know that I am a fantasizer. All I do is fantasize, and I could probably fantasize about anything.

Bill, without confrontation of his belief, shifted his view of himself as a pedophile. As we discussed in Chapter Three, the change-focused therapist made a big deal out of this shift in perspective, amplifying and expanding it with several questions that highlighted Bill's competencies and self-discoveries. The conversation continued, with Bill discussing his plan to talk to women. Bill reported that he has someone in mind, a woman he met at the library. The therapist followed the client's lead, and Bill's excitement about the possibility of dating this woman carried the rest of the session.

SESSION FOUR

BILL: I gave that girl a kiss! I was talking to her, and she put her cheek down, and I gave her a kiss. It was fun and felt good. . . . . I know I'm interested in girls, and I think things are changing. But how can I be sure?

THERAPIST: Have your thoughts decreased?

BILL: I think so, but I'm not sure.

Bill shared his exciting news and his uncertainty about the extent of the change. The therapist again highlighted the change and Bill's contributions, as well as reinforcing the connection between finding a relationship and reducing the thoughts. Although Bill's scores on the ORS had increased, Bill wanted a more specific measurement of the thoughts. Consequently, the therapist asked him to monitor and count his thoughts to see if pursuing a relationship did indeed decrease the thoughts as he suspected.

SESSION FIVE

BILL: I completed the assignment and I found that my thoughts have substantially decreased. Better yet, I found that I can control them when they do occur! If I dream of a kid, I can now immediately transfer my thinking to a woman. I get turned on by my thoughts of women. I've reprogrammed my thinking. It feels great.

Bill had his own theory on how to resolve his problem, and honoring that theory created a space for him to employ his strengths. Throughout the therapy the client's ideas directed the process; the therapist used Bill's theory of change to direct therapeutic actions. The therapist's input directly followed from the client's generated content. The therapist introduced no outside content. Bill's theory evolved throughout the process as he made new discoveries and practiced new behaviors. He changed his self-diagnosis from pedophile to fantasizer and learned that he could change from fantasizing about children to fantasizing about women. The emergent process of the therapy intertwined with Bill's ideas to produce a theory that was helpful for his unique circumstances. Recent follow-up revealed Bill's continued attraction to, and pursuit of, women.

No Outside Content: He Drinks Around Bums

Sometimes therapists face situations that are particularly scary because of the children involved. The following case, of Liz and Bob, illustrates one that immediately raised the therapist's hackles. Bob didn't make a good first impression: his long, dirty, greasy hair looked like it had not been washed in weeks; and his beard could only be described as ZZ Top-ish. He smelled like he hadn't bathed in a while, and his clothes reeked of gasoline. The pièce de résistance of Bob's appearance was multiple tattoos and body piercings. Bob was clearly no stranger to hard times. Liz, on the other hand, looked like she had arrived with the wrong person: a very well–put together woman accompanied by a homeless guy.

SESSION ONE, EXCERPT ONE

LIZ: I don't feel that we are going to be together if it continues.

THERAPIST: Do you know what she means by "if it continues"?

BOB: Yeah, I'm not working. I'm staying home with the baby. I drink during the day, sometimes too much. It's more practical for her to work and me to stay home. There just aren't any good day cares around us. She is going to college, and she's bettering herself, and I just seem to be in a rut. Everything's a catch 22.

THERAPIST: When you say "if it continues," what exactly is the "it"?

LIZ: I mean, like closeness, sex. Unless I start it, we don't have sex. I decided not to start it anymore.

From the first statements of the session, the therapist used the clients' language. The use of "if it continues" enabled the therapist to explore what the clients viewed as relevant and encouraged their meanings to come forth. Although the conversation had just started, Liz already indicated a possible goal in her statement, "We don't have sex."

SESSION ONE, EXCERPT TWO

THERAPIST: How do you think coming here can be helpful?

BOB: When we first got together, I used to hug her and kiss her for no reason. I was much more affectionate. I haven't been doing it, like I used to. . . . It's getting me to talk and maybe could get me to do what I used to do.

LIZ: I don't think when you are watching a child you should be drunk. You have to be sober. And he drinks around bums. And I don't want my daughter around that. I don't understand how he can even do that if he loves her. He looks like a bum. He's still drunk from the day before. . . . I don't give it much hope. When we got married, I trusted him, and I respected him. I don't trust him anymore, and I don't respect him. When that's gone, your marriage is gone.

Yes, it sounded pretty bad, but after direct inquiry about the couple's ideas and expectations, both revealed their theories of change. Bob believed that being affectionate to his wife the way he used to would help the marital problems. For Liz, in addition to closeness and sex, a successful marriage required trust and respect. For Liz to trust and respect Bob, she needed for Bob to be sober while watching their daughter. The two identified the goals and the means to achieve them. After a break with the team, the therapist implemented their theories of change.

SESSION ONE, EXCERPT THREE

THERAPIST: The team and I were very taken by your ability to talk honestly about your marriage. You both want the same things. Bob, you want to be affectionate and that is what you [Liz] are looking for.

But, as Bob said, he is in a catch 22, trying to decide "I'd really like to go back to work, but is putting my child in this day care really the best thing for her?" That is a struggle of a good parent. And it shows, Liz, the responsibility that it takes to be a good father. What you are doing is putting your child before yourself.

LIZ: I never looked at that.

The therapist complimented the couple and validated Bob's struggle regarding working and placing his daughter in an inadequate day care. Highlighting Bob's struggle as a "good parent" provided Liz with a different view of her husband, consistent with her hopes to regain trust and respect for him. The therapist honored Bob's theory of change regarding affection and Liz's desire for closeness and sex. To further encourage a new view of Bob and the possibility of noticing the changes the couple desired, the therapist asked the clients to note the things they wanted to continue in the relationship, what de Shazer (1985) calls the first-session formula task.

SESSION TWO, EXCERPT ONE

LIZ: He has been nicer. He's more attentive. He's kissed me and more.

THERAPIST: He's been more attentive; he's kissed you. Now give me an example. Like, how is he more attentive?

LIZ: Well, like if we pass each other, like walking through the house, he'll stop and give me a kiss or a hug.

BOB: It's been missed for a long time, so I figured the best thing to start with is go back to what I used to do, when we were getting along real good.

LIZ: He hasn't been drunk.

THERAPIST: In two weeks? How have you managed not to get drunk in two weeks?

BOB: Just don't do it. It's no big deal. It's not difficult. Just decided not to do it and didn't, that's all.

THERAPIST: Great!

LIZ: He wants to save the marriage.

The therapist continued using the clients' language to keep their meanings center stage and to validate the clients' beliefs and values regarding their solutions. Bob repeated his theory of change by stating, "So I figured the best thing to start with is go back to what I used to do." Liz was beginning to respect Bob because he hadn't been drunk and he showed signs of wanting "to save the marriage." Since going back to the way things were emerged as a potent solution, the therapist unfolded its meanings to the clients. The therapist decided not to follow up Liz's "and more" comment because of her obvious embarrassment. The team assumed the couple had resumed sexual contact.

SESSION TWO, EXCERPT TWO

THERAPIST: What other things did you do when you first met?

BOB: We used to make each other laugh. We would get into word games. You know, two words that sound the same and don't mean the same.

LIZ: We make fun of the English language.

BOB: *Sun* and *son*.

LIZ: *Maid* and *made*.

The therapist explored the clients' experiences and discovered additional resources to empower the changes the couple had made.

Laughter and word games characterized the rest of the session. After a discussion break with the consulting team, the therapist accommodated Liz and Bob's word games in a final message to the clients.

SESSION TWO, EXCERPT THREE

THERAPIST: The team really enjoyed the word games. A word game for what is going on in your relationship is *light*.

LIZ: Is that *light* or *light*? *[laughing]*

THERAPIST: That's it, exactly. It's light; things have gotten lighter between the two of you. You're laughing, hugging more, kissing more, and talking more. And as your relationship's getting lighter, he's being nicer; he's not drunk; you're trusting and respecting him more. As your relationship continues to get light, the light of your fire is getting brighter. You've rekindled your relationship, and it gets brighter as you give it attention. Yet things happen sometimes, and you can't give a fire as much attention. Kids get sick; adults disagree; and it might look like the fire's gone out. Yet if you stoke it and give it a little bit of attention and start rekindling it and putting more wood on it and doing the loving things you do, the fire will light again.

BOB: You need to pay attention to it.

LIZ: Yeah.

The therapist interspersed the clients' words from both sessions throughout this final segment. After the break the therapist wove all the threads together to form a tapestry of the client's language, meanings, and theories to highlight the noted exceptions, resources, and solutions. The clients' word game provided the framework for validating their ideas to improve their relationship. It is worthy to note that Liz and Bob resolved the drinking problem without the team's intervention, further testament to their inherent resources.

TRUSTING THE CLIENT'S THEORY

That so few dare to be eccentric marks the chief danger of the time.

—*John Stuart Mill,* On Liberty

Despite our well-intentioned efforts in privileging their perspectives, clients hold beliefs and values that at times grate like sharp fingernails on a chalkboard. Women oppressed by male chauvinism sometimes embrace a subservient position. Clients disempowered by victim- or deficit-based views sometimes persist in seeing themselves as damaged goods. Clients deceived by the medical model and wanting to see us as experts sometimes don't see the value of collaboration. These are the situations that test our mettle as therapists. And these are the clients from whom we have learned the most.

As this chapter illustrates, clients have taught us to use their map as the best guide to the therapeutic territory. The therapist is a coadventurer, exploring the landscape and encountering multiple vantage points while crossing the terrain of the client's theory of change. When stuck along the way, we join clients in looking for and exploring alternate routes on their own maps. In the process clients uncover trails we never dreamed existed.

This chapter proposed that the client's theory of change offers ways of integrating multiple therapy perspectives one client at a time. Trusting in the client's theory of change requires taking a leap of faith, risking jumping headfirst into uncharted water with no land in sight. Honoring the client's theory of change is a proactive initiative that requires a focused effort to conduct therapy within the context of the client's unique ideas and circumstances. Because model and technique represent only 15 percent of outcome variance at most, we view them only as content areas, metaphorical possibilities, which may or may not prove useful in the client's unique circumstances.

As a field, we should deemphasize our theories and instead focus on those of our clients. Amplifying the client's voice through routine assessment of the fit and benefit of services would go a long way toward encouraging our client's ideas to take center stage—and toward eschewing process-oriented intellectualizations that occur outside of awareness of those they purport to be of help.

We hope that the field of psychotherapy will move beyond efforts aimed at seeking consensus on how therapy is to be conducted. Instead, clients, counselors, theoreticians, and researchers would be working together to develop the most effective ways to use client ideas and feedback regarding the outcome and process of therapy to improve success; heroic clients would partner with us to improve effectiveness and ensure accountability, restoring faith in psychotherapy services and reestablishing our relational rather than medical identity.

CHAPTER SIX

The Myth of the Magic Pill
The Ethics and Science of Medication

with Grace Jackson, Roger P. Greenberg, and Karen Kinchin

> *He's the best physician who knows the worthlessness of most medicines.*
>
> *—Benjamin Franklin*

his chapter confronts the myth of the *magic pill* and presents evidence that the superior effectiveness of many drugs is largely a presumption, based on an empirical house of cards, driven by an industry that has no conscience about the implications of its ever-growing and disturbingly younger list of consumers. Despite our critical perspective of psychotropic medications, we are not against drugs any more than we are against CBT or any other viable approach to human distress. Similar to our stance toward evidence-based practice, we object to marketing and corporate influence holding sway over public and professional opinion when the data regarding both the theoretical underpinnings and efficacy of drug treatment is at best unconvincing. Further, we fully recognize that medication helps some clients and that they freely choose drugs as a first line of defense. In truth, we honor client preferences, even for medication, and stand against any practice that does not center clients' desires about how they may be helped.

This chapter seeks only to critically examine the research addressing the widely held beliefs about drugs, hoping to replace blind obeisance to the myth of the magic pill with an informed set of options with which to address client concerns. Recognizing that most mental health professionals do not have the time, and sometimes feel ill equipped, to explore the controversy regarding psychotropic drugs, in this chapter we offer the gist of the research about medicating children and adults so that you may draw your own conclusions.

THE ETHICS OF MEDICATING KIDS

During the 1990s, prescriptions for psychiatric drugs to children and adolescents skyrocketed (Olfson, Marcus, Weissman, & Jensen, 2002; Zito et al., 2003). Evaluating the records of almost a million Medicaid and HMO youths, Zito et al., in one of the largest and most comprehensive studies to date, concluded that child and adolescent psychotropic utilization rates nearly tripled from pre-1990s levels. Total psychotropic prevalence for youths reached as high as 6.3 percent, rivaling adult rates. According to an IMS Health survey, between 1995 and 1999, the use of antidepressants increased 151 percent in the seven through twelve age group and 580 percent in the under-six population (Diller, 2000). Children under eighteen saw a nearly 300 percent increase in the use of antipsychotic medications such as Risperdal. According to Diller, Drug Enforcement Administration records and national physician practice surveys indicate that approximately four million children took stimulants in 1998.

Even more alarming rates cluster in certain groups. Zito et al. (2003) found that children in foster care were sixteen times more likely to receive a prescription than were their counterparts outside foster care. The *Boston Globe* reported that, in the Massachusetts Medicaid program, one in eight teens and one in nine children aged six through twelve (8 percent and 13 percent respectively) was taking psychotropic medications (Barry, 2003). Between 1991 and 1995, pediatricians and psychiatrists wrote record numbers of stimulant, tricyclic antidepressant, clonidine, and SSRI prescriptions for preschoolers (Zito et al., 2000). Prescription rates for methylphenidate (Ritalin) for children aged two through four grew by 169 percent. Zito et al. (2000, p. 1026) called such dramatic increases "remarkable in light of the limited knowledge base that underlies psychotropic medication use in very young children."

In most major surveys of child and adolescent psychotropic use, stimulants rank as most popular, with antidepressants second. The research also points to an increasingly commonplace trend, polypharmacy, prescribing two or more medications simultaneously. According to one study, the rate of coprescription rose significantly from 4.7 percent to 11.6 percent during the period from 1987 through 1996 (Olfson et al., 2002). Children on stimulants for diagnoses of attention deficit hyperactivity disorder (ADHD) are frequently prescribed clonidine, an adult hypertensive, to help with insomnia. These kids often take an additional antidepressant along with their amphetamine or methylphenidate. Psychiatrist Joseph Woolston (1999, p. 1455) remarks:

> Unfortunately, the multiple "comorbid" diagnoses may reify the need for multiple medications: a different medication to treat each different "disorder." Almost weekly I am asked to evaluate and treat children who allegedly have 5 or 6 Axis I disorders and who are receiving as many or more different psychotropic medications to treat each disorder.

Out of these diverse studies, surveys, and anecdotal reports a consistent picture emerges. Children and teenagers can hardly be said to live, play, and work in drug-free zones. The use of drugs to fix their own, their parents', or their school's problems is rampant. IMS Health, the pharmaceutical industry's own source of information, estimates that as many as five million children are taking some form of psychotropic medication (Diller, 2000). Given indisputable trends, widespread marketing, and a growing acceptance of medical intervention, current prevalence is likely far greater.

The news of rising psychiatric prescription rates to kids has prompted concern among many. However, reassurance from the medical establishment, including its massive presence in mainstream media, quells much of the public's uneasiness. Popular Web sites, while always advocating therapy interventions, give the most detail for medication treatments. The NIMH Web site reports that childhood "mental disease," contrary to earlier thinking, can begin at very young ages; early diagnosis means a better prognosis. "We used to think children could not be mentally ill . . . ," so the line goes, relegating nonmedicating preferences to the uninformed dark ages, when children were left to suffer without the benefit of today's modern medicines. The logic and the emotional appeal are compelling. Concerned parents should "see your [child's] doctor."

In such a climate, legitimate requests for alternatives often meet with formidable resistance. Reports have surfaced of parents facing accusations of neglect by state child protection agencies because of their refusal to medicate their child. Some mental health workers may fear that openly advocating for nonmedical interventions, especially for what are considered severe or chronic conditions, makes them appear ill-informed, radical, or even unethical. Under such conditions, the road to informed consent and free choice by parents, children, and concerned clinicians becomes more and more perilous.

Until recently, childhood psychiatric medications have largely been used "off-label," meaning without the necessary scientific studies to produce Federal Drug Administration (FDA) approval. Now, this "gap" is closing, with more and more studies, funded almost exclusively by the medication manufacturers, finding their way into journals and granting scientific legitimacy to what already seemed just common sense.

Scientific backing opens the door to more and stronger arguments in favor of child pharmacotherapy in both the lay and professional press. A recent issue of *Family Therapy Magazine,* the quarterly publication of the American Association of Marriage and Family Therapy, is a case in point. This issue devotes itself to exploring family therapists and medications, with a special article on pediatric psychopharmacology (Walkup, 2003). Child and adolescent psychiatrist and psychopharmacology researcher John Walkup lays out the case: the accurate depiction of trends in prescribing practices for children fails to "put the increased use in perspective" (p. 35). He argues that many more children are being prescribed medications because

- Psychiatric medications work for children's problems.
- Destigmatizing psychiatric disorders has freed families and communities to seek medication intervention for troubled kids.
- Medications have become available during the 1990s to serve the needs of untreated children.

Our contention is that both commonsense and scientific grounding for widespread psychiatric drugging of children is at best unconvincing. Let's take each point in turn. First, what evidence do we have for the efficacy of psychotropic medications for safely alleviating children's psychological distress?

Antidepressants and Kids: A Sad Story

What do we know about antidepressants, the second most widely prescribed psychotropic medication for children and adolescents? The failure of tricyclics to effectively treat children is well documented (see Fisher & Fisher, 1997). During the 1990s, there was great hope for the "newer" antidepressants, the SSRIs. However, before 1997, SSRI efficacy studies found little to be hopeful about. A comprehensive ten-year review revealed a dearth of evidence that either tricyclics *or* SSRIs were effective for children and adolescents (Birmaher, Ryan, Williamson, Brent, & Kaufman, 1996). In spite of this, with ever staunch optimism, the reviewers concluded that "psychosocial and pharmacological treatments [for children] are vital" (p. 1581).

Prior to 1997, there was the interesting paradox that at the same time clinicians were prescribing more and more SSRIs for children, researchers were unable to prove that antidepressants were efficacious for this population. All of this changed with the publication of two studies by Emslie et al., one in 1997 and one in 2002. The first Emslie study was an eight-week randomized, placebo-controlled, double-blind trial comparing the efficacy of fluoxetine (Prozac) and placebo. This study found

- A significant difference in response between medication and placebo groups on *one* of five psychometrically sound outcome measures

- *No differences* in outcome between the medication and placebo groups as indicated by self-report scores of participating adolescents and their parents

- *No differences* in outcome between medication and placebo on two other clinician-rated measures

Readers can easily get stuck in the technical quagmire of clinical trial research. The 1997 and 2002 Emslie et al. studies provide ready-made examples for learning how to understand and evaluate the science that underpins psychotropic prescription. Using the Emslie studies, we will illustrate how four fatal flaws doom much of what passes as sound pharmacology research (Duncan & Miller, 2000, Sparks & Duncan, 2003). With the four flaws taken into account, the Emslie studies' already meager results grow even more meager, along with their claims justifying the safety and efficacy of Prozac for children.

The Four Flaws of Drug Research

FLAW NUMBER ONE: CLIENT VERSUS CLINICIAN RATINGS. Studies of antidepressants usually rely on clinician-rated measures of depression (the Hamilton Depression Rating Scale or the Global Assessment Scale, for example) rather than client-rated measures (such as the Beck Depression Inventory or the Outcome Rating Scale). Study outcomes, then, reflect researchers' viewpoints, not clients'. In their provocative tour de force *From Placebo to Panacea,* Greenberg and Fisher (1997) demonstrate that clinicians and clients differ substantially in their reading of how much improvement has actually occurred during clinical drug trials. For example, in 1992 Greenberg, Bornstein, Greenberg, and Fisher published an extensive meta-analysis of twenty-two antidepressant studies involving 2,230 persons and compared the effects of a placebo with both "old" (Elavil, for example) and "new" (Prozac) antidepressants. They found that both old and new antidepressants showed an advantage of about 20 percent over the placebo on clinician-rated measures, but *no advantage* on client-rated measures. In short, when clients rate their *own* responses, they often experience no improvement on antidepressants beyond what can be attributed to hope and expectation. If clients don't feel better after taking medications, how meaningful is any improvement other raters think they see? The 1997 Emslie study found no difference between the placebo and SSRI groups on the two client-rated measures.

The skepticism researchers have for the perceptions of study participants, even if they are children and adolescents, reflects the mistrust of client views deeply ingrained in mental health discourse. Various explanations have been offered to discount client voices: clients are too impaired by their so-called illness to accurately report their condition, or they cannot objectively assess improvement or lack of improvement in the way an observing expert can.

FLAW NUMBER TWO: COMPROMISED BLIND. But how objective are expert observers in drug trials? The validity of controlled studies in which a placebo is compared to a real drug depends on the blind; participants who rate the outcomes should not know who is getting the real drug and who is getting the placebo. Greenberg and Fisher (1997) note that the use of inert sugar pills as the placebo in the vast majority of studies actually makes it possible for most participants and clinicians to tell who is getting the real drug and who isn't. Those taking the active medication are more likely to experience the standard adverse effects such as dry mouth, weight loss or gain, dizziness, headache, nausea, insomnia, and so on—clear signals they are taking a powerful drug—while those taking the sugar pill have few or no reactions. As a result, the alleged double blind study is immediately unblinded for those rating outcomes, a fact that seriously compromises any conclusion that can be drawn. Using active placebos that mimic the side effects of the drug under scrutiny helps studies avert this second fatal flaw.

Other problems hamper the blind in double blind studies. For example, many drug trial participants in placebo groups have previously been on drug regimens, even some just prior to entering the trial, and are therefore familiar with the effects of active medications. One review of blindness in antidepressant trials notes that participants are far from passive—they actively read subtle cues or attempt to discover their treatment status and do so with remarkable accuracy (Evan, Siobud-Dorocant, & Dardennes, 2000). This same review notes that simply asking participants to track side effects compromises the blind from the outset. In all, what is presumed to be blind is at best visually impaired and subject to experimenter and allegiance bias.

No active placebo was used in the 1997 Emslie et al. study. The Emslie study researchers, undoubtedly aware of the many critiques of the study's blind, attempted to salvage its integrity (see Hughes et al., 2000). In their assessment, Emslie and fellow researchers determined that the blind "was clearly maintained" (p. 593). When both the Prozac and placebo groups were considered together, without regard to client response, there was no trend in the prediction beyond what would be expected by chance. However, when clients' responses to treatment were considered, clinicians accurately predicted medication for responders (twenty-seven out of thirty-one) and placebo for nonresponders (twenty-six out of thirty-five). These represent approximately 87 percent and 74 percent rates of accuracy, respectively, far from chance predictions! It is more than interesting that the very efforts to bolster claims about the integrity of the blind ultimately prove that the blind was undermined.

FLAW NUMBER THREE: TIME OF MEASUREMENT. The time researchers choose to make comparisons in controlled clinical trials is critical in determining the actual differences in effectiveness between a medication and placebo. First, antidepressants are almost never prescribed for short periods of time. Second, and more important, taking the last measure at twelve weeks, a typical drug study time frame, provides an inadequate look at the differential efficacy because differences between groups tend to dissolve by sixteen weeks. This major design flaw suggests that longer-term evaluation was avoided, as in nearly all drug studies, not simply because of funding or logistical obstacles, but because of fear that the effects would wash out. The eight weeks of the 1997 Emslie et al. study was obviously an inadequate length of time to draw any conclusions about differences between medication or placebo response. Flaw number three, time of measurement, casts one more shadow of skepticism on Emslie's final conclusions.

FLAW NUMBER FOUR: CONFLICTS OF INTEREST. The importance of the Emslie et al. study (1997) as a justification for prescribing SSRIs to juveniles cannot be underestimated. Keep in mind that until Emslie's 1997 publication, there was virtually *no* evidence supporting the increasingly widespread prescription of antidepressants for children and adolescents. This study provided enough basis for antidepressant prescriptions to youths to continue unabated (albeit off-label) and represented the first of two studies needed to achieve FDA approval of the medication Prozac for this group.

Emslie et al. (2002) completed the Prozac approval sweep with the publication of a second placebo-controlled randomized clinical trial for fluoxetine treatment of child and adolescent depression. The first point of interest is on the first page and illustrates the fourth fatal flaw of drug studies—namely, *who is funding the study and with whom are the authors affiliated.* In May of 2000, the editor of the *New England Journal of Medicine* called attention to the problem of "ubiquitous and manifold . . . financial associations" that authors of drug trials had to the companies whose drugs they were studying (Angell, 2000, p. 1516). Since this time, there has been increasing pressure for medical journals to publicize funding sources and author ties to those sources in order to alert readers to potential conflicts of interest. Under the title of the 2002 Emslie et al. study, readers can note that Drs. Emslie and Wagner were paid consultants for Eli Lilly and Company, which funded the research. The remaining six authors were listed as *employees* of Eli Lilly who "may own stock in that company" (p. 1205).

Beyond that—same study, different day. Lilly and Company pronounced Prozac to be "well tolerated and effective for acute treatment of MDD [major depressive disorder] in child and adolescent outpatients," adding that "Fluoxetine is the only antidepressant that has demonstrated efficacy in two placebo-controlled, randomized clinical trials of pediatric depression" (Emslie et al., 2002, p. 1205). The primary measure of the study failed to show a significant difference in response; all client-rated and two clinician-rated scales showed no difference. Three out of seven clinician-rated measures showed significant differences between the experimental drug and placebo. As a nine-week trial, the study did not assess longer-term outcomes. Once again, the study used no active placebo, seriously calling into question whether the investigators, either employees or consultants of the company whose drug was under investigation, could, with so much at stake, reasonably remain objective.

Nevertheless, the deed was done—two studies allegedly proved the efficacy of Prozac for children and adolescents. Shortly after the second publication, the FDA granted legitimacy to an already well-entrenched prescribing practice. The January 3, 2003, edition of *FDA Talk Paper* prepared by the FDA Press Office announced FDA approval for Prozac for pediatric use to treat depression. The report noted that studies have found side effects similar to those in adult trials. The paper also acknowledged that, after nineteen weeks of treatment with fluoxetine, youths in one clinical trial gained an average of 1.1 centimeter less in height (about half an inch) and about one kilogram less in weight (about two pounds) compared to youths taking placebos. The FDA report added that, although long-term effects on growth are not known, Lilly had agreed to conduct a Phase Four postmarketing study to evaluate this concern. Unfortunately, the track record for pharmaceutical completion of Phase Four follow-up studies is dismal. For example, of 107 new drugs approved between January 1995 and the end of 1999, not one had been classified by the FDA has having completed Phase Four commitments (Sasich, Lurie, & Wolfe, 2000).

What difference does FDA approval make if child and adolescent antidepressant prescription is already a well-established and growing fact of life? FDA blessing allows the unfettered marketing of these drugs to those who may be concerned about their impact in a child's life. Bestowing the governmental seal of approval quells real fears of parents, clinicians, and clients. It allows the matter of efficacy to finally be put to rest. In an era of "evidence-based practice," it can now be said that indeed evidence exists, regardless of how slight, that at least this particular compound works. This "fact" is now repeated in future research articles, mental health Web sites, promotional materials, workshops, classrooms, popular and professional books, ads, and more—media saturation reinforces truth.

For example, Brent and Birmaher (2002), in their most recent review of adolescent depression, unequivocally state the case for SSRIs for adolescent depression. "SSRIs are the most commonly used treatment for adolescent depression, because of the proven efficacy of fluoxetine, citalopram, and paroxetine in placebo-controlled trials, with a response rate of approximately 60 percent and a favorable side-effect profile" (p. 668). And this "truth" virtually halts inquiry into the actual soundness of the evidence that undergirds a massive child and adolescent pharmaco-mental health industry.

In contrast, but not supported by multibillion dollar corporate entities, psychotherapy for children and adolescents has a strong tradition of proven efficacy (Mufson, Weissman, Moreau, & Garfinkel, 1999; Asarnow, Jaycox, & Tompson, 2001; Michael & Crowley, 2002; Curry, 2001; Lewinsohn & Clarke, 1999). Nevertheless, the political and economic clout of medical psychiatry has allowed childhood psychopharmacology to take its place at the head of the treatment table.

Stimulants and Kids: The Wrong Kind of Attention

Attention Deficit Hyperactivity Disorder (ADHD) is arguably the most controversial topic in recent mental health history because the ADHD diagnosis is not defined by a biological marker (Leo & Cohen, 2003), is quite subjective, and is not easily distinguished from the everyday behavior of children (recall our validity discussion of diagnosis in Chapter Two). Despite the guidelines of diagnostic prevalence of 3 to 5 percent established by the 1998 NIH consensus panel, diagnostic rates are as high as an astounding 33 percent in some locations (LeFever, Arcona, & Antonuccio, 2003). And despite the lack of evidence for long-term safety and effectiveness, stimulant medication treatment for ADHD has increased an astronomic 700 percent in the 1990s (Mackey & Kipras, 2001).

Without consideration of design flaws, stimulants—primarily Ritalin—have unequivocally established their efficacy over placebo in small, short-term randomized clinical trials on narrowly defined ADHD symptoms (not on social or academic measures). To counter the criticism that short-term efficacy studies do not address the more important issue of effectiveness—or the success of stimulants on a wider range of outcome measures in real settings over a longer period of time—researchers conducted the Multimodal Treatment Study of Children with ADHD (MTA) (MTA Cooperative Group, 1999). The MTA compared four treatments for ADHD: behavioral treatment (BT), medication management (MM), combined BT and MM, and a community comparison treatment control group. The MTA has already been touted, in both popular and professional publications, as proving that stimulants are more effective than behavioral intervention. Given the significance of the study for policy implications, it is important to scratch a little below the surface to understand its conclusions.

First, on the positive side, the most unique element of the study is its large sample. Previous studies of ADHD treatment have generally been small, with 1 to 20 subjects in each condition. With 144 subjects in each group, the MTA was far superior in numbers alone. The MTA also surpassed its predecessors because it evaluated treatment for fourteen months instead of the customary twelve to sixteen weeks. Another impressive aspect is the comprehensive nature of the assessments conducted. Rather than the simple clinician-rated outcome measures that characterize most studies, the MTA selected a total of nineteen measures from multiple sources (parents, teachers, child, peers, and objective tests and observations) in multiple domains of functioning (ADHD symptoms, peer and parent-child relationships, classroom behavior, and academic achievement).

Before looking at the specific problems with the MTA, consider the results collected at the fourteen-month endpoint, as one of the principle investigators (Pelham, 1999, p. 982) summarized them:

- All four groups showed dramatic improvement.

- MM was superior to BT on parent and teacher ratings of inattention and teacher ratings of hyperactivity *but not on any of the other sixteen measures.*

- Combined treatment and MM did not differ on any dependent measure; combined treatment was better than BT on parent and teacher ratings of inattention and parent ratings of hyperactivity, oppositional behavior, and reading achievement.

- Both MM and combined treatments were superior to community treatments on parent and teacher symptom ratings and

teacher-rated social skills, whereas BT was equivalent to community treatments; the two conditions with BT were superior to
community treatment on parent-child relationships.

Let's examine these results in light of drug studies' usual design flaws.
First, as Breggin (2000a) articulates, the study was not placebo controlled or double blinded. The MTA not only lacked a pill placebo
control group but also relied only on evaluations made by teachers
and parents who were not blinded to the treatment conditions. Adding
emphasis to this criticism, Breggin suggests, is the fact that the *only*
double-blind measure (blinded classroom raters) *found no difference
among any of the treatment groups.*

Next, consider the issue of client versus other ratings. Neither the
subjects themselves (the seven- to nine-year-old children) nor their
peers rated the children as more improved when using medication
than when using behavioral or community alternatives. Breggin
(2000a) suggests that the negative findings from the blinded
classroom observers, the children themselves, and their peers indicate that stimulant drugs offer no advantages over nonmedication
alternatives.

Finally, recall that the time of measurement is a crucial factor to
consider. Here is the kicker of this study: assessment occurred at the
fourteen-month endpoint while subjects were actively medicated but
after the fading of therapy. The researchers took endpoint measures
four to six months after the last, face-to-face, therapeutic contact!
Thus, the endpoint MTA treatment comparison was for active MM
treatment versus withdrawn BT. The study's slightly drug-favoring
results were a foregone conclusion, based on the very way the study
was designed (Pelham, 1999).

Given that the results reflect medication versus withdrawn therapy,
the lack of difference on sixteen of nineteen measures (comparing
MM with BT) and on nineteen of nineteen measures (comparing community treatment of mostly medicated children with BT) is
even more telling. Also impressive, given the withdrawal, is that
75 percent of the children in the BT condition were maintained without medication for fourteen months, including one-half of those who
were medicated at study entry (Pelham, 1999).

Two papers addressing the twenty-four-month follow-up data are
under review (Pelham, personal communication, April 21, 2003). They
show that the group differences are even smaller because the MM

and combined groups have lost much of their effect, whereas the BT and community groups have retained their gains. Further, at twenty-four months, the majority of parents in the BT group thought their kids were doing well enough that they did not medicate them even after the study had ended (Pelham, personal communication).

Moreover, the MTA reported that parents significantly preferred the behavioral and combined treatments over medication alone. Even when a preference for medication exists, most parents desire not to medicate their children for the long term, as evidenced by the fact that most ADHD-diagnosed individuals stop taking stimulant medication during late childhood or adolescence (Pelham, 1999). This makes non-medical intervention particularly important in light of the fact that effects of stimulant medication, though beneficial in the short term, do not last beyond medication termination. This is of course why the endpoint measure in the MTA was of active medication and withdrawn BT and not vice versa.

Perhaps parental concern about long-term stimulant use is most fueled by adverse drug reactions. A whopping 64 percent of the children in the MTA were reported to have some adverse drug reactions: 11 percent were rated as moderate, and 3 percent as severe, with this category representing largely depression, worrying, and irritability. In his review of the research, Breggin (1998) reports that these troubling reactions to stimulant medications are common across clinical trials.

Finally, to emphasize the importance of parental preference, consider the recent revelation made by one of the principal investigators of the MTA, psychiatrist Peter Jensen. Jensen has been traveling the globe extolling the virtues of stimulants over behavioral interventions. With an audience at a recent APA meeting, Jensen shared that his son is diagnosed with ADHD and that he and Mrs. Jensen, ironically, opted for behavioral treatment instead of medication (O'Connor, 2001).

The MTA, as well as all the available evidence regarding stimulants, says nothing that indicates that medication should be privileged over any other option, especially as guided by client preferences. Moreover, and more troubling, the overuse of stimulants is a stopgap measure that locates the problem exclusively in the child (LeFever et al., 2003) and creates an "attention deficit" in professionals to responding more creatively to behaviorally demanding children and the less-than-perfect learning contexts to which they are expected to adapt. Mental health professionals need to challenge business as usual and encourage a broader discussion of the socioeconomic and cultural issues affecting children and their success in the schools.

On balance, given the less than overwhelming empirical support and apparent medical risks as well as the nebulousness of the ADHD diagnosis itself (Leo, 2000), the judicious use of stimulants seems warranted. LeFever et al. (2003, p. 12) make the following (edited) recommendations:

- Before any treatment, a suspected case of ADHD requires a thorough evaluation that establishes that the symptoms cannot be better explained by other factors and are inconsistent with developmental level.
- If a child receives a diagnosis of ADHD during the preschool years, stimulants should be avoided because many behavioral problems are resolved by the first or second grade.
- Behavioral interventions ought to be tried first because of their comparable efficacy and lower medical risks than drug treatment.
- If the child has not responded adequately after six months of therapy, then drug treatment may be considered.
- Psychotropic medications should not be combined until there are existing data from controlled studies supporting the safety and efficacy of the combination in children.

Destigmatization and Helping the Suffering Masses

Putting aside the underwhelming efficacy of both stimulants and antidepressants, Walkup (2003) also argues that destigmatization has freed caretakers to use medical means to address children's psychological needs. Destigmatization would be a good thing, but we find the logic that mental illness is not stigmatizing a bit hard to swallow. Peter Breggin (2000b, p. 27) states it well:

Nothing is more stigmatizing than carrying the label of "mental illness" for the rest of your life. It is especially unfair and demoralizing to tell children that they suffer from "brain diseases," "biochemical imbalances," or "crossed wires" when they simply don't.

How benign is a psychiatric label when it means a child must take medicine and must rely on experts rather than his or her own resources to solve problems? How harmless is it when a diagnosis means a child can forget pursuing a job or career in the armed forces, or may be ineligible to run for political office in the future? Instead, we concur with Breggin (2000b) that psychiatric diagnosis and its sidekick, medication, *create* stigma. We prefer to understand children's problems from almost any other frame—lack of maturity, individual temperament, life trauma, or difficulties with relationships—situations that are amenable to time or to the effort of the child guided by those closest to him or her. We also prefer to take into consideration the impact of social conditions beyond the child, family, or school that inhibit the best efforts of all. What might be seen as a brain disease may, in fact, be better described as diseases of poverty, racism, or other forms of marginalization.

Walkup and others, often by omission, paint a relatively benign picture of the side effects of child psychiatric medications. One parent we know questioned the possible effects of Geodon, an antipsychotic, combined with Zoloft for her fifteen-year-old son. The prescribing psychiatrist responded by suggesting that she not read the warnings on the drug insert because "it would just make you crazy." Although most professional organizations, including the National Institute of Mental Health (NIMH), encourage parents to read and to be informed when considering medication for their child, we wonder how often adverse events get lost in the discourse of drug efficacy and benefit.

In reality, the side effects of psychotropic medications for children warrant serious examination. Primarily, the impact of earlier and longer chemical intervention on not yet developed brains represents a significant concern (Vitiello, 1998). There is evidence that the use of neuroleptic and other psychotropic medications makes long-term, if not permanent, changes in brain structure (Breggin & Cohen, 1999). Second, too many warning signals point toward an *increased* risk of mania and suicide brought on by psychotropic medications, specifically the SSRIs (e.g., see Breggin, 2000b). Emslie et al. (1997) failed to discuss the implications of the 6 percent dropout rate due to manic reactions in the 1997 study of adolescents and Prozac. If this rate were extrapolated to the general population (as were the study's efficacy claims), for every hundred thousand children on Prozac, six thousand would likely experience this serious adverse effect.

Moreover, in a study of paroxetine (Keller et al., 2000), also called Paxil in the United States, twenty-one out of ninety-three (23 percent) Paxil takers reported manic-like symptoms, including hostility, emotional lability, and nervousness. (Ten in the Paxil group reported tremor, none in the placebo group.) In real practice, when these medications are taken for much longer periods of time than in clinical trials, rates of serious adverse responses are likely to be even more pronounced. Nevertheless, both of the previously mentioned studies proclaim the investigative drugs well tolerated and safe. Meanwhile, reports of children becoming either more violent or more depressed due to medications designed to produce the opposite are abundant and growing (e.g., see Breggin 2000b; Breggin & Cohen, 1999; Fisher & Fisher, 1997).

Recently, the United Kingdom's Medicine and Healthcare Products Regulatory Agency (MHRA) stated that Seroxat (paroxetine) must not be prescribed for anyone under the age of eighteen (Bosely, 2003). According to MHRA, clinical trials have failed to demonstrate the compound's efficacy for childhood and adolescent depression. More important, these trials indicate harmful outcomes as much as 3.2 times greater in the paroxetine group compared to children and adolescents taking placebo, including increased agitation, aggression, self-harm, and suicidality. Glaxo, the drug's manufacturer, denied covering up studies suggesting the drug might cause damage to children under eighteen. Earlier in the year, *The Guardian* revealed that members of the first working group investigating the safety of SSRIs had shareholdings in Glaxo, leading to the group's eventual disbanding.

Nine days later, the FDA issued a similar warning. Stating that it was reviewing reports of possible increased risks of suicidal thinking and suicide attempts in children and adolescents being treated with Paxil, the FDA recommended that Paxil not be used by this age group (*FDA Talk Paper,* June 19, 2003). The FDA's announcement also took note of the fact that three well-controlled trials in pediatric patients with MDD failed to show that the drug was more effective than placebo. Once again, how does this sit with the following claim made by the authors of one highly touted trial: "Paxil is generally well tolerated and effective for major depression in adolescents" (Keller et al., 2001, p. 762)? No surprise, this study was funded by GlaxoSmithKline.

The final argument Walkup (2003) and others make is that, instead of questioning current prescription rates, we should in fact be asking whether *enough* children are "receiving treatment." Fretting over design flaws or even a few unpleasant side effects is missing the bigger picture. This argument cites the Surgeon General's 2001 National Action Agenda for Children's Mental Health (NAACMH), claiming a virtual epidemic of child mental disorders. According to NAACMH, one in ten children or adolescents in the United States suffers from mental illness enough to impair their life functioning. Sadly, this initiative proclaims, only about one half of these "receive necessary treatment" (Mitka, 2001, p. 398).

In light of these messages, parents and other caretakers are understandably anxious, nervously watching for the telltale signs that their child might be the next to succumb. According to Walkup (2003, p. 35), the most relevant question here is "not the increased use per se, but what percentage of children and adolescents with pharmacologically responsive conditions are actually getting medication treatment?" In other words, if only half are being treated, and if evidence now indicates responsiveness for the largest categories of disorders, then current prescription rates for children should practically double. Instead of the five million plus children taking psychiatric medications, there should be as many as ten million or more receiving treatment.

Missing in the explanations offered by Walkup (2003) and others, besides the questionable efficacy of these drugs, are several key questions. How do we know that so many children are supposedly sick? Have the numbers of disturbed children and mental disorders all but remained constant in past generations, and only now are we able to locate, diagnose, and treat them? If increases in so-called childhood mental disorders are a more recent phenomenon, how might we make sense of this? Why are poor children—those on Medicaid, in the foster care system, or in residential settings—more often diagnosed and medicated? What role do simple cultural differences take when the psychiatric establishment is composed mostly of white American men (Zito, Safer, dosReis, & Riddle, 1998)? Finally, instead of diagnosable illnesses, are we seeing reasonable reactions to oppressive conditions by those most likely to be under the gaze of the system? If so, should we be focusing our time, energy, and resources toward larger social agendas rather than toward pills that subdue and stigmatize the very victims of these conditions?

One thing we do know. Pharmaceutical marketing took on new life in the 1990s, and at the same time, so did a host of mental disorders. With the population "educated" to the symptoms of silent epidemics, the everyday business of living, with its diversity of temperaments and emotional cycles, became subject to disordering. Who stands to gain the most from promoting a medical versus nonmedical story for children in trouble? We believe that an ethical path requires posing this question and those raised earlier to the scientific and broader communities in ways that invite clarification of the true options available to children and their families. Our ethical position is that families should make the decisions they believe will be most helpful for their youngest members. However, we believe that the information caregivers and young clients receive is often weighted in favor of corporate rather than therapeutic interests, disallowing adequate informed consent. We recommend a vigorous critique of what has come to be everyday understanding of what works for children and teenagers as they navigate the sometimes difficult paths to adulthood. We assert that heroic kids and heroic parents should have a full range of options for making this journey on their own terms.

MEDICATION NATION

One should treat as many patients as possible with a new drug while it still has the power to heal.

Sir William Osler

Five psychotropic drugs (three SSRIs and two antipsychotics) appear on the list of the top twenty drug sellers of 2002 (IMSHealth, 2003): antipsychotic Zyprexa ranked sixth with sales of $2.9 billion; ninth was Zoloft, with sales of $2.5 billion; coming in tenth and selling $2.3 billion was Paxil; fifteenth was antipsychotic Risperdal, selling over $1.8 billion; and, finally, Celexa placed twentieth, with sales of 1.6 billion. Prozac, once the gold standard, has fallen out of the top twenty, but is still a contender. If antidepressants were books, they would be runaway bestsellers. More than 150 million prescriptions were written for them in 2002, and consumers spent more than $9 billion.

The use of psychotropic drugs for human suffering has become our culture's conventional wisdom despite the fact that neither the latest discoveries of neuroscience nor outcome research have confirmed their efficacy or strongly supported their use. Mass-market advertising has succeeded in its intention to make the taking of antidepressants, for example, seem as normal and pervasive as swallowing aspirin. Sure, the popular press regularly criticizes the pharmaceutical companies for questionable marketing strategies and nefarious research practices, but most people have now come to expect occasional excesses from businesses competing for market share in the capitalistic society in which we live.

And although most mental health professionals would acknowledge that the explanation given to clients is a gross oversimplification of actual brain functioning and recognize that drugs never quite live up to the hype, few reject the biochemical model altogether. Fewer still question the effectiveness of the drugs, for children or adults, and virtually no one challenges the idea that combining medication with therapy is the best of all treatment options. At least it includes what talk therapists have to offer. The problem with these common beliefs and practices emerges, however, when we examine them in the light of research. Empirically, there is little support for

- The ubiquitous biochemical imbalance
- The superior effectiveness of drug treatment
- Better outcomes when therapy is combined with drugs

The Mantra of Psychiatry: The Biochemical Imbalance

Antidepressants broke new television ground during the 1999 World Series in a commercial asserting the power of Paxil to cure social anxiety. An avalanche of ads aimed directly at the public has since smothered the advertising landscape. Perhaps the most impressive job of public awareness and product identification has been accomplished by the advertisers of Zoloft: cute little oval-shaped guy initially mopes and frowns while a narrator tells us about chemical imbalances; the oval then starts bouncing around, cheerfully smiling, presumably after taking Zoloft. "Biochemical imbalance" is now an irrepressible part of the American vernacular.

To understand the controversy around the biochemical imbalance theory is to appreciate both the history of drug treatment and drugs' proposed mechanisms of action. The present era of biological treatments for mental maladies was ushered in by the compound reserpine, a high-blood-pressure remedy originating in India. In 1952 psychiatrist Nathan Kline experimented with reserpine in persons diagnosed with schizophrenia, obtaining what he perceived to be significant results.

Some years later, researchers found that reserpine depleted catecholamines (dopamine, norepinephrine, epinephrine) within presynaptic nerve endings. This finding contributed to the dopamine excess theory of schizophrenia, which surprisingly persists today. Recall that a neurotransmitter, like dopamine, is synthesized and stored within a presynaptic nerve ending. When the neuron is stimulated by an electrochemical signal, it triggers neurotransmitter release from the nerve ending into the synaptic cleft. Here, it diffuses to make contact with receptors on the pre- or postsynaptic neurons, or it is removed from the synapse by enzymatic degradation (in the case of acetylcholine) or reuptake (for the bioamines, like dopamine).

Shortly after reserpine was presented to the world as a treatment for schizophrenia, researchers discovered its propensity to cause depression. Noting a 15 percent incidence of depression among those taking reserpine for hypertension, researchers advanced the theory that catecholamine depletion must be the "cause" of mood disorders. The irony here, of course, was that reserpine had just been touted as a highly effective therapy for schizophrenia. Scientists didn't seem to notice the implications of their new theory, which suggested that a drug that caused depression was now a remedy for schizophrenia. Moreover, scientists failed to explain why 85 percent of the persons who received reserpine (for high blood pressure) did *not* manifest signs or symptoms of depression, which the drug was expected to engender because of purported neurotransmitter reduction.

The second new compound, chlorpromazine, was a surgical sedative adopted by French psychiatrists as a "treatment" for anxiety, agitation, and psychosis. Ultimately, the antipsychotic properties of the drug were attributed to its ability to block dopamine receptors (Barondes, 1993; Snyder, 1986). One of the pioneers in modern psychopharmacology was the Swedish researcher Arvid Carlsson, who studied neurochemical changes in the brains of rats following the administration of chlorpromazine. On one hand, the levels of *dopamine* remained unchanged; on the other hand, the levels of *dopamine metabolites* were raised. To account for these findings, Carlsson proposed that postsynaptic receptor blockade resulted in a feedback message to the first neuron, triggering the synthesis of more dopamine. Thus, the levels of dopamine appeared to be constant, as the cell made new quantities of the neurotransmitter to replace what the administration of the drug had depleted.

What Carlsson did not appreciate was the theoretical inconsistency of these first schizophrenia drug "cures." Reserpine suggested that psychosis responded to dopamine *depletion*. Conversely, chlorpromazine suggested that psychosis responded to just the opposite, dopamine enhancement (enhanced turnover and secretion). Biopsychiatry has still not accounted for this discrepancy, which is actually just one among many pertaining to the biogenic amines.

The Elusive Biological Marker: The Bioamine Theories

Despite fifty years of research, the invention of electron microscopy, the advent of radiolabeling techniques, the revolution of molecular biology, and the merger of computers with neuroimaging machines, *no* reliable biological marker has ever emerged as the definitive cause of any psychiatric "disease." What many fail to appreciate is that biochemical imbalances and other so-called functional mind diseases remain the only territory in medicine where diagnoses are permitted without a single confirmatory test of underlying pathology.

The lack of a neurobehavioral diagnostic test, however, is not for lack of trying. For example, once heralded as the gold standard for delineating endogenous versus reactive depressions, the dexamethasone suppression test (DST) was abandoned in the 1980s after its disappointing performance. Less than half of depressed persons failed to suppress cortisol following the administration of a synthetic steroid, while many nondepressed subjects tested positive on the same procedure (Nathan, Musselman, Schatzberg, & Nemeroff, 1995). Ultimately, the DST failed to live up to its promise and was rejected due to its low predictive validity. Other highly touted markers unceremoniously fell off the landscape for similar reasons.

The biogenic amine theory of depression was so named because the earliest chemicals believed to have antidepressant effects were found to modify the body's major amines: dopamine, norepinephrine, and serotonin (Barondes, 1993). Enthusiasm about serotonin, the queen of all chemical imbalance theories of depression, did not emerge until the early 1970s, when researchers believed that there might be differences among drugs based upon the selectivity for one of the bioamines. According to Healy (1997), the first SSRI (zimelidine, or Zelmid) was patented in April 1971 and released in Europe in 1982. However, the drug was never marketed or licensed in the United States because of case reports linking it to serious neurological disease. Since that time, of course, a variety of SSRIs have been marketed worldwide. Notwithstanding the fact that SSRI responders are scarcely distinguishable from those who respond to placebo, the medical establishment and public continue to embrace the serotonin theory of depression (Antonuccio, Danton, DeNelsky, Greenberg, & Gordon, 1999; Kirsch, Scoboria, & Moore, 2002).

The search for the serotonin imbalance, like all neurotransmitter imbalances, has involved studies of human brain tissue, body fluids, and blood cells. First, it is important to appreciate that serotonin is a ubiquitous chemical distributed throughout the body. Over 90 percent of it is produced *outside* the brain, by the enterochromaffin cells of the digestive tract. Platelet cells bind serotonin within the blood vessels of the gut and carry it throughout the body for other purposes (Gilman, Rall, Nies, & Taylor, 1990). A second important property of serotonin—as with all of the biogenic amines—is its size. As a relatively large molecule, the serotonin that flows through blood vessels is too large to penetrate the blood-brain barrier. This is why serotonin cannot be given orally or intravenously to replace "low levels" in the brain; and this is also why serotonin blood levels cannot be used as barometers of serotonin in the brain.

However, in the 1980s, researchers proposed platelets as models for brain activity, based upon the hypothesis that blood cell receptors would echo the receptor properties of neurons themselves. In 1990, however, the World Health Organization rejected the validity of this approach, disallowing the use of platelet-binding assays as biological markers for depression (Nathan et al., 1995).

Recognizing these limitations, a number of researchers have tried to quantify neurotransmitter levels within the brain. For primarily technological reasons, sampling these chemicals directly in humans has not been feasible. Indeed, with over a hundred billion cells, each extending thousands of connections, and with neurotransmission events that last milliseconds, there is no reason to believe that direct measurement would be either possible or meaningful. Although researchers have used animal models, no consensus exists about the presence of chemical abnormalities in animal brains, unless or until outside substances (such as reserpine or imipramine) have first provoked them.

Following thirty years of failure in establishing the existence of a neurochemical *imbalance,* researchers turned their attention away from bioamine *levels* to a more global concept of disrupted bioamine *regulation* and neurotransmission. The emphasis has shifted to neuron receptor properties (number and sensitivity), which are presumed to interrupt the functioning of postsynaptic cells. The evidence presented in postmortem analyses of brain tissue and live neuroimaging techniques has proven highly variable, with no consistent findings to support theories of abnormal receptor density (Hales, Yudosky, & Talbott, 1999; Healy, 1997; Fogel, Schiffer, & Rao, 1996).

In defense of biological psychiatry, despite the oft-heard story of the biochemical imbalance, theory has advanced to the point of no longer attributing mental illness to deficits or excesses of any one chemical. A consensus is building that supports mental illness as the product of disrupted homeostasis within the entire neuroglial soup. Given the fact that the human brain consists of over two hundred chemicals, a hundred billion neurons, and thousands of connections between each one of them, one must wonder if a biological model that attributes pathology to all chemicals devolves to no particular theory at all.

On Balance

Before there can be a neurochemical theory of mental pathology, there must be a neurochemical theory of mental health. Medical science has yet to explain the homeostatic mechanisms through which the brain regulates chemical and receptor processes. Without a fundamental understanding of how the brain *controls* these functions, it remains futile to discuss the chemical substrates of mental distress as the basis of treatments presumed to correct them. Maybe there *is* no evidence of a biochemical imbalance because there can *be* no evidence. Maybe human behavior cannot be defined or determined solely in physical terms, without relational and contextual considerations.

Whereas research has fervently but fruitlessly pursued the elusive biological marker that will unlock the mysteries of mental illness, little information about the long-term neurological consequences of psychoactive drug therapies has surfaced—even in the face of evidence that these medications commonly induce changes in receptor function that could aggravate both the severity and chronicity of mental health-related symptoms. Indeed, as neuroscientist Elliot Valenstein (1998) points out in his book *Blaming the Brain*, the arguments supporting biochemical imbalances are not only unconvincing but ignore the possibility that psychotropic drugs create, not cure, biochemical problems because of the brain's plasticity and rapid adaptation to pharmaceuticals.

Nevertheless, we are left with the darling little Zoloft guy's words of wisdom. Despite the paucity of evidence, in the evolving biological narrative, depression and other human problems are not a bundle of miseries shaped by many forces: a sedentary, lonely, impoverished life; the loss of love, health, or community; feelings of powerlessness arising from unsatisfying work, oppressive socioeconomic or cultural factors, troubled children, or a difficult relationship; or frustrated ambitions. No, it is a chemical imbalance. Its resolution does not require one to get meaningful support from others, to establish a collaborative relationship with a therapist, to change attitudes and actions, or to make any personal effort. There is only one solution needed: the passive consumption of a magic pill.

Demystifying Magic Pills

The idea that drugs are not one therapeutic tool among many but rather are universal panaceas has appeal to mental health practitioners and the public alike. Many therapists seem to have embraced drug company publicity and accepted their second-class status, assuming the primacy of pharmaceuticals is based not on great marketing but good science. They have become acolytes, worshiping before the altar on which the magic pill is displayed. For example, the American Psychological Association, suffering from prescription envy, continues to fight for prescription privileges bolstered by its recent victory in New Mexico. Other professional organizations seem reluctant to offer any critical counterpoint to the meteoric rise in drug consumption.

Greenberg (2002) suggests that solving problems with pills relieves people of the responsibility for having to do much to subdue their discomfort while separating them from the need to link negative emotions with ongoing life events. Simultaneously, pills offer clinicians an easy-to-provide, medically respectable treatment that is well supported by drug companies and an insurance industry eager for approaches that require ever briefer interactions with clients. A closer look, however, has raised major questions about the true level of benefit medicinal solutions provide and dimmed their luster as unique answers for depression and other emotional problems. For example, looking at recent scientific studies, Moncrieff (2001) concluded that despite their increasing use, antidepressants give no indications that they have lessened the burden of depressive experiences. Her observation was partially fueled by an inspection of prevalence rates of depression over a forty-year period (Murphy, Laird, Monson, Sobol, & Leighton, 2000). That analysis showed that rates of depression had not changed since the 1950s. Antidepressants, Moncrieff reasoned, are overrated. She is not alone in coming to this conclusion.

Others have determined that the difference in outcome between antidepressants and chemically inert pills called placebos is much smaller than the public has generally been led to believe (e.g., Antonuccio et al., 1999; Greenberg & Fisher, 1989, 1997; Kirsh & Sapirstein, 1998). For example, Greenberg and Fisher (1997) cite a number of reviews showing that antidepressant outcomes exceeded placebo in only 18 percent of cases. Similarly, a 1999 report from the Agency for Health Care Policy and Research reviewing more than three hundred randomized trials of the newer SSRI antidepressants indicated that the drug outperformed placebo pills by only 18 percent (Mulrow et al., 1999). Moreover, even this relatively modest difference in outcome between antidepressants and placebos may turn out to be an overestimate of the benefits attributed to antidepressants. As discussed previously, most drug studies favor the drug under investigation when the study's design includes inactive placebos, primary clinician-rated measures, and abbreviated study time lengths.

Relatedly, side effects *by themselves* may predict the results seen in antidepressant studies. A review examining the thirteen then-available studies on Prozac (Greenberg, Bornstein, Zborowski, Fisher, & Greenberg, 1994) found that side effects were highly correlated with improvement. The greater the number of side effects participants experienced, the better the outcome was judged to be by both clients and clinicians. These results suggest that a sudden nudge to clients' physical perceptions seemed to jump-start their own capacity for emotional regeneration. Alternatively, revealing through side effects who was taking the real medication may simply have unblinded studies and allowed participants to rate improvement based on a bias that real drugs should produce more benefit than sham pills.

Kirsch and Sapirstein (1998) make a persuasive case that side effects and the power of the placebo may account for the lion's share of effects attributed to antidepressants. Their meta-analytic review of nineteen studies involving 2,318 people showed that 75 percent of the response to antidepressants was duplicated by placebo. They speculated that even the remaining 25 percent of the positive antidepressant effect might turn out to be attributable to the unblinding power of side effects. The review also echoed a point made by others (Greenberg & Fisher, 1997; Moncrieff, Wessely, & Hardy, 1998), namely, that by using *active* placebos (those that mimic the side effects of the real drug), studies might show the advantage for antidepressants to be quite small or possibly even nonexistent. The Kirsch and Sapirstein (1998) paper created quite a flurry of emotional responses from critics and supporters alike, heightened by its arrival during a time of psychology's push for prescription privileges (Beutler, 1997). Yet the credibility of these preeminent scientists planted a seed of doubt in many skeptical of previous reviews.

The controversy about the benefits of antidepressants heated up even more when Kirsch, Moore, Scoboria, and Nicholls (2002) responded to some of their critics with a paper titled "The Emperor's New Drugs." This paper analyzed the efficacy data submitted to the U.S. Food and Drug Administration (FDA) for the six most widely prescribed antidepressants approved between 1987 and 1999. Once again, the results were provocative. Approximately 80 percent of the response to medication was duplicated by placebo control groups. Moreover, the drug-placebo difference was less than *two points* on the physician-rated measure of outcome! FDA memoranda intimated that the clinical significance of such a small difference was questionable.

As with the previous paper, a series of commentaries debated the meaningfulness of the results. However, this time Kirsch et al. (2002) responded that they were heartened to see that there was now unanimous agreement among the commentators that the mean difference between response to antidepressants and placebos is very small—so small that most of the drug studies funded by the pharmaceutical industry (57 percent) failed to show a drug-placebo difference. One group of commentators (Hollon, DeRubeis, Shelton, & Weiss, 2002) noted that until recently the small drug-placebo response difference had been a "dirty little secret" known only to researchers who conduct clinical trials, FDA reviewers, and a small group of critics who inspected the published data.

The main points of debate about the Kirsch et al. paper (2002) centered around whether even the small differences found might reflect the usefulness of drugs for some minority of people, whether clients with more severe depressions would do better than those with milder versions, and whether a variety of design problems could account for the troubling findings. Kirsch and his colleagues addressed each of these issues, dismissed most as inconsistent with the data and decided that, in the main, their results still cast doubt on the power of the pill. They acknowledged that other questions remained to be addressed but suggested that given the existence of other potent nondrug treatments for depression, antidepressants, because of their side effects, might be best considered as a last resort to offer only to those refusing or failing to respond to other therapies.

Drugs Versus Therapy: Are Two Treatments Better Than One?

Given the miniscule differences between placebo and antidepressant outcome, therapists need never undervalue psychotherapy or kowtow to drug treatment, especially when they consider long-term follow-up. Shea et al. (1992) conducted an eighteen-month follow-up study of clients in the original 1989 NIMH multisite project and reported that the psychotherapies outperformed the medications and placebo on almost every outcome measure. More therapy clients than drug clients recovered without a subsequent major depressive relapse, whereas those receiving the antidepressants sought treatment more often during the follow-up period, showed a higher probability of relapse, and experienced fewer weeks of minimal or no symptoms than either the two therapy groups or the placebo group.

But wouldn't the best of all worlds be one in which medications were *combined* with therapy, for a kind of double-whammy treatment effect? The idea that both together must be better than either one alone for addressing mental health problems has become the newest orthodoxy. In fact, this sensible-sounding compromise solution actually promotes the use of medications, by implicitly suggesting that virtually anybody who enters therapy could usefully take them. And yet little evidence supports the two-is-better-than-one approach. For example, Greenberg and Fisher (1989) identified eleven trials focusing on the question of whether combining drugs with psychotherapy for depression produces increased benefits. In nine of the trials, no added benefits were obtained. One of the two trials suggesting that the combination might have some advantages noted that drugs and psychotherapy had their impacts on different aspects of the clinical picture. Drug effects mainly influenced sleep and appetite while psychotherapy effects were more wide-ranging, affecting mood, apathy, work, suicidal ideation, and interest. Another relevant paper

(Robinson, Berman, & Neimeyer, 1990) presented a meta-analysis of fifteen studies comparing psychotherapy, antidepressants, or the two in combination. Results revealed that the combination was no more effective than either treatment alone. Still another review of seventeen research reports concluded that combining drugs with psychotherapy most often showed no advantage over delivering either treatment alone (Conte, Plutchik, Wild, & Karasu, 1986).

A large study by Keller et al. (2000) provides a contrast to the finding of little benefit accruing from combination treatments. This multicenter work compared outcomes for 681 chronically depressed persons randomly assigned to receive an antidepressant, cognitive behavioral psychotherapy, or a combination of the two. At the end of twelve weeks, about three-quarters of those in the combined treatment condition showed a positive response, compared to approximately half the participants in each of the individual treatments. The authors stated that the results demonstrated that the combination treatment was more efficacious than either treatment alone for clients with chronic forms of depression. Critics of the study raised questions about the lack of a placebo control group and about using only a single clinician-rated measure of outcome (The Hamilton Depression Rating Scale). Finally, the researchers did not know at the time of publication whether the difference in treatment outcomes would still be evident at a follow-up point beyond the twelve weeks of study. Nonetheless, this project perhaps stands as a hint that under some circumstances, with certain kinds of chronic conditions, combination treatments may afford some advantages, at least in the short run.

A similar point of view emerges from a project carried out by Thase et al. (1997) in Pittsburgh. They used a "mega-analysis" to examine the results on 595 persons enrolled in six treatment protocols conducted over a ten-year period. The researchers were looking for correlates of response to treatment for depression. Clients had been treated for sixteen weeks with either psychotherapy alone or a combination of interpersonal psychotherapy and antidepressants. The researchers acknowledged that most studies had failed to find significant differences between monotherapies and combined treatment regimens. Indeed, this study too showed that most persons with moderate or low levels of depression gained nothing by adding medications to the psychotherapy provided. However, they did find the combination offered advantages for the minority of persons suffering with severe, recurrent depressions.

To sum up, research evidence indicates that for most experiences of depression, combination treatments do not provide added benefits and may unnecessarily subject clients to unpleasant side effects and extra costs. Clinicians should, in other words, consider psychotherapy first. At the same time, the studies make some suggestion that a minority of clients—those with chronic, recurrent, severe bouts of depression—may gain some benefits from combined treatments. Yet it is not known at this point if the benefits observed in research studies are either long-lasting or carry over to the real-world experience of people who are not part of controlled research trials. It is also possible that enhanced outcome ratings may derive solely from the pills' effects on participants' sleeping and eating. A more pessimistic interpretation of the limited benefits of combined treatments is that they are illusory and based on the biases of outcome raters who are not shielded from knowing which clients are receiving which kinds of treatment.

Although we have focused on antidepressants because of their prevalence, similar points can be made about other drugs; closer inspection reveals compromises of the double blind, a bias toward clinician-rated measures, and short-term measurement of outcome. This is not to say that these drugs are not useful at times, but rather that they need not be worshipped as the one true god of change.

WHERE DOES THIS LEAVE US?

When money speaks, the truth keeps silent.

Russian Proverb

With all this largesse and publicity raining benevolently down, is it any wonder that people become hypnotically fixated on the brouhaha about a "revolution" in pharmaceuticals and overlook the boring fine print of the drug studies, with their more negative implications? Is it any wonder that mental health professionals, who do not have the time to sift through the doublespeak (e.g., the Emslie et al. and MTA studies: the fact that Prozac only outperformed placebo on a few clinician-rated measures; the sleight-of-hand presentation of the integrity of the double blind; or the interesting design choice of withdrawing behavior therapy long before endpoint measurement in the MTA), become beguiled into believing that privileging drugs is a matter of scientific fact?

To be trigger-happy to bring medication into the discussion automatically is to be under the influence of bad science and great marketing. When clients are stuck or desperate, the medication solution is easy to whip up; like ready-made dinners, it takes the work and anxiety out of "What's for supper?" What is required is a shift to, or more likely a reconnection with, what therapists know and have experienced over and over, both in their clients and in themselves—that most people can and will develop solutions to even the most daunting dilemmas given support and encouragement, that the impetus to health has many avenues and sometimes takes unorthodox routes, and that change will and does occur naturally and universally. At the core is a faith in change and the human tendency to find a way even out of the heart of darkness.

We privilege this stance as way to level the playing field, to compete with the powerful and boisterous medical ideologies promoted by profiteers and championed by factions within our own professions. When we can hang on to these beliefs in our hearts, emboldened by personal, anecdotal, and empirical evidence, we and our clients can hear, loud and clear, other possibilities in times of crisis, where once there was only the seductive chant to medicate.

Having said that, we would never stand in the way of a client considering medication if the client believed his or her problems were of biological origin and thought the drugs might be helpful. It is up to therapists to privilege clients' wishes in the therapy conversation, including their trains of thought, their brainstorming, and their talk. When clients put talk of medication on the table, then therapists can naturally help them explore it as an option. When clients believe medication will help, feel more hopeful at the possibility of trying medication, and are in the driver's seat in making an informed choice (including information about side effects, length of treatment, and possibilities of relapse), then medication can be beneficial. To follow the client's lead is to maximize client participation, strengthen the therapeutic bond, and enhance therapeutic outcomes.

The only exception to this would be with children. Given that drugs are essentially foisted on kids without their consent and that the efficacy and safety of most drugs has yet to be established, we consider the practice of prescribing drugs to kids as clearly the last resort, and in many cases, unethical, until other options have been discussed.

Whatever approach evolves from the dynamic moment-to-moment synthesis of ideas, the measure of its helpfulness is the client's view. We must know when to say when—whether the approach is medication or one of the four hundred methods and techniques of therapy. Therapy must have an evaluative component that enlists the client's help in determining the adequacy of any approach—a partnership that involves the client's voice in every juncture and decision.

In a country that has come to expect and even demand miracles from the pharmaceutical companies, it is little wonder that the chronic problems of drug therapy and the excesses of corporate marketing have been largely ignored. We hope against hope that some pill, some simple and painless solution, will be the cure-all for our emotional and familial woes. Finally realizing that psychiatric drug therapy is a profit-driven industry, built on a flimsy science, may be the bad-tasting medicine we've needed. Although it may be hard to swallow, it is time for therapists to learn the data, reinvigorate their belief in therapy, and offer clients real choices for addressing their concerns.

CHAPTER SEVEN

Planet Mental Health

*Daring as it is to investigate the unknown, even more so it
is to question the known.*

—Kaspar

Ask a fish, "How's the water?" and the fish says,
"What water?" Ask psychotherapists, family therapists, psychologists,
psychiatrists and people using their services to step back and evaluate "mental health" and you're likely to get uncomprehending silence.
"Mental health" is a term that has become so commonplace, so everyday, it rolls off the tongue or off the page without a moment's thought.
We literally cannot make out the motives, theories, power, and economic underpinnings of "mental health" that surround us every day.
Consider how "mental health" pervades our daily lives. There are
degrees in mental health; books about mental health (and its corol-
lary, mental illness); mental health Web sites, conferences, brochures,
databases, projects, programs, and congressional bills. Our mental
health is discussed, rated, named, treated, assessed, diagrammed, and
monitored. Mental health is as taken for granted as apple pie—how
dare one question what it is or what it means! Securely entrenched in
our thoughts and practice, "mental health" offers little opportunity to
compare and contrast other ways of thinking or doing; it is invisible,
unquestioned, and unquestionable.

In this chapter we invite the reader to read with a critical eye and to question the unquestioned. Through an alien's look at the talk and texts that ensure the dominance of "mental health," the reader can examine taken-for-granted ideas and decide his or her preferred course. Taking a step back, we see "mental health" come into focus as an object in question versus sacrosanct institution, a choice versus a given. Capitalizing it as Mental Health, as we will in this chapter, highlights it as a representation of certain ways of thinking and practicing. At the same time, it denotes the prominence of those thoughts and practices in our day-to-day lives. Mental Health stops the eye on the page and spurs the mind to examine and to question. Similarly, if we consider ourselves as inhabitants of Planet Mental Health, we can appreciate how much Mental Health permeates our professional and personal lives. We then can begin to ask whether other planets might offer more agreeable environments, or whether and how we might transform Planet Mental Health.

The Neurology of Mental Health

Mental Health is discourse, a set of beliefs about the nature of who we are and how we live in our world. The discourse of Mental Health speaks to such fundamental issues as what is the human mind, how should it function, what is the mind's health, how might it become "sick," who might help get it well and how (Gergen & Kaye, 1992). The word *mental*, of course, refers to the mind and *health* to the absence of disease or disability. With its emphasis on illness, Mental Health adopts a scientific, medical perspective. As with science, Mental Health's history and development is often taken for granted; it "just is." However, from a critical perspective, we see Mental Health as the product of a particular place, time, and way of thinking; it has a history, has authors with specific biases, and serves certain political and social needs.

Our place and time, as was discussed in previous chapters, privileges a biological perspective over the social and psychological. The "Decade of the Brain" continues into the twenty-first century, featuring the "medicalization of human pain and emotional suffering in which genes and neurotransmitters are the focus of ... interest" (Sluzki, 1998, p. 417). In a curious body-mind blend, human emotions are thought of as products of neurotransmitter amounts and flow. Images of clouded brains in before-and-after magnetic resonance imaging scans proclaim the final demolition of boundaries between mental and physical. Despite its holistic veneer, the biological take on emotional distress has led to an illogical conclusion—that there is only one best way to intervene. Medical interventions are considered "best practice" for a host of behavioral and psychological problems; talk and social intervention take on adjunct, supportive, often dispensable roles.

Biological fundamentalism requires a medical model and medical script, including assessment, diagnosis, and the treatment of ill or disabled persons by expert clinicians. A number of assumptions support this script:

- Psychological distress indicates a problem with an individual, even if in response to social trauma or stress.

- Psychological distress must be scientifically named and categorized to be understood and treated.

- Persons experiencing distress are dysfunctional and must resign themselves to the hands of experts.

- The client's perspective and understanding of his or her problem is suspect.

- The ill person's resources are useful to the extent they promote the doctor's orders.

Unseen and unquestioned, these assumptions inflate medical authority and diminish "local" expertise—the client's wisdom, strength, resiliency, and natural healing capacities.

A medical script and its underlying assumptions are not always benign in their implications. The various practices that follow this script often affect the basic rights of consumers and undermine their participation in getting over their problems. For example, in the name of Mental Health, the more extreme methods of restraint (electroconvulsive therapy, lobotomy, physical restraint, and social isolation) have been historically carried out. In the name of Mental Health, persons of diverse sexual orientations have been prohibited from pursuing careers, obtaining housing, or creating families. Mental Health has benevolently pushed Valium, Xanax, and other medications on women speaking out, and acting out, the pain of abusive relationship and intolerable social conditions, their silence and addiction under medication's influence reinforcing beliefs in their own pathology. In the name of Mental Health, children in record numbers are medicated for diverse learning styles, so-called overactive temperaments, or behavioral acting out. In Mental Health's name, elderly citizens languish, lifeless and joyless, from pill to pill.

Mental Health scripts and assumptions dominate the daily workings of psychotherapy. In most psychotherapeutic contexts, doctor-patient relationships in which the powerful minister to the disabled flourish. Such relationships necessarily curtail clients' contributions to change. Psychotherapy's sellout to a medical model has the full backing of a powerful industry. Pharmaceuticals wield their dollars and advertising clout to bolster Mental Health's move toward biology. The circle is complete as drug-funded studies manufacture so-called evidence for the necessity of Prozac. The strong arm of Mental Health—with its special knowledge, special money, and specialized clinicians—rules.

Swimming in Pathology

Surely such a picture of control is fiction, like Ken Kesey's novel *One Flew Over the Cuckoo's Nest*. Maybe there are isolated situations, or isolated institutions, where Mental Health takes a radical, repressive form. Should a parent, for example, really be that concerned about having a child seen at the local mental health clinic because her grades are failing? Or should anyone hesitate to tell a doctor about periods of depression? Should clinicians hold suspect years of training in diagnosis and assessment or question their own and their colleagues' desire to help?

Disclosing and critically looking at the underpinnings of Mental Health does not discount the helpfulness of psychotherapy and most therapists. Therapy succeeds because of the motivation and resources brought to the endeavor by clients, combined with the natural desire of therapists to support these, despite pressures to do otherwise. Many clinicians tolerate mandatory agency requirements so they can start to listen to clients and what they really want. These therapists instinctively attune their talk and their therapy in ways that match and bring forth the client's own language, energy, and ideas for solutions. And many clinicians cringe at thumbing through the *DSM* to find the least stigmatizing diagnosis to put on the insurance form. Where Mental Health business as usual prevails, clients still manage to turn therapy to their best advantage. One might say that clients are masters at getting what they need, even in less than favorable circumstances.

Despite these triumphs, therapists and clients face daunting odds. Client participation may sound good in theory, but day-to-day talk and action in the majority of Mental Health settings reveal more strongly rooted beliefs in client incompetence. For example, testing, diagnosis, and expert prescription reinforce client disability, while professional language and work protocols reinforce therapist power. Therapists more often treat believing in and building on client strengths as just an add-on to what they consider the real work for the real, underlying problems.

In this milieu therapists' efforts to highlight client ideas and resourcefulness (e.g., in supervision meetings or case staffings) take on a subversive quality—small acts of insurrection in a professional Mental Health climate. Client-directed therapists may find themselves practicing in the closet or perhaps questioning their strongest instincts. At the same time, clients learn to doubt their most valuable assets. Instead, they may learn a "sick" identity, becoming increasingly subject to its revolving door of disability. Planet Mental Health locks clinicians and clients alike inside an inscrutable reality that defines what is wrong with people and how they can be helped; it's just the way it is.

Despite recognition by many that something is wrong, that there's got to be a better way, business as usual prevails. We seek to raise clinicians' and consumers' threshold of consciousness by exposing how everyday language, including case notes, case supervision talk, case descriptions in books and workshops, and the vast array of media text (Internet, TV, brochures, etc.) perpetuate Mental Health discourse. However, a client-directed perspective's most subversive aspect is its insistence on privileging the local knowledge of persons seeking assistance—their goals, their strengths, and their motivations—in actual practice.

The following illustrates one real-life example of how typical therapeutic language reveals its roots in standard Mental Health discourse. A critical look at this example challenges Mental Health thinking and implications, offering a counterview and alternatives for practice.

JAN AND MARK ENCOUNTER MENTAL HEALTH

A word carries far—very far—deals destruction through time as the bullets go flying through space.

—*Joseph Conrad,* Lord Jim

Recently, we contributed a chapter to an edited book on the comparative treatment of couples (Duncan, Sparks, & Miller, 2000). This book presents how different models conceptualize and treat a single case of a couple seeking marriage counseling (Dattilio & Bevilacqua, 2000). The editors gave the invited authors a sixteen-page compendium of the issues to explore, as well as everything about the couple anyone would ever want to know, and asked the authors to comment.

We applaud the editors' efforts to highlight many ways to slice the therapy pie—that a couple seeking therapy will encounter different experiences depending on whom they choose from the yellow pages. However, writing the chapter presented a considerable dilemma: How could we articulate what client-directed, outcome-informed therapy looks like if we followed the preset categories and instructions given by the editors? If we conformed to writing about our model, mode of assessment, preferred interventions, time line for therapy, and strategies for termination—then we would be agreeing that these categories were essential to any therapy. Further, if we addressed these categories based on the information provided in the "Case Study"— including "Psychiatric History," "Medical History," "Mark's Social History," "Jan's Social History," "Substance Abuse History," "Child Abuse," "Criminal History," "Presenting Problem," "History of Presenting Problem," and "Critical Life Events Time Line"—then we have accepted, again, a priori, the assumptions these categories reflect. Our account of therapy, then, would be predestined to meet Mental Health's requirements.

This is how much, if not most, therapy is shaped, whether in writing or in real life. The categories, areas of inquiry, method, and scope of therapy are preset by basic ideas about therapy and the therapist's role. In all the sixteen pages of "information" sent to us, no real information to describe a client-directed, outcome-informed therapy even existed—no information provided by real clients in real therapy situations, their voice and descriptions of their problem, their goals, and their ideas about change. We lacked the heart and soul of therapy— the moment-to-moment encounter between therapist and client, the flow of ideas and reflections back and forth in which each turn of the conversation takes its direction from the client's choice of content and goals. In essence, the information we had received was just so much disembodied clinical language, much like traditional case notes, assessments, "biopsychosocials," or case descriptions in journals and books—lifeless words on a lifeless page.

Writing, of course, necessarily limits communication. Neverthe-less, there are ways to moderate writing's limitations and stay true to the client's voice in case descriptions. Therapists can include tran-scripted case material or actual client descriptions. Most important, therapists can make sure they write from the client's perspective.

Because we had no real access to Jan and Mark and no chance to learn their perspectives, we had to improvise. We decided to describe how to be client-directed not by following the categories or case mate-rial as given but instead by creating the missing piece, the clients' voices. To do this, we invented Jan and Mark's therapy, as though it were happening in the present. In this way we were able to describe an imaginary therapy that unfolded based on each step of the therapy process and not on some preconceived therapy model. Our chapter became more of a video in which the reader could hear and see Jan and Mark and know how the therapist responded to her understand-ing of their problem and their responses to her.

The following contrasts excerpts from the editors' case informa-tion with our account of Jan and Mark's therapy, highlighting the assumptions that underlie each. This gives readers the opportunity to experience an alternative to Mental Health's privileged view.

—*vw*—

Question: What is your treatment model?

Asking to define one's model already situates the questioner in a tra-ditional medical model. In modern psychotherapy the model reigns. Models are the basis for defining competency, specialized knowl-edge, and specialized practice. What are clinical training programs about if not to acquaint students with an array of models and then assist them to develop competence in a preferred approach? Model knowledge separates "the men from the boys," the para- from the pro-, the expert from the armchair psychologist. The medical model, because of its affiliation with science, represents the model of models. To the degree that psychotherapy models imitate medi-cine, they assume an aura of credibility unavailable to alternative approaches.

Merriam-Webster's Collegiate Dictionary (1993, p. 425) defines *model* as "1. a standard or example for imitation or comparison" and "2. a representation, usually in miniature." A therapy model is a representation (in someone's head or on paper in a book) of how therapy should go—a preconceived framework for therapy. Models spring from many sources, including theory, research, personal preference, or simply what's in vogue. What's important is to think of a model as just that—a frame for working. Understanding how models come into fashion and the role they actually play in therapy helps put their importance and their validity into perspective.

As we discussed previously, models and their techniques account for a modest proportion of therapy outcome. Nevertheless, models do have their place (if only they would stay there). Research indicates that clients prefer working with therapists who provide structure and a certain amount of direction to a therapy session (Mohl, 1995). Models can do this. To the degree that models jump-start therapy or provide a sense of order, they may be helpful. However, from an outcome-informed perspective, there are several problems with models and the worship of them.

Models can take on the trappings of truth; their proponents denounce competitors as heretics and champion favored ways of working as more progressive or more enlightened than others. The truth status that models attain belies their origins as constructions, necessarily subject to the whims of political or cultural mores of their place and time. In addition, models simply are not getting better at pointing the way to succeed at a given problem. Despite the hype, rates of improvement in, for example, substance abuse, substance-abuse relapse, depression, anxiety, or other psychological complaints remain unchanged.

Most importantly, therapists' love affair with models blinds them to the roles clients play in bringing about change. When models crowd therapists' thinking in their interaction with clients, there is little room left for the client's model to take shape—the client's ideas about his or her predicament and what it might take to fix it. If the therapist molds client input into the shape of a favored model, the client's model becomes distorted beyond recognition. For example, when refusal to attend AA meetings is framed as "denial" or parental concern as enmeshment, key communications about what the client thinks, wants, or values are not only left unexplored, they are denigrated as harmful. The hallowed act of interpretation, a direct offspring of the almighty model, nullifies therapy's most valuable raw material for change, the client's own ideas and participation.

The tendency to assume model superiority and effectiveness and the exclusion of client voice and participation through model enforcement reinforces standard notions of clinical expertise. As models proliferate and flourish, so do their specialized languages, systems of categories, and arsenal of techniques. The knowledge gap gets wider, and the division between those in the know and those out of the know congeals. At the top of the heap are the medical doctors and psychiatrists, steeped in layers of medical and psychoanalytic theory. Psychologists, social workers, family therapists, and mental health workers each add their own repertoires of specialized language and theories, churning out model upon model.

Last, of course, are consumers, those who are in the dark. Their language, their ideas are at best quaint, to be mimicked for the sake of friendliness or to elicit compliance. At worst, client ideas are part and parcel of the problem, those very elements needing to be eradicated or transformed into problems that the model can now fix. Once clients see the light and give up their erroneous notions of what is wrong and what is needed, change can begin. All in all, from a client-directed point of view, the model and worshipers of the model are the golden calf, the false path away from a true source of therapeutic change.

Answer: Therapists do not, cannot, enter their work as blank slates. We all have ideas, theories, both formal and informal, about the best ways for change to occur. We don't leave these ideas at the door but bring them into the therapy encounter. If one must use the term *model,* then being client-directed is a model that privileges the client's model. When asked to detail our model, we chose to describe outcome-informed work by introducing Jan and Mark to the reader through constructed dialogue. We wanted their voices from the outset to be louder than all the information about Jan and Mark's history that the editors had provided; in a sense we politely declined to review Jan and Mark's case file prior to seeing and hearing their story. By leaving predetermined model categories and "information" at the door, we showed how the therapist ensured space for Jan and Mark's own models to emerge and be vital in the course of therapy.

———

Question: What type of assessment does client-directed, outcome-informed therapy do to structure treatment?

The request to write about how we would assess Jan and Mark's marriage based on a host of historical information revealed its allegiance to traditional Mental Health assumptions. Expert assessment is the centerpiece of a medical script—the basis upon which the patient-doctor relationship is fashioned. Let's spell it out. You're not feeling well, mentally or physically. You seek the opinion of someone trained to recognize the cause of your problem and the ways it manifests in your body or mind. The trained person, by virtue of this understanding, then knows how to get rid of the problem. He or she tells you what to do or what to take to alleviate your suffering. Your cure depends on your faithful giving over of yourself to this process and adherence to its findings and prescription. You are, more or less willingly, the subject of power inherent in this system of belief and wielded by its keepers, the doctors.

We are all familiar with this script, most likely participating in it in a variety of ways throughout our lives. And each of us has had more or less success with getting the help we sought within its confines. Indeed, there are times when putting oneself in a doctor's care is "just what the doctor ordered"; the comfort and trust we place in certain people and their skill and talent at helping produce a winning combination. At the same time, while we attribute the cure to the wise doctor, we fail to credit our own belief and wisdom and their mysterious power to heal. We may not recognize the forces really at play when we invariably assign improvement to professional expertise.

Others experience assessment in less benign ways. For example, diagnosis, a form of distilled assessment, and evaluations, such as those common in criminal or court settings, differentially affect various cultural subgroups (Kutchins & Kirk, 1997; Parker, Georgaca, Harper, McLaughlin, & Stowell-Smith, 1995; Whitaker, 2002). In these cases assessments frequently serve political purposes, such as the suppression of complaints or forced isolation, rather than the real needs and concerns of those assessed. The doctor-patient relationship, when paired with marginalized groups, reaches its greatest power disparity and its greatest potential for abuse.

"Assessment" is steeped in our most basic ways of understanding any phenomenon, specifically cause and effect. Though notions of circular causality have long made their appearance in clinical texts, let's face it, we think about clinical situations in much the same way we think about day-to-day events. A leads to B, and to know A is to know something about B. Linear causality coupled with Freudian theory has deeply embedded notions of past trauma as causal of present-day problems and of present-day problems as amenable to change through knowledge of and intervention into the past. Intervention into the past, a curious notion when held to light, has assumed various clinical guises, including catharsis, awareness, and "working it through." A past and problem causal framework permeates Mental Health. We know the earth is round, yet we think and live on it as though it were flat; we may know that the past may be irrelevant to present-day solutions, but we still instinctively talk and treat it as though it were king.

As illustration, let's take the information given to us as a basis for assessing Jan and Mark and their marriage. We believe the editors' choices in what was relevant exemplifies the way many case studies, case notes, and reports reflect Mental Health assumptions, specifically biases toward the past, problems, and expert assessment.

Of the editors' eleven categories of information, all but one and a portion of another dealt with historical issues. The opening "Case Study" included information about Mark and Jan's current employment, hobbies, and routines. The "Presenting Problem" category described their statement, presumably obtained at a first therapy meeting, of their current relationship difficulty and what precipitated the call for an appointment for counseling. "Presenting Problem" and part of "Case Study" amounted to, at most, three pages. The remaining twelve pages delved into Jan and Mark's social, psychiatric, medical, presenting problem, and critical life event histories. The editors apparently favored the importance of history in assessment over the present by a ratio of four to one. It is likely that the editors offered a wide range of information in order to accommodate the various models of authors contributing to the book. Nevertheless, the four-to-one ratio not only limited choice for more present- or future-focused approaches, it necessarily channeled assessments to reflect standard Mental Health parameters.

Let's take a look at the descriptions within the sections to see how supposed neutral language in fact betrays a Mental Health bias. In the section "Presenting Problem," the editors described the interaction between Jan and Mark:

> At times, Mark will avoid being around the house, particularly when Jan is at home. He does this to avoid tension in the relationship. This conflict avoidance pattern of interacting has led to a lack of trust and emotional distance between them, greatly affecting their level of intimacy.

The reader is left in the dark as to how this information has been learned—over the phone at the initial intake, at a first session, or from review of a past case file? Whose perspective is it—Jan's, Mark's, or the therapist's? Many case reports and documents are written in ways that fail to reveal the author. The default understanding is to assume that either everyone agrees that this is the case or that the assessor has inside accurate knowledge, even if clients hold a different view.

The phrase *conflict avoidance pattern* casually sneaks its way into a seemingly neutral description. The reader is likely caught off guard; and the assessment implicit in this phrase, with all its attendant judgment and implication for practice, becomes a foregone conclusion. In absence of presenting actual client dialogue, client perspectives, and video language (detailed description) in the clients' own words, the words and phrases used to report client interaction become inextricably laced with labels and judgments that reflect the observer or writer's own point of view and background.

Presumably neutral or client-reported information, when framed in particular ways, bears the stamp of another Mental Health bias, a problem focus. The author writes, "Their sex life has deteriorated to the point where they now sleep back-to-back." Again, the sentence rolls off the page unnoticed. The reader is left with the bleak picture of a cold, distant relationship. The pronouncement overrides any critical look at the fact that many couples sleep back-to-back yet have lively sex lives. In the hands of the expert, proclamations of dysfunction become unquestioned truth.

Answer: The relationship between Jan and Mark and their therapist, by virtue of occurring in our time and place, necessarily entails traditional boundaries between helper and helped, assessor and assessed; in short, Jan and Mark entered therapy on Planet Mental Health. As part of a traditional Mental Health culture, Jan and Mark sought the help of someone they believed possessed an inside connection to what they needed to get their marriage back on track. At the same time, they each possessed a wealth of understanding about the problems they had experienced in the past, both individually and as a couple, and how they had overcome them. They also knew what were the real sticking points in their current dilemma and had at least a ballpark idea of what needed to happen for things to get better. In actuality, they were already on the inside track.

Unfortunately, Mental Health's standard medical script downplays these significant resources. Jan and Mark, as have many, came into therapy uncertain about their own ideas and more than willing to have someone give them the real scoop on what was wrong. They were pre-programmed to doubt and discount their own knowledge. This preprogramming can get in the way of what we know to be the most critical factor in any therapeutic change, the client's expertise and resources.

Nevertheless, client-directed therapy works with what the client wants and the client's expectations, even if those desires and expectations appear unfriendly to client strengths. To work in true collaboration means trusting in and counting on clients' abilities to make the most of the therapy encounter when that encounter values their perspectives, hopes, and expectations. Aligning with a client's desire to access expertise or to have an expert take charge paradoxically puts the clients in the driver's seat and maximizes their collaboration. Our desire to step off the throne must not blind us to clients' desire for us, at times, to be there.

From a client-directed perspective, therapist expertise does not exist at the expense of clients'. Nor does a desire to privilege clients diminish therapist expertise or prevent working collaboratively with those seeking an expert assessment. However, how the therapist considers and exercises that expertise does matter. In outcome-informed work assessment is coassessment, incorporating client input and voice and diminishing traditional power alignments based on expert knowledge. Coassessments are evolving, mutual struggles to reach a joint description of the problem and a path to enter for solving the problem. A client-directed therapist's assessment expertise consists of his or her ability to draw forth, expand, and focus client resources in the interest of change.

Absent from coassessments are the constant internal dialogue, interpretation, and reformulation of client accounts in the therapist's thoughts based on preset theoretical frameworks. Internal scripts and ongoing evaluations are part of the human process of thinking. Client-directed therapists, as we mentioned, are not blank slates; they too carry with them evaluative notions that constantly interplay with client input. Nevertheless, the process of coassessment differs significantly from traditional modes of assessment; internal evaluations and dialogue consist of constant attention to the clients' language and meaning. Therapists engaged in a process of coassessment assume a posture of open listening, questioning, and exploring based on client input that strives to clarify client meanings and expectations.

Assessment dialogue between therapists and clients is not an attempt to funnel client information toward an understanding that makes sense to the therapist but an attempt to follow clients' leads toward directions that ultimately make sense to them. The reformulations that occur in a client-directed therapist's mind during any assessment procedure consists of an internal search of his or her reservoir of experience for matches to or expansions of client ideas. The evolving, revolving conversation that ensues results in a jointly constructed understanding (assessment) with client material dominant. In a client-directed assessment, client participation and contribution, the gold standard for a positive outcome, is a given.

In the chapter we wrote for the edited volume, we attempted to articulate how a client-directed assessment differed from traditional assessments by manufacturing snippets of dialogue that reflected the back-and-forth nature of assessment from a client-directed point of view. Bringing the clients' voices onto the page helped to depict a client-focused assessment and to decentralize our own expert voice as authors of an approach or model.

How might readers be more in tune with Jan and Mark and less in tune with pronouncements of conflict avoidance patterns if an assessment read this way:

> At the first interview, Mark stated that he didn't like to "hang around the house very much" because it always seemed to end with him and Jan "getting into it." Jan complains that his absence from the home has resulted in her feeling mistrustful of his whereabouts and feeling "cold" toward him. Nevertheless, Mark and Jan both report a desire to regain the closeness they once had.

Simply assigning who believes what (based on accurate listening and recording) clarifies differences and similarities of opinion. Including actual quotations helps ensure that client perceptions and understandings are not subtly altered by therapist interpretation. There are three voices in this assessment. Reporting the "facts" in this way puts the clients' voices on an equal (or greater) footing with the therapist's.

Given a range of choices, how might we understand and describe the following words from Jan: "We used to be hugging all the time . . . you know; now he just rolls over and goes to sleep. At least he hasn't started sleeping on the sofa every night, like when we fight." There are choices that a reporter of therapy makes, just as there are choices that a therapist makes in every response to client input. In this case the therapist-writer could hear "deteriorated sex life" or could hear a continued desire to maintain some emotional and physical proximity. The therapist might report this situation by the following, "Despite stating that their sex life is not what they would prefer, they continue to sleep together." This rewriting includes both the clients' complaint and the reality of their decision to sleep together. Mental Health bias tunes out the latter and focuses on the complaint. The bias in outcome-informed work is toward both a recognition of the problem and a forward-looking, hopeful attitude. This attitude is based on a realistic faith in clients' abilities to change and on the importance of communicating that faith in the interest of heightening hope and expectancy for a positive outcome.

In case writing and in therapy, the client can confirm or reject this choice. Should Mark and Jan prefer to recognize their decision to continue sleeping together as noteworthy, perhaps even useful in helping their relationship, then they incorporate it into the gradually evolving story of Jan and Mark. Should Jan feel the therapist "doesn't get it," she can reiterate "Look, our sex life has really gone downhill. It's a problem for me." The therapist's willingness to ask and to change horses midstream is the hallmark of not only client-directed assessment but client-directed therapy itself. Client-directed work continuously evaluates and realigns the direction of therapy to match client meanings and preferences. Assessment is, therefore, not a distinct phase of treatment that precedes intervention but a pivotal component of change itself. To the degree that therapists gear their questions and therapy to clients' preferred views of what they need and want, answers to client dilemmas naturally take shape.

―⁓―

Question: What are client-directed, outcome-informed therapy's goals?

The editors asked us, "What would be your goals for this couple?" This followed questions about treatment model and assessment. The medical script unfolds in predictable fashion. Goals in Mental Health are the natural products of the therapist's determination (through the model's lens) of what is wrong. It's only logical: if the therapist determines the problem, the therapist determines what isn't the problem or how the situation should be when the problem is gone. Again, asking us to discuss goals is really an apparently innocuous request. It is the insinuation of the word "your" that gives away Mental Health's bias toward therapist privilege in therapy.

It is important to realize that goals, those imagined end points that help focus therapy's energy and keep it on track, are particularly laden with favored cultural mores. For example, psychiatrists in the 1950s and 1960s established acceptable goals for women in therapy, including the acceptance of status as helpmates to their partners and unselfish giving in the home, whether in the service of household chores or the sexual demands of their spouses. The keepers (and enforcers) of the norm just happened to be men; their picture of end points reflected their own biases as members of a dominant cultural group. Other favored norms have subtly influenced therapy goals, including preferences for material wealth and achievement, the superiority of two-parent (opposite-sex) households, and the separation of extended family from core parenting. Each takes its end point from preferences of the prevailing culture. Even so-called enlightened views, such as equally shared parental roles or the importance of traditional education, can take the form of oppressive dictates when pushed on families with different cultural backgrounds and different expectations. The insistence on therapist-defined goals puts therapy in danger of being just one more arm of social control and social conformity rather than a vehicle for the realization of personal hopes and dreams.

Answer: Recall that research on the alliance points to the importance of therapist accommodation to the client's goals for therapy (Bachelor & Horvath, 1999). When clients perceive that therapists accept and help focus therapy around what they want, they engage in and stay with therapy to its conclusion. The question then becomes, in what ways do outcome-informed therapists listen for, elicit, understand, accept, and pursue client goals in therapy?

On Planet Mental Health, the tendency to be sidetracked is great. If you spend four years of your life studying how men suppress their emotions to their detriment and the detriment of their partners, your eyes and ears—your goals—will be keenly attuned to how men express or fail to express themselves in therapy; your natural desire will be to point out the error of their ways and to coach them in correcting them. It's really OK, you may think, because you're still going with what they want, more respect from their wives or partners. When they drop out of therapy after the second session, your viewpoint is confirmed: men who can't express themselves withdraw when you get too close. The problem is theirs, not yours. At best, you can say, "He just wasn't ready to change."

After returning from the latest narrative conference, it seems only sensible to help your adolescent client externalize her eating problem. What she really wants to know is how to break up with her boyfriend. We can get to that later (if she comes back). We all know, on Planet Mental Health, that multiple personalities need to be integrated and voices are not something that are OK to carry around in your head. Ideas about those "others" being resources, special gifts, are just something that help the unfortunates feel better so they can get about the task of becoming normal—like us! We know she asked for assistance in dealing with an abusive boss, but, "first things first."

Families and individuals have been more or less subjected to a host of therapeutic shoulds and shouldn'ts, dos and don'ts and their accompanying techniques, with more or less success. Indeed, videos and books depicting dramatic therapeutic change attest to the match of certain approaches and techniques for certain clients. Nevertheless, the amount of client dropout or therapy failure attributable to lack of agreement on goals, probably substantial, is not likely to hit the headlines. Indeed, it's not even likely to be seen as news but as something to chalk up to client disability or lack of client motivation.

It has taken the formation of radical, grassroots consumer contingents and a growing body of critical therapists, including outcome-informed therapists, to counter the automatic enforcement of preset therapeutic goals through preset means. From a client-directed, outcome-informed perspective, clients are not only the ones paying, they know best. When it comes to goals, we are at their service.

—∿—

Question: What specific techniques or interventions does your model implement during the treatment process?

And now for the really big show, The Intervention—the acid test for any self-respecting clinician. Let's not just point fingers at psychiatrists with the one-size-fits-all intervention—namely, the pill. Psychologists, not to be outdone by their rival gang, are equally enamored of the almighty power of therapeutic technique. But it doesn't stop with psychologists.

No, it took the renegades, the family therapists, to perfect the intervention to its highest art form. What swashbuckling enactments, what breathtaking chair moving, what heartrending sculpting! From falling off chairs to invariant prescriptions, to symptom prescription, to washing floors at 3:00 A.M., family therapy's interventions rose to new heights of . . . entertainment. Audiences thrilled, readers gasped. And what about clients? Perhaps helped, perhaps bewildered, perhaps angry—on Planet Mental Health, they just figure it's what you do in therapy. And they take it, find a way to use it, and move on with their lives, mere blips on old masters' workshop tapes from long-forgotten conferences in long-forgotten hotels.

Let's go to the dictionary again. According to *Merriam-Webster* (1993), to intervene means the following: (1) to come between disputing people, groups, etc.; (2) to interfere with force or threat of force; (3) to occur incidentally so as to modify. *Intervene* and *intervention* connote an active coming between, a type of interference, often forceful, that changes the state or course of something. Therapists, as intervenors, are active agents coming between people and their problems, people and their patterns of acting and living, or coming between an internal problem (illness) and health. Intervention classically situates therapists and clients in alignment with Mental Health tenets. People with problems request assistance from someone who can do something, to them or to the problem, that changes the problem's course, changing their lives. A causes B. A does something to B and changes B. Clinical experts are *A*s; clients (and their problems) *B*s.

Therapists, in this light, carry with them a kind of imaginary black satchel in which they store their tools, their interventions. They have the know-how to reach in and pull out the best one for fixing the problem. For Jan and Mark, we might pull out "I-statement" strategies; or "odd-day, even-day" homework assignments; or perhaps that old war horse, the miracle question. Take two and call me in the morning.

The application of interventions for interventions' sake, divorced from client input, plays into all those factors that dampen client participation and construct client passivity or resistance, specifically, ignoring client goals, expectations, and resources. Clients have their own black satchel of tricks—those ideas about what they want and their own creativity to suggest and fashion interventions—if only therapists took the time to look in and decide with clients what's best to try.

Interventions may, at a minimum, give clients a sense that at least something is being done; they can serve to generate some hopefulness for change. In these cases clients most likely will take a therapist's intervention and make it their own—transform it into what they believe will work for them. Jan and Mark's therapist might send them home with the assignment to go out for a candlelight meal in a romantic restaurant. When they report putting candles on the kitchen table and opening a special bottle of wine (in the middle of the week!), the therapist can scold them for avoiding improvement. Or she can take it and run with it, seeing their creative adaptation of the assignment as what best suits their lives and preferences and is more likely to engender change.

To the degree that intervention takes shape outside client frames of reference, they at best give hope and the raw material for client-generated intervention. At worst, they stifle client creativity, constructing therapy relationships where the learned helpless seek guidance from the powerful or the disempowered seek a voice through resistance.

Answer: Need *intervention* be a dirty word? Must we tiptoe around the *I* word, politely offering reflections, engaging in conversation, and declining to give advice? Do clients need to hit us over the head, "Read my lips . . . what do *you* think?" Intervention phobia has reached epidemic proportions in some therapeutic circles. From a perspective that truly honors client input, such avoidance is untenable; at worst, it mirrors the same elitism that permeates the pro-interventionists. Outcome-informed therapists reject both. Yes, we believe we can have our cake and eat it too. Clients, with good reason, seek outside assistance with their problems when, and usually only when, they feel they have exhausted all reasonable, known avenues of problem resolution within their natural helping networks. In a word they're stuck. They come to us for a very particular kind of service—help with getting unstuck. Our job is to have the range and flexibility of knowledge and skills to match their expectations and preferred modes of learning and changing. If clients want to "work the AA program," we'll oblige;

if they want to explore the past, we'll go there. If they have a hankering to try systematic desensitization, why not. After all, when you deconstruct special, expert knowledge, it's not rocket science (but don't tell). It's up to us to be trained and adept at determining what is wanted and then giving it—to be not a jack of all trades and master at none but a jack of all trades and master at finding, honoring, and giving clients what they want.

With Jan and Mark, the therapist fashioned her interventions based on their moment-to-moment input. Jan believed that she and Mark had to deal with the past; there needed to be some reparation for past wrongs in order for her to move forward. Mark felt that the past got in the way with moving forward into the future. He didn't want to go there. Here were two different, conflicting theories of change. The therapist in this case respected each view, framing the problem in therapy conversation in ways that validated both positions. Two different views can exist side by side, and a solution can still emerge.

The therapist doesn't always (most often) know how solutions will emerge. The therapist trusts, first and foremost, the power of maintaining a strong therapeutic bond with all participants, keeping the conversation going in ways respectful to everyone's point of view and letting the magic of client motivation and creativity do its thing. It's really a matter of trust—trust in your own ability to listen, feel, respect, and struggle; trust in clients' ability to struggle and to find a way. It's not rocket science, and it's not easy. Going the client-directed route is not anything goes, fly by the seat of your pants. It's a thoughtful and knowledgeable endeavor that calls on considerable therapist expertise and repertoire. What it isn't is the blind implementation of theory-driven strategies aimed at fixing theory-framed problems.

Eventually, Jan and Mark came into therapy and related a particular "barn conversation," those conversations they traditionally had in a neutral territory (the barn) while doing a mutually enjoyable task (caring for their animals). Somehow, the barn conversation had "lifted a cloud." They each felt they were in a different place. Somehow, the issue of the past and the importance of the past had been dealt with, put to rest, along with forking piles of hay and shoveling manure. The therapist's real intervention here was to hear it, ask for more detail, and expand it for all its worth. A therapist's best intervention is recognizing a diamond in the rough and, with clients, setting it off nicely to its best, most resplendent advantage. This process most notably reflects the circular, evolving, and mutual intervention that defines client-directed, outcome-informed therapy.

Looking from Orbit: New Views of Planet Mental Health

Most people resolve their difficulties on their own, using their own and extended networks of resources. Only a small portion of the population experiencing the natural adjustments of living—including personal trauma, loss, grief, life transitions, and ranges of emotion and mood—resort to what many think of as professional help (Bohart & Tallman, 1999). Left to their own devices and given adequate social support, the "mentally ill" get over their problems, at a minimum to the extent that their lives no longer need revolve around drugs and hospitalization (Haley, 1989; Karon & Vanderbos, 1994; Whitaker, 2002). Despite this, therapists and clinicians on Planet Mental Health, tend to see pathology lurking behind every door. We see ourselves living in a tenuous, dangerous world populated with vulnerable mental constitutions. In such a world, Mental Health services become indispensable.

Such a perspective is understandable when the daily work of helpers is filled with stories of trauma and distress—stories all the more demoralizing when framed and set apart from stories of resiliency. However, Mental Health's insistence on a paradigm of disability fills another function. Ensuring persons' fragility and ensuring persons' acceptance of their fragility ensures the continuance (and growth) of the so-called helping professions.

The tendency to secure the market is a predictable aspect of a free-market system, operating generally outside the immediate awareness and intentions of the system's individual members. But when the need for pathology is deliberately cultivated for the benefit of certain institutions or structures, these tendencies take a malevolent turn. Whose interests are really being served when citizens are accosted in supermarkets to test their depression (during Depression Awareness Week, for example), an allegedly insidious ailment that can lurk beneath awareness, only to manifest full blown, possibly when it's too late and more long-term treatment is needed? Whose interests are being served when full-page drug advertisements fill professional journals and when pharmaceutical money and personnel infiltrate professional conferences, research institutions, and "educational" forums? Who benefits when women, adolescents, children, and minorities are funneled into Community Mental Health, often through probation, schools, state departments of children and families, or other social service (enforcement) agencies. It's literally a multibillion dollar industry, and everyone vies for a piece of the profits. Unfortunately, Mental Health thrives to the degree that mental illness thrives. The fox is guarding the coop, and with the hens' full blessing.

Critiques of Mental Health are not just about cynicism with market mentality, greed, or the quest for status and power. Psychotherapy, psychotherapists, and drugs have their usefulness and their place in society. Special healers and helpers have practiced their craft throughout history in most cultures of the world. There appears to be a niche, a social need, for the relationship that people seek and form at certain times and for certain purposes with those believed to possess special knowledge and capacities to help. Unique qualities of helpers, including empathy, selflessness, and a strong belief in people and the power of relationships strike a clear, strong resonance amid less noble din. Purity of intent persists, and succeeds, despite opposing forces. Critiques of Mental Health seek not to deflate or disparage this spirit but instead to champion it so that it can grow stronger and louder.

RESPONSIBILITY ON PLANET MENTAL HEALTH

It's not terribly difficult to tame a lion, but is there anyone who has learned to make the lamb roar?

—Old Viennese saying

What becomes the obligation of any who perceive Mental Health in a new light, for both its benevolence and misuse of benevolence? We're all implicated, and we all own a piece of sorting out what works from what perpetuates the very problems we oppose. From a client-directed point of view, escape from such a quagmire lies in one avenue: a true partnership in research, theory, and practice, with the greater half of the therapeutic equation being client-consumers. There must be fifty ways (at least) to leave old familiar ways. From quiet moments of clear, thoughtful questioning of business as usual in staffings, classrooms, or professional gatherings to a more vocal protest in print or talk, client-directed ideas can take hold.

Clinicians in centers, hospitals, and offices may respectfully challenge everyday practices that exclude clients from treatment decisions (Sparks, 2002). They may insert the client's voice and the client's wishes into supervision and case discussions, as well as case records. They may take a more vocal stance by insisting that clients attend staffings and that medical options not go automatically unchallenged as treatments of choice for "more severe cases." They may resist calling clients by case numbers, diagnoses, or pet case names. When clients cannot be present for case discussions, therapists can challenge themselves to speak as though the clients were present. Simply put, clinicians resist when they refuse to participate in professional jargon, labeling, and preset treatment protocols that do not involve clients as equal, indeed essential, and worthy members of the treatment team.

Therapist resistance perhaps takes its most subversive form when practiced in the one-on-one encounter with clients. Here, therapists can go out of their way to support the client's resistance to standard procedures—to struggle and to devise plans of action that uniquely fit client preferences and goals. Therapists can encourage clients to make use of their natural networks first and foremost above "professional" intervention. Therapists can be willing to take chances—go beyond the bounds of the office and standard procedure—to involve the client's natural supports. Finally, they can have an abiding faith in their clients' abilities to find a way, even in extreme and sometimes dangerous circumstances.

In how we read, what we choose to take at face value, and what we choose to examine more closely, clinicians and consumers can become more active and more effective in making changes on Planet Mental Health. Most importantly, clinicians can truly collaborate in their face-to-face encounter with those seeking help, seeking their help in return, to fashion philosophies and practices that work. From critique to change and back again, collaboration is a revolving, evolving mutuality—not supplanting Mental Health but making sure that all who have a stake have a say in defining "best practice."

—ᵐ— Epilogue: A Tale of Two Therapies

Until lions have their historians, tales of hunting will
always glorify the hunter.

—*African proverb*

Emma couldn't quite figure out what was happening. She should be
on top of the world. After all, here she was, one of the elite freshmen
at Yale, away from home for the first time in a new and wondrous
world. The best part—she was here on full scholarship. Finally, the
dream she and her family had long worked for—that someone from
their modest South Florida household might stroll the historic quad-
rangle alongside classmates from the upscale suburbs of Boston and
New York—was coming true. Yet what seemed at first like a fairy tale
had gradually taken on an ominous character. She found herself more
and more isolated in her dormitory room, reluctant to venture out
into the city for social times with new friends. Even the classroom,
once as comfortable as her backyard, had now become a place of
uncertainty, with term projects uncompleted and grades unfamiliarly
slipping. Calls to home only heightened everyone's anxiety. Sometimes
Emma imagined she heard voices (of her parents, teachers, friends,
self—did they caution, advise, or simply keep her company?). Aware
that all was not well in the Cinderella picture, Emma sought help from
the university psychologist.

THERAPY ONE

February 12: Met with patient, an eighteen-year-old female, attending her
second semester. Patient describes feelings of panic, anxiety, and phobic responses and
claims to hear voices. Discussed options for therapy and medication. Referred to
Dr. N——— for medication. Diagnosis: Psychotic disorder not otherwise specified.
Follow-up appointment scheduled in one week.

February 13: Patient, female, age eighteen presents with psychotic features and mixed affect. Prescribed Geodon, 20 mg. twice daily. Dx: Schizophrenia. Med. review two weeks.

By March, the dream seemed in jeopardy. Emma, unable to concentrate, increasingly anxious and isolated, returned to her home on medical leave. Here, she grew restless, depressed; she spoke of hurting herself. One afternoon, her younger sibling found her in the garage, threatening to accomplish this end.

March 15: Patient actively suicidal and psychotic. Depression mixed with periods of agitation. Patient refuses attempts to sedate during disruptive outbursts. Continue inpatient until reduction in symptoms. Schedule sessions with mental health counselor. Medication review with increase to 60 mg. twice daily.

In the course of six months, Emma had gone from being the pride of her family and friends to a patient in the psychiatric wing of the local hospital. Where once she saw her future before her, she now saw only darkness. Every attempt of every professional she had encountered—the university psychologist and psychiatrist, the hospital nurse and psychiatrist—failed to relieve her distress. Emma's family was just as dismayed and bewildered. Then, through a twist of fate, Emma encountered someone and something different.

While hospitalized, Emma worked with Jean, a counseling intern from the local university.

THERAPY TWO

March 16: Met with Emma for one hour. She seemed groggy but talked about her experiences at school. She relates feeling confused but does not believe she is psychotic. She is concerned about how she feels on the medication. She states she feels like she has lost her ability to think and to connect with others and this makes her more depressed. Reviewed her options and the supports she needs to go home and to return to school. Assured her that she would get better. Scheduled next meeting to construct time line.

March 24: Emma is going home today. She has complained about the medication and does not believe it is helping her. Her parents are concerned about the medication. Gave reading material and made referrals for outpatient counseling.

Jean spent time with Emma, listened to her, and took her concerns about the medication and her desire to go home seriously. Jean had information about client-directed therapy as well as research on medications; she was happy to oblige Emma's and her parents' curiosity about what other options might be available to help Emma safely get back into her life. Due to Jean's and the family's collaboration, the referral to work with Emma upon her return home from the hospital eventually landed at Barry and Jacqueline's office.

Working with Emma was not exactly smooth sailing. Initially, Emma felt that she might never get the self she knew back. She made the decision to discontinue all medications and was feeling the rebound effects of this, despite her measured withdrawal. She simply could not make sense of the events that had so dramatically altered the shape of her current and future life. Emma's initial Outcome Rating Scale (ORS) scores were consistently at the lowest ends (a total of a whopping 2 to be precise), indicating an extreme discomfort in all areas of her life. Blaming herself, she sometimes thought about ways to leave her circumstances, whether by taking off with a truck driver across country or by some other even more drastic means.

Emma's parents and brother were understandably fraught with worry. At the same time, they fully supported her decision to take a nonmedication route and set up a round-the-clock safety watch for her. During this time, our team of four therapists formed our own safety net supporting the family's, through 24/7 on-call coverage. Barry, as Emma's therapist, was the first line of contact in an emergency. At the same time, Emma and her family met the team during a live consultation. This consultation provided the family with a sense of having many allies; they were truly not alone in the fight. During the course of the next two months, Barry or Jacqueline got calls when Emma would try to leave the house, threatening to "take off," or when family members simply needed the support to continue to have hope for change. We each were prepared to do whatever it took for Emma to regain a hold on life in the way she preferred.

Meanwhile, Barry worked weekly with Emma in therapy. During this time, they kept track of progress using the ORS and monitored the alliance with the Session Rating Scale (SRS). After nine sessions, Emma's ORS ratings remained a distressing 4. Although the SRS indicated a positive alliance, clearly Emma and Barry were stuck. They had tried many different things. The early checkpoint conversation included a more detailed discussion about the SRS and resulted in a decision for Barry to be more suggestive of ideas. Another conversation revealed Emma's desire to be hypnotized, which in turn was implemented. Later discussion about the lack of progress culminated in a consult with the team. But despite many good ideas, Emma's enthusiasm at the time, and good SRS scores, no appreciable difference emerged on the ORS; it seemed to stay stuck on the page at a paltry 4.

At this point Barry walked the walk. In a difficult but important last-chance discussion, he commented that things were not moving as they had hoped and he feared that he was becoming an obstacle to Emma's returning to Yale. Then he inquired about what she thought they could do to help her move forward. Although similar discussions had taken place at earlier sessions when no progress was forthcoming, it had a greater sense of urgency this time. After brainstorming options with Barry, Emma decided that shifting to a female therapist from the team might help loosen the gridlock.

Emma and Jacqueline worked together over the course of approximately four months. During the first three sessions, Jacqueline made some adjustments based on feedback from Emma on the SRS, specifically offering some concrete suggestions for dealing with the emotional cycles she was experiencing. Although the SRS remained on target, the ORS still hovered in the lower regions across all domains, ranging from total scores of 4 to 6. Then things started to happen. By the fourth session, the ORS showed some gains, albeit slight, moving to an 8, with most gains in the interpersonal and individual scales. By session six, all the scales showed noticeable increases, bringing the total score to 10. Emma was starting to talk about taking a course at a local university! The shift from the first session score of 4 to the 10 indicated a greater than 5 increase, enough to call it reliable change and enough change to warrant continued work with Emma.

By the eleventh session, Emma had moved forward to a total score of 22. She scored high on all scales with the exception of the social (a much lower score of 1). That session revolved around the variety of things Emma was doing that contributed to her sense of individual and interpersonal well-being and what she needed to do to jump-start her social life. Canceling the next session, Emma announced she no longer needed to come to therapy. This is of course what the ORS and Emma were saying about change in the previous meeting, although termination had not been discussed.

When the work concluded, Emma was working at a local nonprofit organization, exercising with her mom at their health club, and had set up a plan for reentering school within the next year. She was no longer attempting to take off and felt she had strategies for handling the times when she was down. The most dramatic shift on the ORS had occurred during a weeklong visit from family, when Emma made a strong reconnection with an uncle. Jacqueline's contacts with Emma after ending therapy confirmed her reclaiming of her self and her life (even though in many ways those aspects were not always parts of the self she had known before). Jacqueline and Barry learned several months later that she continued taking courses at a local college, was working at a beachfront café, and had a boyfriend. She was well into the process of gaining reinstatement at Yale and proudly told Jacqueline she thought she could graduate with her class by doing extra summer coursework. Although she had journeyed into, in her words, "a dark world" and was now dealing with the aftermath of that journey, she was more or less a young woman figuring out how to become a healthy adult, with all the heartache and ups and downs that entails.

EMMA'S TALE

Tales of Therapy One and Therapy Two are, of course, our stories. Emma has her own to tell. In the interest of adding her voice to the previous account, we asked Emma to share with us her version of this time in her life. The following are excerpts from her written response to this request.

> The experience at Yale when I was first having problems was pretty frightening. I felt very alone in the process, and I don't think my particular counselor was the greatest fit. I would have preferred somebody else, but I didn't really have a choice because the first time I saw her was during the clinic's walk-in hours.

The system Emma encountered, although accommodating walk-ins, had no way of checking on her experience and matching her with someone she could feel comfortable with. The emphasis here was on delivering competent service without having client feedback inform that service.

> I also think that the psychiatrist that I was assigned to was also unhelpful in terms of giving advice about medication and its side effects. She mostly told me about physical effects such as muscle cramping and that this type of medication was administered to me in a very low dose, so I thought it would just be a quick fix. Her explanation of what

was wrong with me also didn't really sink in because I didn't really understand or have any familiarity with the very abstract psychiatric definitions that are used. She said that I had had a psychotic episode, and I had heard the adjective before, but I really couldn't see how it could be related to me, so it just really didn't sink in, and it confused me even further.

The doctor's explanations, esoteric for Emma, heightened her uncertainty and made her even less sure of what was happening and of her ability to cope. When we asked what was and wasn't useful about the professional help she received when she returned home, here is what Emma wrote:

If a psychiatrist can be considered a helper, I would say my experience was negative. The conventional psychiatric route I took: a psychiatrist, taking a prescribed psychotropic medication, and then being hospitalized thwarted what would have probably been a much speedier recovery. The psychiatrist, Dr. N———, whose office I visited really regarded me as person who couldn't make my own decisions. I think he viewed me as subhuman, and he was also probably racist or had a racist philosophy of psychiatry and how illnesses affect certain groups more. He made me leave the room when he told my father that I should be hospitalized, which I believe was a violation of patient rights since I should have been notified first.

In this part of her tale, Emma describes her continued alienation arising not from her original problem but from the system's response to it. The fact that she now writes about this with more than a hint of outrage speaks to personal strengths that would not be subdued, either by her distress or by a system that devalued them. She speaks about being hospitalized:

The psychiatrist who I was assigned to in the psychiatric hospital I stayed in was also very degrading. She treated me like an animal. I was very edgy due to my antipsychotic overmedication, and I am convinced I acted obsessively because of it, and I kept insisting that I wasn't sick or schizophrenic. I was continuously badgering her to change the diagnosis and find out what was wrong with me, and she screamed at me and told me to go away.

From one encounter to another, Emma's own resources and wishes were ignored, much like the experience with Ann that Barry recounted in the Preface. At the same time, Emma experienced unwanted effects from neuroleptic medication. Understandably, she took her resistance to another level, attempting other tactics to draw attention to her desire to be heard and to be treated like a reasonable thinking person—like a human being. One can guess that what others often view as psychotic behavior may, in fact, be desperate efforts to confront a dehumanizing context.

> All of the decisions that were made for me during this time period just worsened my mental state. I turned into a zombie because of the drugs, and I really was not the same person at all. I have never seen anything like what those drugs can do to you. Nobody should ever have to take those drugs. I was in a hospital for nine days, and I didn't go outside, and I was so zombified I didn't care that I hadn't been exposed to natural sunlight and fresh air.

When a person is defined as psychologically sick, then the confines of a hospital are deemed as being only in order. Instead, Emma points to the net effect of months of medication and hospital isolation and the subsequent segregation from natural elements that work synergistically with our bodies and our moods to keep us on an even keel—particularly sunlight and outdoor air.

> My therapist in the hospital who was against my hospitalization and medication was most helpful during this period because she made us aware of the dangers and potency of becoming dependent on psychiatric medication.

Emma responded to someone who shared information that could help her make sense of what she was experiencing and gave her different options for dealing with it. Here are some of her observations about her first few sessions at our office:

> My experience with Barry was a good starting point, but I believe that during this time, I was so severely depressed I didn't have faith in anything that could possibly aid my recovery. The progress scale indicated that Barry and I weren't a good fit at the time, but I believe that

I probably wasn't a good match for anybody back then. I think it was a good example of how slow recovery is when the problem is mental and not physical.

Emma's explanation for why things weren't moving conformed with our own. She stated that, although Barry might not have been the best fit, her own process of recovery may simply have been on its own timetable. What we hoped to do was not interfere with that timetable. Continuing in the same format for much longer with no change could construct a sense of hopelessness and self-blame. Instead, we understood the problem as one of Emma's needing a change of scene, so to speak. Changing therapists here simply meant that we would once again do whatever it took, even if that meant getting out of the way.

Mental health culture often blames clients for not getting better. In such a climate, clients can come to see themselves as so beyond hope that no one can help. Perhaps we need to work harder to counter this construction of hopelessness. We could instead spread the word that research tells us the opposite: when clients are not achieving results in one format, it is not because of the severity of their problem or a lack of what it takes to get better. Rather, it is due to a less than optimal fit between the helper and the client; with a better fit, clients readily achieve results. Continuing in a therapy where change is not happening may contribute to a problem's chronicity, short-circuiting the natural progression from crisis to more or less problematic everyday life.

We asked Emma to complete her therapy tale by describing her process of change:

> Initially the experience was something that felt self-defeating because I wasn't getting better or didn't see myself getting better, but then towards the end it was good that I was beginning to tackle issues that were important to me such as moving ahead with the future as I began to feel more positive with myself. . . . My experience of change is in many ways inexplicable and very simple. One day I was in the bathroom, and I just started thinking ahead for the future, like "Oh, I need to get my driver's license soon," and from there it just got better. Before there had been absolutely no positive thoughts associated with my future. Things always seemed very bleak. I had no positive thoughts or energy directed toward the future. That seemed so simple, yet it was so life-changing because it planted the seed for something greater in my mind.

Emma's description of change tells us nothing and tells us everything. It tells us that change is an essentially highly idiosyncratic process; it remains one of the most mysterious and widely studied events in all of psychotherapy. People's descriptions of their experiences of change underscore its enigmatic nature. The body of empirical data we have about change takes nothing away from this mystery. It gives us nothing about the unique content of change as personally experienced. What it does do, however, is point to common themes. These themes might best be summarized as follows: (1) change does happen; and (2) it's about the client.

IT'S ABOUT THE CLIENT

For us the question is this: To what extent do our theories and practices support change and the client's rightful role as its primary author? The paradigm shift we envision is committed to a relational rather than medical model. It embraces a client-directed rather than theory-driven process. And it emphasizes client-defined outcome rather than competence as a measure of effectiveness.

A relational model means therapists work *with* rather than *on* clients. In a with-therapy, clients have the most important voice about what they want and how they prefer to get it. As Emma wrote:

> You have to let the client know that they are the sole people that can begin to change because things like this come only from within. People can help and guide you, but at the end of the day it is your choice. You have to decide to get better.

Our vision rejects exclusive and expert-derived theory as a basis for practice. Instead, it is interested in client ideas of change, client-initiated topics, client priorities, and client views of the therapy's progress. It elevates, without reservation, local, client theories over all those that the therapeutic community previously held sacrosanct. As Emma put it:

> She [the psychiatrist] just wanted to put everything into medical terms since I had been hospitalized and medicated, and she said that she wanted to help me with what had triggered everything, and she thought that that was anxiety. But even if it was anxiety that started everything all those months before, I needed help with

something else because I was so numb at the time because I was still being medicated, and anxiety had nothing to do with my emotional problems.

Finally, our preferred future equates therapist competence with client-defined outcomes. Clients, not supervisors, directors, licensing boards, insurance companies or agency CEOs, are the final arbiters of whether service is effective. Practice shifts from an emphasis on competent service delivery, as defined by the rote provision of evidence-based treatment and professional procedures, to outcome-informed practice, where clients guide the process by telling us what works and what doesn't. Therapists no longer serve theories disconnected from the immediate therapy process. Instead, they serve clients, gauging each step based on systematic, in the moment, collection of client feedback.

In a relational, client-directed, outcome-informed system, some of the things you do may go against the grain of what is considered "best practice." Emma wrote:

> Well of course, you and Barry share a unique philosophy when it comes to mental healthcare. You could have put me in a hospital due to my actions and my words, and I would have been medicalized and taken two steps back again, but you didn't, and for that I am forever grateful.

You also may have to step outside the usual bounds of practice in order to accomplish client-preferred goals and methods. As Emma wrote: "I would say that people should *always* have someone to talk to at anytime of the day or be with them. That is extremely important if they are a danger to themselves and others."

Most of all, you may have to suspend an ingrained devaluing of client knowledge, courage, and will to overcome even the most distressing circumstances. Believing in clients undergirds the heroic client project. We acknowledge that most helpers, including those who came in contact with Emma, are committed to ethical and caring service. How have we, then, as a profession, come to abandon our instincts to believe in and be responsive to our clients? How have we come so far from the idealistic impulses that attracted many of us to this work? The roots of mistrust in clients lie in our history, including assumptions about madness and its cure. They also have much to do with money and power. We challenge beliefs and practices that hinder our best intentions, diminish clients, and distort the process of change. We invite those who share a hope for and vision of a different future to learn from the clients in these pages and in our memories and to remain creative and resolute in our quest for change.

As Emma wrote: "I would also say they should be patient and encourage the client that they *will* get better, but they have to believe because I got better, and I'm living proof."

APPENDIX I: A First-Person Account of Mental Health Services

Ronald Bassman

In 1969, at the age of twenty-five, I was admitted to a psychiatric hospital for the second time in three years. The first diagnosis, schizophrenia, paranoid type, was followed by schizophrenia, chronic type. My treatments included electroshock, insulin comas, and massive doses of medication. After I recovered from my "treatments" and began addressing the identity issues that had triggered my excursion into "madness," I returned to graduate school at the University of Southern Mississippi and earned my doctorate. I have worked as a licensed psychologist in a state hospital and private practice, been a consultant to numerous schools and state agencies, and have been the director of a seven-county comprehensive mental health center. Working as a clinician and an advocate, I hid my psychiatric history for over twenty years. About five years ago, I chose to identify myself as a psychiatric survivor in order to draw from all of my experience. Currently, I am involved in advocacy, retraining of state hospital staff using a recovery model, and self-help project development for the New York State Office of Mental Health Division of Recipient Affairs. I am vice

---

Note: This article originally appeared in the *Psychotherapy Bulletin* (Bassman, R. [1999]. The psychology of mental illness: The consumers/survivors/ ex-mental patients' perspective. *Psychotherapy Bulletin, 34*(1), 14–16) and is reprinted here with permission.

president of the National Association of Rights Protection and Advocacy and also serve on the American Psychological Association Task Force on Serious Mental Illness and Children with Severe Emotional Disturbance.

Defeated and dejected, I was too weak to resist the psychiatrist's argument to my parents at my discharge meeting. His job was to convince us that I was an incurable schizophrenic. I was twenty-three years old when that prosecuting doctor, serving also as judge and jury, sentenced me to a life of, at best, controlled madness. With the smug certainty of a bookie, the doctor told my family that my chances of making it without being hospitalized again were very slim. His medical orders were stated with an absolute authority that discouraged any challenge.

Barely acknowledging my presence, he nodded toward me and declared, "Your son has to take medication for the rest of his life and must return to the hospital for weekly outpatient treatment. He should not see any of his old friends. If his behavior changes or he gets upset, let me know."

Discharged from a psychiatric hospital in 1970 for the second time and labeled a chronic schizophrenic, many years elapsed before I could rid myself of a name that curses the bearer—a name that robbed me of the right to respect myself.

What is *crazy?* Does it have an edge, an invisible boundary one steps over, or is it like falling off a mountain cliff? Falling onto the craggy ledges of the cliff may provide temporary porches of respite. Some may tumble into that black hole propelled by the pushes of seen and unseen forces from within and without. Those unlucky enough to fall to the bottom suffer a hell that eludes description to all but the gifted artist. Once trapped, the slippery shiny sides of that imaginary yet real hole rebuff and taunt one's attempts at escape. Family, friends, and doctors drop ropes and ladders to offer their help, but absolute obedience is too steep a price for that assistance. Passion, drive, self-respect, and long-held dreams should not be regarded as excess baggage to be discarded before the ascent.

Alone and surrounded by others, painful silence punctuated by unbearable noise, nothing is predictable. The confused darkness of dread, terror, and loneliness make night and day indistinguishable. Reality's laws have exploded. The self has disintegrated. All is possible. Nothing is doable. Yet for those who are able to look into and see beyond their distorted reflections in the magical shiny stone walls of their mad confinement, hope can illuminate a vision of possibility for a better tomorrow.

Today, having earned the "credentials" and some degree of respect from my professional peers and my consumer/survivor peers, I have the opportunity to speak out and advocate for those who have lost their voices. Too many of us have been made to accept the too strongly promoted, most current beliefs about mental illness with its pronouncements of lifetime disability and its associated demand to downsize one's dreams and aspirations. Others define realistic expectations for us as low stress jobs in the 4F fields: Filth, Filing, Food, and Fetching. Too many have learned to survive by becoming helplessly and hopelessly compliant. I join with my consumer/survivor peers in an expanding social movement, a rights movement that has never before existed. Always in the past, mental health reform has been driven by the passion and leadership of a few special individuals; and when their time has passed, the reform and progress has ended. The hope now is that through the discovery of each other, the bonding and alliances, the once isolated closeted recovering, recovered, and transformed will find validation with others who have shared their experience of confusion, pain, and oppression. Having rediscovered the personal truths of their experience, they will no longer allow themselves to be defined by labels that deny their dignity and value as whole people with diverse strengths and weaknesses.

Within the consumer/survivor movement, the once frightened and beaten down, the voice-hearers, the traumatized, the victims of tardive dyskinesia are banding together with their peers to advocate and lobby for rights, to create self-help alternatives, to share successful coping strategies, and to inspire and instill hope through the personal examples of their lived lives. Activist consumer/survivors speak of empowerment and liberation. They are refusing to allow others to speak for them and are reclaiming ownership of their experience. When we look for therapy or help, we are looking for active collaborative relationships where power inequities are minimized. We have learned that we thrive on choice, hope, and possibility. And we wither and atrophy from force and coercion. Having learned from personal experience that all of our rights can be taken away from us, we know that we must fight to keep our rights, and thus we may be suspicious of those who offer themselves as helpers. We resonate with the insight of an unknown aboriginal woman who said, "If you're coming to help me, you are wasting your time. But if you have come because your liberation is bound up with mine, let us work together."

Now is an excellent time for psychologists to join consumer/survivors in reforming a medically based, drug-dominated oppressive mental health system that is harmful to people who have been diagnosed with major mental illness. Genuine allies are welcome. You are invited to learn about the rich diversity of projects and consumer/survivor literature and research that has been emerging during the past twenty years, yet remaining virtually absent from academia, major publications, and mainstream practices.

I deeply appreciate the psychologists who are willing to shed the hierarchical role of expert helper in favor of open person-to-person collaboration in a mutually beneficial developmental journey. As a consumer/survivor and a psychologist, I am disappointed and embarrassed by the almost complete absence of psychologists from the political arenas where consumer/survivors have had to speak out without allies but with no shortage of those who would elect themselves as their caretakers. I urge you to educate yourself. Find out how a self-identified consumer differs from a self-identified psychiatric survivor. Learn the differences between the consumer/survivor groups and family advocacy groups (NAMI) and how they often have opposing advocacy issues. I ask you to do some introspection to see if your beliefs are supported by the willingness to take the risks inherent in the actions required to remove the barriers to empowerment for the most disenfranchised among us: the person diagnosed and treated for major mental illness.

How much of our individual freedoms are available for sacrifice to society's surveillance in its quest to maintain the illusion of control, predictability, and safety? Will the "mentally ill" continue to serve as the "not us" scapegoat which conveniently diverts people from confronting the always possible terror of life and death? As I watch the growing numbers of people who are diagnosed with some form of mental illness, and even more sadly, the number of children being prescribed Ritalin and whose diagnoses are preparing them to become the new group of "chronic mentally ill," I shudder at the price exacted to feed our community's need for predictability and safety.

I urge psychologists to learn how they can use their education, talents, and skills in new ways by engaging in an exciting collaborative journey of creativity and personal growth where people support each other as equals and speak of what is in their hearts. To be effective in the service you provide for a consumer/survivor, it is imperative that you see the individual and value that special individual by engaging in a collaborative search to find understanding, meaning, and connection in this person's unfolding life narrative.

—ᴬᴬᴬ— APPENDIX II: Consumer/ Survivor/Ex-Patient Resource Information

Compiled by Ronald Bassman

To learn to pick and choose what works best for you often requires investigation outside the mainstream medical model. Expertise developed by peers—consumers/survivors/ex-patients (C/S/X)—is usually cited as significant in people's self-development and emergence from a role of passivity and dependence. What follows are some helpful resources for people who question the validity of their diagnosis and treatment for serious mental illness and want to take on more personal responsibility and control in their lives:

National Empowerment Center: http://www.power2u.org
Federally funded, peer-run technical assistance center

MadNation: http://www.madnation.org
C/S/X activism and information

Support Coalition: http://www.efn.org/~dendron/index.html
Coalition of international C/S/X activism groups

Knowledge Exchange Network: http://www.mentalhealth.com
Federally funded C/S/X initiative for information

Mind: http://www.mind.org.uk/
C/S/X advocacy and activism in Great Britain

National Association of Rights Protection and Advocacy: http://
www.connix.com/~narpa
Advocacy alliance of lawyers, C/S/X, and mental health professionals

National Mental Health Self-Help Clearinghouse: http://www.
mhselfhelp.org/
Federally funded C/S/X technical assistance center

For announcements, information, and newsletters, contact the following groups:

National Empowerment Center: (800) 769-3728
National Mental Health Consumers Self-Help Clearinghouse: (800) 553-4539

~~~ APPENDIX III: Five Questions About Psychotherapy

1. What practice directions should the field take?

Psychotherapy has all but been reduced to medical diagnoses and evidence-based treatments. The key figure, the client, has been left out, and the search for the magical processes that produce change distracts us from the critical variable of outcome. Therapists do not need to know what approach to use for a given diagnosis as much as whether the current relationship is producing results and, if not, how to adjust therapy to maximize the chances of success. Therapists must routinely monitor the benefit of services with reliable, valid, and feasible measures of client-defined outcomes. The field must embrace outcome management from the client/consumer point of view as the central practice direction and eschew process-oriented intellectualizations of psychotherapeutic work.

2. What research directions should the field take?

Study after study has confirmed the Dodo Bird Verdict—indeed, all approaches are about equally efficacious. Consequently, the field should abandon the research of models and techniques because it will not improve the effectiveness of psychotherapy one scintilla. Conversely, studies have shown that outcome feedback increases effectiveness up to 65 percent, and that clients whose therapists had access to outcome and alliance information were less likely to deteriorate, more likely to stay longer, and twice as likely to achieve change. The best hope for improving effectiveness will be found in researching outcome management.

3. What theoretical directions should the field take?

For all the claims and counterclaims and the thousands of theoretical formulations, psychotherapy has not identified a single construct or specific ingredient that reliably produces change. The love affair with theory takes place outside the purview of those most affected and blinds the field to the roles clients play in bringing about change. Having a "theoretical direction" only supports the quest for the Holy Grail—we have surely been there and done that. As a field, we should deemphasize theory and instead amplify the client's voice via formalized feedback about outcome, improving effectiveness one client at a time.

4. What education and training directions should the field take?
Research documents a complicated relationship between training and outcome. At best, the data indicate a small correlation. At worst, other research finds that increasing the amount of training most therapists receive may actually lessen effectiveness. Manualizing so-called empirically supported treatments has not proved helpful in improving outcome and has the potential for negatively impacting the relationship and decreasing clinical innovation.

Becoming outcome-informed directly addresses the limitations of training and offers the first "real-time" protection to consumers and payers. Instead of empirically supported therapies, consumers would have access to empirically validated therapists. Training might be spent helping clinicians listen for, master, and respond to formal client feedback. Creativity and ethics would be stressed over mastery of particular methods. Emphasis would shift from competence to effectiveness, the ultimate determinant of graduation being an ability to actually help rather than simple regurgitation of the current "state of knowledge" in the field.

5. What would you like the field of psychotherapy to look like in twenty-five years?
Given the empirical evidence, seeking improvement in treatment in terms of therapeutic process is a mistake—indeed, more of the same kind of thinking that spawned the very rivalries that seem to cripple us. In twenty-five years, we hope that the field would have moved beyond efforts aimed at seeking consensus on how therapy is to be conducted. Instead, clients, clinicians, theoreticians, and researchers would be working together to develop the most effective ways to use client feedback regarding the outcome and process of treatment to improve success. Heroic clients would partner with us to improve effectiveness and ensure accountability, restoring faith in psychotherapy and reestablishing our relational rather than medical identity.

APPENDIX IV: Outcome Rating Scale and Session Rating Scale; Experimental Versions for Children

Outcome Rating Scale (ORS)

Name: _____ Age (yrs.): _____
ID # _____ Sex: M/F _____
Session # _____ Date: _____

Looking back over the last week, including today, help us understand how you have been feeling by rating how well you have been doing in the following areas of your life, where marks to the left represent low levels and marks to the right indicate high levels.

Individually
(Personal well-being)

I————————————————————————————I

Interpersonally
(Family, close relationships)

I————————————————————————————I

Socially
(Work, school, friendships)

I————————————————————————————I

Overall
(General sense of well-being)

I————————————————————————————I

Institute for the Study of Therapeutic Change

www.talkingcure.com

© 2000, Scott D. Miller and Barry L. Duncan

Session Rating Scale (SRS V. 3.0)

Name: _____ Age (yrs.) :____
ID # _____ Sex: M / F ____
Session # ____ Date: _____

Please rate today's session by placing a hash mark on the line nearest to the description that best fits your experience.

Relationship

I did not feel heard, understood, and respected.   I————————————I   I felt heard, understood, and respected.

Goals and Topics

We did *not* work on or talk about what I wanted to work on and talk about.   I————————————I   We worked on and talked about what I wanted to work on and talk about.

Approach or Method

The therapist's approach is not a good fit for me.   I————————————I   The therapist's approach is a good fit for me.

Overall

There was something missing in the session today.   I————————————I   Overall, today's session was right for me.

Institute for the Study of Therapeutic Change

www.talkingcure.com

© 2000, Lynn D. Johnson, Scott D. Miller, and Barry L. Duncan

Child Outcome Rating Scale (CORS)

Name: _____ Age (yrs.): ____
Sex: M / F ____
Session #____ Date: _____

How are you doing? How are things going in your life? Please make a mark on the scale to let us know. The closer to the smiley face, the better things are. The closer to the frowny face, things are not so good.

Me
(How am I doing?)

I————————————————————————I

Family
(How are things in my family?)

I————————————————————————I

School
(How am I doing at school?)

I————————————————————————I

Everything
(How is everything going?)

I————————————————————————I

Institute for the Study of Therapeutic Change

www.talkingcure.com

© 2003, Barry L. Duncan, Scott D. Miller, and Jacqueline A. Sparks

Child Session Rating Scale (CSRS)

Name: _____Age (yrs.): _____
Sex: M / F _____
Session # _____ Date: _____

How was our time together today? Please put a mark on the lines below to let us know how you feel.

Listening

Did not always
listen to me.   I———————————I   Listened to me.

How Important

What we did and
talked about were   I———————————I   What we did and
not really that   talked about were
important to me.   important to me.

What We Did

I did not like what
we did today.   I———————————I   I liked what we
                                                                      did today.

Overall

I wish we could do   I hope we do the
something different.   I———————————I   same kind of things
                                                                          next time.

Institute for the Study of Therapeutic Change

www.talkingcure.com

Young Child Outcome Rating Scale (YCORS)

Name: _____ Age (yrs.): _____
Sex: M / F _____
Session #_____ Date: _____

Choose one of the faces that shows how things are going for you. Or, you can draw one below that is just right for you.

Institute for the Study of Therapeutic Change

www.talkingcure.com

© 2003, Barry L. Duncan, Scott D. Miller, Andy Huggins, and Jacqueline A. Sparks

Young Child Session Rating Scale (YCSRS)

Name: _____ Age (yrs.): _____
Sex: M / F _____
Session #_____ Date: _____

Choose one of the faces that shows how it was for you to be here today. Or, you can draw one below that is just right for you.

Institute for the Study of Therapeutic Change

www.talkingcure.com

© 2003, Barry L. Duncan, Scott D. Miller, Andy Huggins, and Jacqueline A. Sparks

~~~ References

Addis, M. E., Wade, W. A., & Hatgis, C. (1999). Barriers to dissemination of evidence-based practices: Addressing practitioners' concerns about manual-based therapies. *Clinical Psychology, 6*, 430–441.

Ahn, H., & Wampold, B. (2001). Where oh where are the specific ingredients? A meta-analysis of component studies in counseling and psychotherapy. *Journal of Counseling Psychology, 38*, 251–257.

Albee, G. (2000). The Boulder Model's fatal flaw. *American Psychologist, 55*, 247–248.

American Association of Marriage and Family Therapy. (2001). *AAMFT Code of Ethics* [On-line]. Available: http://www.aamft.org/ethics/2001code.htm.

American Counseling Association. (1995). *Code of ethics.* [On-line]. Available: http://www.counseling.org/site/resources_ethics.html.

American Healthcare Institute. (2003). *Approved, state of the art seminars for mental health professionals* [Advertisement]. Baltimore: Author.

American Psychiatric Association. (1952). *The diagnostic and statistical manual of mental disorders.* Washington, DC: Author.

American Psychiatric Association. (1980). *The diagnostic and statistical manual of mental disorders* (3rd ed.). Washington, DC: Author.

American Psychiatric Association. (1987). *The diagnostic and statistical manual of mental disorders* (3rd ed. revised). Washington, DC: Author.

American Psychiatric Association. (1994). *Diagnostic and statistical manual of mental disorders* (4th ed.). Washington, DC: Author.

American Psychological Association. (1993). *Task force report on promotion and dissemination of psychological practices.* Washington, DC: Author.

American Psychological Association. (1998a). Take part in national anxiety disorders screening day. *APA Monitor, 29*(1), 39.

American Psychological Association. (1998b). *Communicating the value of psychology to the public.* Washington, DC: Author.

American Psychological Association. (2002). Ethical principles of psychologists and code of conduct. *American Psychologist, 57,* 1060–1073.

Anastasi, A. (1982). *Psychological testing* (5th ed.). New York: Macmillan.

Anderson, T. (1987). The reflecting team: Dialogue and metadialogue in clinical work. *Family Process, 26,* 415–428.

Angell, M. (2000). Is academic medicine for sale? *The New England Journal of Medicine, 342*(20), 1516–1518.

Angold, A. E., Costello, J., Burns, B. J., Erkanli, A., & Farmer, E.M.Z. (2002). Effectiveness of nonresidential specialty mental health services for children and adolescents in the "real world." *Journal of the American Academy of Child & Adolescent Psychiatry, 39,* 154–160.

Anker, M., & Duncan, B. (2003). Using the Outcome Rating Scale with couples. Manuscript in preparation.

Antonuccio, D. O., Danton, W. G., DeNelsky, G. Y., Greenberg, R. P., & Gordon, J. S. (1999). Raising questions about antidepressants. *Psychotherapy and Psychosomatics, 68,* 3–14.

Arneill, A. B., & Devlin, A. S. (2002). Perceived quality of care: The influence of the waiting room environment. *Journal of Environmental Psychology, 22*(4), 345–360.

Asarnow, J. R., Jaycox, L. H., & Tompson, M. C. (2001). Depression in youth: Psychosocial interventions. *Journal of Clinical Child Psychology, 30*(1), 33–48.

Asay, T. P., & Lambert, M. J. (1999). The empirical case for the common factors in therapy: Quantitative findings. In M. A. Hubble, B. L. Duncan, & S. D. Miller (Eds.), *The heart and soul of change: What works in therapy* (pp. 33–56). Washington, DC: American Psychological Association.

Asay, T. P., Lambert, M. J., Gregersen, A. T., & Goates, M. K. (2002). Using patient-focused research in evaluating treatment outcome in private practice. *Journal of Clinical Psychology, 58,* 1213–1225.

Bachelor, A. (1995). Clients' perception of the therapeutic alliance: A qualitative analysis. *Journal of Counseling Psychology, 42,* 323–337.

Bachelor, A., & Horvath, A. (1999). The therapeutic relationship. In M. A. Hubble, B. L. Duncan, & S. D. Miller (Eds.), *The heart and soul of change: What works in therapy* (pp. 133–178). Washington, DC: American Psychological Association.

Barondes, S. (1993). *Molecules and mental illness.* New York: Scientific American Library.

Barry, E. (2003, March 9). Guidelines pushed on child medication: Romney aide questions use of psychiatric drugs in Mass Health program. *Boston Globe*, pp. 26.

Belar, C. (2003). Competencies for quality health care. *Monitor on Psychology, 34,* 38.

Berg, I. K., & Miller, S. D. (1992). *Working with the problem drinker: A solution-focused approach.* New York: Norton.

Berman, P. (1998). Psychotherapists' income plummet! *The Maryland Psychologist, 16,* 22–28.

Beutler, L. (1997). Facts and fiction about prescription privileges. *Psychotherapy Bulletin, 32,* 4–6.

Beutler, L., & Clarkin, J. (1990). *Systematic treatment selection: Toward targeted therapeutic interventions.* New York: Brunner-Mazel.

Beutler, L. E., Malik, M., Alimohamed, S., Harwood, T. M., Talebi, H., Noble, S., & Wong, E. (2004). In M. J. Lambert (ed.), *Bergin and Garfield's handbook of psychotherapy and behavior change* (5th ed., pp. 227–306). New York: Wiley.

Birmaher, B., Ryan, N. D., Williamson, D. E., Brent, D. A., & Kaufman, J. (1996). Childhood and adolescent depression: A review of the past 10 years. Part II. *Journal of the American Academy of Child Psychiatry, 35*(12), 1575–1583.

Blatt, S. J., Zuroff, D. C., Quinlan, D. M., & Pilkonis, P. (1996). Interpersonal factors in brief treatment of depression: Further analyses of the NIMH Treatment of Depression Collaborative Research Program. *Journal of Consulting and Clinical Psychology, 64,* 162–171.

Bohart, A., & Tallman, K. (1999). *What clients do to make therapy work.* Washington, DC: American Psychological Association.

Bordin, E. S. (1979). The generalizability of the psychoanalytic concept of the working alliance. *Psychotherapy: Theory, Research, and Practice, 16,* 252–260.

Borduin, C., Mann, B., Cone, L., Henggeler, S., Fucci, B., Blaske, D., & Williams, R. (1995). Multisystemic treatment of serious juvenile offenders. *Journal of Consulting and Clinical Psychology, 63,* 569–578.

Bosely, S. (2003, June 10). Seroxat warning over risk to young. *The Guardian,* available www.guardian.co.uk/uk_new/story/0,3604,974175/00.html.

Breggin, P. (1998). *Talking back to Ritalin.* Monroe, MA: Common Courage Press.

Breggin, P. (2000a). The NIMH multimodal study of treatment for attention-deficit/hyperactivity disorder: A critical analysis. *International Journal of Risk & Safety in Medicine, 13,* 15–22.

Breggin, P. (2000b). *Reclaiming our children: A healing plan for a nation in crisis.* Cambridge, MA: Perseus Books.

Breggin, P., & Cohen, D. (1999). *Your drug may be your problem: How and why to stop taking psychiatric medications.* Cambridge, MA: Perseus Books.

Brent, D. A., & Birmaher, B. (2002). Adolescent depression. *New England Journal of Medicine, 347,* 667–671.

Brickman, P., Rabinowitz, V., Karuza, J., Coates, D., Cohn, E., & Kidder, L. (1982). Models of helping and coping. *American Psychologist, 37,* 368–384.

Brown, J., Dreis, S., & Nace, D. K. (1999). What really makes a difference in psychotherapy outcome? Why does managed care want to know? In M. A. Hubble, B. L. Duncan, & S. D. Miller (Eds.), *The heart and soul of change: What works in therapy* (pp. 389–406). Washington, DC: American Psychological Association.

Carroll, L. (1962). *Alice's adventures in Wonderland.* Harmondsworth, Middlesex: Penguin. (Original work published 1865)

Carson, R. C. (1997). Costly compromises: A critique of the *Diagnostic and Statistical Manual of Mental Disorders.* In S. Fisher & R. P. Greenberg (Eds.), *From placebo to panacea: Putting psychiatric drugs to the test* (pp. 98–114). New York: Wiley.

Castonguay, L. G., Goldfried, M. R., Wiser, S., Raue, P., & Hayes, A. M. (1996). Predicting the effect of cognitive therapy for depression: A study of unique and common factors. *Journal of Consulting and Clinical Psychology, 64,* 497–504.

Clement, P. W. (1994). Quantitative evaluation of 26 years of private practice. *Professional Psychology: Research and Practice, 25,* 2, 173–176.

Connors, G. J., DiClemente, C. C., Carroll, K. M., Longabaugh, R., & Donovan, D. M. (1997). The therapeutic alliance and its relationship to alcoholism treatment participation and outcome. *Journal of Consulting and Clinical Psychology, 65*(4), 588–598.

Conte, H. R., Plutchik, R., Wild, K. V., & Karasu, T. B. (1986). Combined psychotherapy and pharmacotherapy with treatment of depression: A systematic analysis of the evidence. *Archives of General Psychiatry, 43,* 461–479.

Cummings, N. A. (1986). The dismantling of our health system: Strategies for the survival of psychological practice. *American Psychologist, 41,* 4, 426–431.

Cummings, N. A. (2000). A psychologist's proactive guide to mental health care: New roles and opportunities. In A. Kent & M. Hersen (Eds.), *A psychologist's guide to managed mental health care* (pp. 141–161). Hillsdale, NJ: Erlbaum.

Curry, J. F. (2001). Specific psychotherapies for childhood and adolescent depression. *Biological Psychiatry, 49*(12), 1091–1102.

Dannon, P. N., Iancu, I., & Grunhaus, L. (2002). Psychoeducation in panic disorder patients: Effect of a self-information booklet in a randomized, masked-rater study. *Depression & Anxiety, 16*(2), 71–76.

Dattilio, F. M., & Bevilacqua, L. J. (Eds.). (2000). *Comparative treatments for relationship dysfunction.* New York: Springer.

de Shazer, S. (1985). *Keys to solutions in brief therapy.* New York: Norton.

de Shazer, S. (1994). Essential, non-essential: Vive la difference. In J. K. Zeig (Ed.), *Ericksonian Methods: The essence of the story.* New York: Brunner-Mazel.

Diller, L. H. (2000). Kids on drugs: A behavioral pediatrician questions the wisdom of medicating our children. [On-line]. Available: http://www.salon.com/health/feature/2000/03/09/kid_drugs/.

Duncan, B. (2002). The legacy of Saul Rosenzweig: The profundity of the dodo bird. *Journal of Psychotherapy Integration, 12,* 32–57.

Duncan, B., Hubble, M. A., & Miller, S. D. (1997). *Psychotherapy with "impossible cases": The efficient treatment of therapy veterans.* New York: Norton.

Duncan, B., & Miller, S. (2000). *The heroic client: Doing client-directed, outcome-informed therapy.* San Francisco: Jossey-Bass.

Duncan, B., Miller, S., Johnson, L., Brown, J., & Reynolds, L. (in press). The Session Rating Scale: A preliminary study of reliability, validity, and feasibility. *Journal of Brief Therapy.*

Duncan, B., Miller, S., & Sparks, J. (2003). Interactional and solution-focused brief therapies: Evolving concepts of change. In G. Weeks, T. Sexton, & M. Robbins (Eds.), *The handbook of family therapy* (pp. 101–123). New York: Brunner-Routledge.

Duncan, B., & Moynihan, D. (1994). Applying outcome research: Intentional utilization of the client's frame of reference. *Psychotherapy, 31,* 294–301.

Duncan, B., Solovey, A., & Rusk, G. (1992). *Changing the rules: A client-directed approach to therapy.* New York: Guilford Press.

Duncan, B., & Sparks, J. (2002). *Heroic clients, heroic agencies: Partners for change.* Fort Lauderdale, FL: ISTC Press.

Duncan, B., Sparks, J. A., & Miller, S. D. (2000). Recasting the therapeutic drama: Client-directed, outcome-informed therapy.

In F. M. Dattilio & L. J. Bevilacqua (Eds.), *Comparative treatments for relationship dysfunction* (pp. 301–324). New York: Springer.

Duriez, S. (1999). *Constructivism, mythology, and management: The art of escaping Procrustes or the practice of constructivism.* Unpublished manuscript.

Elkin, I., Shea, T., Watkins, J. T., Imber, S. D., Sotsky, S. M., Collins, J. F., Glass, D. R., Pilkonis, P. A., Leber, W. R., Docherty, J. P., Fiester, S. J., & Parloff, M. B. (1989). National Institute of Mental Health Treatment of Depression Collaborative Research Program: General effectiveness of treatments. *Archives of General Psychiatry, 46,* 971–982.

Emslie, G. J., Heiligenstein, J. H., Wagner, K. D., Hoog, S. L., Ernest, D. E., Brown, E., Nilsson, M., & Jacobson, J. G. (2002). Fluoxetine for acute treatment of depression in children and adolescents: A placebo-controlled, randomized clinical trial. *Journal of the American Academy of Child and Adolescent Psychiatry, 41*(10), 1205–1215.

Emslie, G. J., Rush, A. J., Weinberg, W. A., Kowatch, R. A., Hughes, C. W., Carmody, T., & Rintelmann, J. (1997). A double-blind, randomized, placebo-controlled trial of fluoxetine in children and adolescents with depression. *Archives of General Psychiatry, 54*(11), 1031–1037.

Erickson, M. H. (1980). The use of symptoms as an integral part of hypnotherapy. In E. Rossi (Ed.), *The collected papers of Milton H. Erickson on hypnosis* (Vol. 4). New York: Irvington.

Erickson, M. H., & Rossi, E. L. (1979). *Hypnotherapy: An exploratory casebook.* New York: Irvington.

Eron, J., & Lund, T. (1996). *Narrative solutions in brief therapy.* New York: Guilford Press.

Evan, C., Siobud-Dorocant, E., & Dardennes, R. M. (2000). Critical approach to antidepressant trials: Blindness protection is necessary, feasible and measurable. *British Journal of Psychiatry, 177,* 47–51.

FDA Talk Paper. (2003). FDA approves Prozac for pediatric use to treat depression and OCD. Retrieved August 2, 2003, from: U.S. Food and Drug Administration: http://www.fda.gov/bbs/topics/ANSWERS/2003/ANSO1187.html.

Fisch, R., Weakland, J., & Segal, L. (1982). *The tactics of change: Doing therapy briefly.* San Francisco: Jossey-Bass.

Fisher, R. L., & Fisher, S. (1997). Are we justified in treating children with psychotropic drugs? In S. Fisher & R. P. Greenberg (Eds.), *From placebo to panacea: Putting psychiatric drugs to the test* (pp. 307–322). New York: Wiley.

Fisher, S., & Greenberg, R. P. (Eds.). (1997). *From placebo to panacea: Putting psychiatric drugs to the test.* New York: Wiley.

Flexner, J. T. (1974). *Washington: The indispensable man.* New York: Little, Brown and Company.

Fogel, B., Schiffer, R., & Rao, S. (1996). *Neuropsychiatry.* Baltimore: Williams & Wilkins.

Frank, J. D. (1973). *Persuasion and healing.* Baltimore: Johns Hopkins University Press.

Frank, J. D. (1995). Psychotherapy as rhetoric: Some implications. *Clinical Psychology: Science and Practice, 2,* 90–93.

Frank, J. D., & Frank, J. B. (1991). *Persuasion and healing: A comparative study of psychotherapy* (3rd ed.). Baltimore: John Hopkins University Press.

Freud, S. (1990). In W. Boehlich (Ed.), *Letters of Sigmund Freud to Edward Silverstein.* Boston: Harvard University Press.

Garb, H. N. (1998). *Studying the Clinician.* Washington, DC: American Psychological Association.

Garfield, S. (1986). Problems in diagnostic classification. In T. Millon & G. Klerman (Eds.), *Contemporary directions in psychopathology.* New York: Guilford Press.

Gaston, L. (1990). The concept of the alliance and its role in psychotherapy: Theoretical and empirical considerations. *Psychotherapy, 27,* 143–152.

Gaston, L. (1991). Reliability and criterion-related validity of the California Psychotherapy Alliance Scales—Patient version. *Psychological Assessment: A Journal of Consulting and Clinical Psychology, 3,* 68–74.

Ger, L. P., Ho, S. T., Sun, W. Z., Wang, M. S., & Cleeland, C. S. (1999). Validation of the Brief Pain Inventory in a Taiwanese population. *Journal of Pain & Symptom Management, 18*(5), 316–322.

Gergen, K. E., & Kaye, J. (1992). Beyond narrative and the negotiation of therapeutic meaning. In S. McNamee & K. J. Gergen (Eds.), *Therapy as social construction* (pp. 166–185). Thousand Oaks: Sage.

Gilman, A., Rall, T., Nies, A., & Taylor, P. (1990). *Goodman and Gilman's the pharmacological basis of therapeutics* (8th ed.). New York: Pergamon Press.

Goldman, A., & Greenberg, L. (1992). Comparison of integrated systemic and emotionally focused approaches to couples therapy. *Journal of Consulting and Clinical Psychology, 60,* 962–969.

Goolishian, H., & Anderson, H. (1987). Language systems and therapy: An evolving idea. *Psychotherapy, 24,* 529–538.

Greenberg, R. P. (2002). Reflections on the emperor's new drugs. *Prevention & Treatment, 5,* Article 27 [On-line]. Available: http://www. journals.apa.org/prevention/volume 5/pre0050027c.html.

Greenberg, R. P., Bornstein, R. F., Greenberg, M. D., & Fisher, S. (1992). A meta-analysis of antidepressant outcome under "blinder" conditions. *Journal of Consulting and Clinical Psychology, 60,* 664–669.

Greenberg, R. P., Bornstein, R. F., Zborowski, M. J., Fisher, S., & Greenberg, M. D. (1994). A meta-analysis of fluoxetine outcome in the treatment of depression. *Journal of Nervous and Mental Disease, 182,* 547–551.

Greenberg, R. P., & Fisher, S. (1989). Examining antidepressant effectiveness: Findings, ambiguities, and some vexing puzzles. In S. Fisher & R. P. Greenberg (Eds.), *The Limits of biological treatments for psychological distress: Comparisons with psychotherapy and placebo* (pp. 1–37). Hillsdale, NJ: Elrbaum.

Greenberg, R. P., & Fisher, S. (1997). Mood-mending medicines: Probing drug, psychotherapy, and placebo solutions. In S. Fisher & R. P. Greenberg (Eds.), *From placebo to panacea: Putting psychiatric drugs to the test* (pp. 115–172). New York: Wiley.

Grunhaus, L., Dolberg, O. T., Polak, D., & Dannon, P. N. (2002). Monitoring the response to TMS in depression with visual analog scales. *Human Psychopharmacology Clinical & Experimental, 17*(7), 349–352.

Haas, E., Hill, R. D., Lambert, M. J., & Morrell, B. (2002). Do early responders to psychotherapy maintain treatment gains? *Journal of Clinical Psychology, 58*(9), 1157–1172.

Hales, R., Yudosky, S., & Talbott, J. (1999). *The American Psychiatric Press textbook of psychiatry* (3rd ed.). Washington, DC: American Psychiatric Press.

Haley, J. (1976). *Problem-solving therapy.* New York: HarperCollins.

Haley, J. (1980). *Leaving home.* New York: McGraw-Hill.

Haley, J. (1989). The effect of long term outcome studies on the therapy of schizophrenia. *Journal of Marital and Family Therapy, 15,* 127–132.

Hansen, N. B., Lambert, M. J., & Forman, E. V. (2002). The psychotherapy dose-response effect and its implications for treatment delivery services. *Clinical Psychology, 9,* 162–169.

Hansen, N. B., & Lambert, M. J. (2003). An evaluation of the dose-response relationship in naturalistic treatment settings using survival analysis. *Mental Health Services Research, 5*(1), 1–12.

Harding, C., Zubin, R., & Strauss, D. (1987). Chronicity in schizophrenia: Fact, partial fact or artifact. *Hospital and Community Psychiatry, 38,* 477–484.

Hardman, J. G., Limbird, L. E., & Gilman, A. G. (Eds.). (2001). *Goodman and Gilman's the pharmacological basis of therapeutics.* New York: McGraw-Hill.

Hatcher, R. L., & Barends, A. W. (1996). Patients' view of the alliance in psychotherapy: Exploratory factor analysis of three alliance measures. *Journal of Consulting and Clinical Psychology, 64,* 1326–1336.

Hay Group. (1999). *The Hay Group study: Health care plan design and cost trends (1988–1997)* [On-line]. Available: http://www.naphs.org/news/haygroupreport.html.

Healy, D. (1997). *The antidepressant era.* Cambridge, MA: Harvard University Press.

Held, B. S. (1991). The process/content distinction in psychotherapy revisited. *Psychotherapy, 28,* 207–217.

Henggeler, S., Melton, G., & Smith, L. (1992). Family preservation using multisystemic therapy. *Journal of Consulting and Clinical Psychology, 60,* 953–961.

Hiatt, D., & Hargrave, G. E. (1995). The characteristics of highly effective therapists in managed behavioral providers networks. *Behavioral Healthcare Tomorrow, 4,* 19–22.

Hill, C. E., Nutt-Williams, E., Heaton, K., Thompson, B., & Rhodes, R. H. (1996). Therapist retrospective recall of impasses in long-term psychotherapy: A qualitative analysis. *Journal of Counseling Psychology, 43,* 207–217.

Hoch, P. (1955). Aims and limitations of psychotherapy. *American Journal of Psychiatry, 112,* 321–327.

Hollon, S. D., DeRubeis, R. J., Shelton, R. C., & Weiss, B. (2002). The emperor's new drugs: Effect size and moderation effects. *Prevention & Treatment, 5,* Article 28 [On-line]. Available: http://www. journals.apa.org/prevention/volume 5/pre0050028c.html.

Holloway, J. D. (2003). U.S. mental health system needs less stigma, more consumer input. *Monitor on Psychology, 34,* 20–22.

Horvath, A. O., & Greenberg, L. S. (1989). Development and validation of the Working Alliance Inventory. *Journal of Counseling Psychology, 36,* 223–233.

Horvath, A. O., & Symonds, B. D. (1991). Relation between working alliance and outcome in psychotherapy: A meta-analysis. *Journal of Counseling Psychology, 38,* 139–149.

Howard, K. I., Kopte, S. M., Krause, M. S., & Orlinsky, D. E. (1986). The dose-effect relationship in psychotherapy. *American Psychologist, 41*(2), 159–164.

Howard, K. I., Lueger, R. J., Maling, M. S., & Martinovich, Z. (1993). A phase model of psychotherapy outcome: Causal mediation of change. *Journal of Consulting & Clinical Psychology, 61,* 678–685.

Howard, K. I., Moras, K., Brill, P. L., Martinovich, Z., & Lutz, W. (1996). Evaluation of psychotherapy: Efficacy, effectiveness, and patient progress. *American Psychologist, 51*(10), 1059–1064.

Hubble, M. A., Duncan, B. L., & Miller, S. D. (1999a). Introduction. In M. A. Hubble, B. L. Duncan, & S. D. Miller (Eds.), *The heart and soul of change: What works in therapy* (pp. 1–32). Washington, DC: American Psychological Association.

Hubble, M. A., Duncan, B. L., & Miller, S. D. (1999b). Directing attention to what works. In M. A. Hubble, B. L. Duncan, & S. D. Miller (Eds.), *The heart and soul of change: What works in therapy* (pp. 407–448). Washington, DC: American Psychological Association.

Hubble, M. A., Duncan, B. L., & Miller, S. D. (1999c). *The heart and soul of change: What works in therapy.* Washington, DC: American Psychological Association.

Hughes, C. W., Emslie, G., Kowatch, R., Weinberg, W., Rintelmann, J., & Rush, A. J. (2000). Clinician, parent, and child prediction of medication or placebo in double-blind depression study. *Neuropsychopharmacology, 23*(5), 591–594.

IMS Health. (2003). http://www.imshealth.com/ims/portal/pages/home.html.

Jacobson, N., Dobson, K., Truax, P., Addis, M., Koerner, K., Gollan, J., Gortner, D., & Prince, S. (1996). A component analysis of cognitive-behavioral treatment for depression. *Journal of Consulting and Clinical Psychology, 64,* 295–304.

Johnson, L. D. (1995). *Psychotherapy in the age of accountability.* New York: Norton.

Johnson, L. D., Miller, S., & Duncan, B. (2000). *The Session Rating Scale version 3.0* [On-line]. Available: http://www.talkingcure.com/measures.htm.

Johnson, L. D., & Shaha, S. (1996). Improving quality in psychotherapy. *Psychotherapy, 35,* 225–236.

Johnson, L. D., & Shaha, S. H. (1997, July). Upgrading clinicians' reports to MCOs. *Behavioral Health Management,* pp. 42–46.

Johnson, S. M. (2003). The revolution in couple therapy: A practitioner-scientist perspective. *Journal of Marital and Family Therapy, 29,* 365–384.

Johnson, S. M., & Greenberg, L. S. (1985). The differential effects of experiential and problem-solving interventions in resolving couple conflicts. *Journal of Consulting and Clinical Psychology, 58,* 175–184.

Johnson, S. M., Hunsley, J., Greenberg, L., & Schindler, D. (1999). Emotionally focused couples therapy: Status and challenges. *Clinical Psychology Science and Practice, 6,* 67–79.

Kadera, S. W., Lambert, M. J., & Andrews, A. A. (1996). How much therapy is really enough: A session-by-session analysis of the psychotherapy dose-effect relationship. *Journal of Psychotherapy: Practice and Research, 5,* 1–20.

Karon, B., & Vanderbos, G. (1994). *The psychotherapy of schizophrenia: The treatment of choice.* New York: Aronson.

Keller, M. B., McCullough, J. P., Klein, D. N., Arnow B., Dunner, D. L., Gelenberg, A. J., Markowitz, J. C., Nemeroff, C. B., Russell, J. M., Thase, M. E., Trivedi, M. H., & Zajecka, J. (2000). A comparison of nefazodone, the cognitive behavioral-analysis system of psychotherapy, and their combination for the treatment of chronic depression. *New England Journal of Medicine. 342*(20), 1462–1470.

Keller, M. B., Ryan, N. D., Strober, M., Klein, R. G., Kutcher, S. P., Birmaher, B., Hagino, O. R., Koplewicz, H., Carlson, G., Geller, B., Kusumakar, V., Papatheodorou, G., Sack, W. H., Sweeney, M., Wagner, K. D., Weller, E. B., Winters, N. C., Oakes, R., & McCafferty, J. P. (2001). Efficacy of paroxetine in the treatment of adolescent major depression: A randomized, controlled trial. *Journal of the American Academy of Child & Adolescent Psychiatry, 40*(7), 762–772.

Kelly, G. (1955). *The psychology of personal constructs.* New York: Norton.

Kendell, R., & Zablansky, A. (2003). Distinguishing between the validity and utility of psychiatric diagnoses. *American Journal of Psychiatry, 160,* 4–12.

Kiesler, C. (2000). The next wave of change for psychology and mental health services in the health care revolution. *American Psychologist, 55,* 481–487.

Kirk, S., & Kutchins, H. (1988). Deliberate misdiagnosis in mental health practice. *Social Service Review, 62,* 225–237.

Kirk, S. A., & Kutchins, H. (1992). *The selling of* DSM: *The rhetoric of science in psychiatry.* New York: Aldine.

Kirsch, I., Moore, T. J., Scoboria, A., & Nicholls, S. S. (2002). The emperor's new drugs: An analysis of antidepressant medication data submitted to the U.S. Food and Drug Administration. *Prevention & Treatment, 5,* Article 23 [On-line]. Available: http://www.journals.apa.org/prevention/volume 5/pre0050023a.html.

Kirsch, I., & Sapirstein, G. (1998). Listening to Prozac but hearing placebo: A meta-analysis of antidepressant medication. *Prevention & Treatment, 1,* Article 0002a [On-line]. Available: http://journals.apa.org/prevention/volume1/pre0010002ahtml.

Kirsch, I., Scoboria, A., & Moore, T. J. (2002). Antidepressants and placebos: Secrets, revelations, and unanswered questions. *Prevention & Treatment, 5,* Article 33 [On-line]. Available: http://www.journals.apa.org/prevention/volume 5/pre0050023a.html.

Kong, D., & Bass, A. (1999, October 8). Case at Brown leads to review: NIMH studies tighter rules on conflicts. *Boston Globe,* p. B1.

Kremer, T. G., & Gesten, E. L. (1998). Confidentiality limits of manage care and clients' willingness to self-disclose. *Professional Psychology, 29*(6), 553–558.

Krupnick, J. L., Sotsky, S. M., Simmens, S., Moyer, J., Elkin, I., Watkins, J., & Pilkonis, P. A. (1996). The role of the therapeutic alliance in psychotherapy and pharmacotherapy outcome: Findings in the National Institute of Mental Health Treatment of Depression Collaborative Research Project. *Journal of Consulting and Clinical Psychology, 64,* 532–539.

Kutchins, K., & Kirk, H. (1997). *Making us crazy:* DSM: *The psychiatric bible and the creation of mental disorders.* New York: Free Press.

Lambert, M. E., & Bergin, A. E. (1994). The effectiveness of psychotherapy. In A. E. Bergin & S. L. Garfield (Eds.), *Handbook of psychotherapy and behavior change* (4th ed., pp. 143–190). New York: Wiley.

Lambert, M. J., & Barley, D. E. (2001). Research summary on the therapeutic relationship and psychotherapy outcome. *Psychotherapy, 38*(4), 357–361.

Lambert, M. J., & Brown, G. S. (1996). Data-based management for tracking outcome in private practice. *Clinical Psychology, 3,* 172–178.

Lambert, M. J., Burlingame, G. M., Umphress, V., Hansen, N. B., Vermeersch, D. A., Clouse, G. C., & Yanchar, S. C. (1996). The reliability and validity of the Outcome Questionnaire. *Clinical Psychology and Psychotherapy, 3,* 249–258.

Lambert, M. J., & Hill, C. E. (1994). Assessing psychotherapy outcomes and processes. In A. E. Bergin & S. L. Garfield (Eds.), *Handbook of psychotherapy and behavior change* (4th ed., pp. 72–113). New York: Wiley.

Lambert, M. J., & Ogles, B. (2004). The efficacy and effectiveness of psychotherapy. In M. J. Lambert (Ed.), *Bergin and Garfield's handbook of psychotherapy and behavior change* (5th ed., pp. 139–193). New York: Wiley.

Lambert, M. J., Ogles, B., & Masters, K. (1992). Choosing outcome assessment devices: An organization and conceptual scheme. *Journal of Counseling and Development, 70,* 527–539.

Lambert, M. J., Okiishi, J. C., Finch, A. E., & Johnson, L. D. (1998). Outcome assessment: From conceptualization to implementation. *Professional Psychology: Practice and Research, 29*(1), 63–70.

Lambert, M. J., Whipple, J. L., Hawkins, E. J., Vermeersch, D. A., Nielsen, S. L., & Smart, D. W. (2003). Is it time for clinicians routinely to track patient outcome? A meta-analysis. *Clinical Psychology, 10,* 288–301.

Lambert, M. J., Whipple, J., Smart, D., Vermeersch, D., Nielsen, S., & Hawkins, E. (2001). The effects of providing therapists with feedback on patient progress during psychotherapy: Are outcomes enhanced? *Psychotherapy Research, 11*(1), 49–68.

Lawson, D. (1994). Identifying pretreatment change. *Journal of Counseling and Development, 72,* 244–248.

Lee, L. (2000). *Bad Predictions.* Rochester, MI: Elsewhere Press.

LeFever, G., Arcona, A., & Antonuccio, D. (2003). *ADHD among American school children: Evidence of overdiagnosis and misuse of medication.* Manuscript submitted for publication.

Leo, J. (2000). Attention deficit disorder: Good science or good marketing. *Skeptic, 8,* 63–69.

Leo, J., & Cohen, D. (2003). Broken brains or flawed studies? A critical review of ADHD neuroimaging research. *Journal of Mind and Behavior, 24,* 29–55.

Levitt, T. (1975, September–October). Marketing myopia. *Harvard Business Review,* pp. 19–31.

Lewinsohn, P. M., & Clarke, G. N. (1999). Psychosocial treatments for adolescent depression. *Clinical Psychology Review, 19*(3), 329–342.

Luborsky, L., Barber, J., Siqueland, L., Johnson, S., Najavits, L., Frank, A., & Daley, D. (1996). The revised Helping Alliance Questionnaire (HAQ-II). *The Journal of Psychotherapy Practice and Research, 5,* 260–271.

Luborsky, L., Singer, B., & Luborsky, L. (1975). Comparative studies of psychotherapies: Is it true that "everyone has won and all must have prizes"? *Archives of General Psychiatry, 32*, 995–1008.

Mackey, P., & Kipras, A. (2001). *Medication for attention deficit/ hyperactivity disorder (ADHD): An analysis by federal electorate.* Unpublished manuscript.

Madigan, S., & Epston, D. (1995). From "Spy-chiatric Gaze" to communities of concern: From professional monologue to dialogue. In S. Friedman (Ed.), *The reflecting team in action: Collaborative practice in family therapy* (pp. 257–276). New York: Guilford Press.

McCall, R. (1980). *Fundamental statistics for psychology* (3rd ed.). New York: Harcourt, Brace, and Jovanovich.

McGuire, W. (2002). Dear colleague. In UnitedHealth Foundation *Clinical evidence mental health.* London: BMJ Publishing.

Merriam-Webster's Collegiate Dictionary (10th ed.). (1993). New York: Merriam-Webster.

Messer, S., & Wampold, B. (2002). Let's face facts: Common factors are more potent than specific therapy ingredients. *Clinical Psychology, Science, and Practice, 9*, 21–25.

Michael, K. D., & Crowley, S. L. (2002). How effective are treatments for child and adolescent depression? A meta-analytic review. *Clinical Psychology Review, 22*(2), 247–269.

Miller, L., Bergstrom, D., Cross, H., & Grube, J. (1981). Opinions and use of the *DSM* system by practicing psychologists. *Professional Psychology, 12*, 387.

Miller, S. D., & Duncan, B. (2000a). *The Outcome Rating Scale* [On-line]. Available: http://www.talkingcure.com/measures.htm.

Miller, S. D., & Duncan, B. L. (2000b). Paradigm lost: From model-driven to client-directed, outcome-informed clinical work. *Journal of Systemic Therapies, 19*, 20–34.

Miller, S. D., Duncan, B., Brown, J., Sorrell, R., & Chalk, M. (in press). The Outcome Rating Scale and the improvement of effectiveness in a telephonic EAP setting. *Journal of Brief Therapy.*

Miller, S. D., Duncan, B., Brown, J., Sparks, J., & Claud, D. (in press). The reliability, validity, and feasibility of the Outcome Rating Scale. *Journal of Brief Therapy, 2*(2).

Miller, S. D., Duncan, B., & Hubble, M. (2004). Outcome-informed clinical work. In J. Norcross & M. Goldfried (Eds.), *Handbook of psychotherapy integration.* New York: Oxford University Press.

Miller, S. D., Duncan, B. L., & Hubble, M. A. (1997). *Escape from Babel: Toward a unifying language for psychotherapy.* New York: Norton.

Miller, S. D., Duncan, B. L., Johnson, L. D., & Hubble, M. A. (2000). Client-directed, outcome-informed treatment. In J. K. Zeig (Ed.), *Ericksonian Foundations.* Redding, CT: Zeig, Tucker.

Mitka, M. (2001). Mental health agenda now set for U.S. children. *JAMA, 285*(4), 398–399.

Mohl, D. C. (1995). Negative outcome in psychotherapy: A critical review. *Clinical Psychology: Science and Practice, 2,* 1–27.

Moncrieff, J. (2001). Are antidepressants overrated? A review of methodological problems in antidepressant trials. *Journal of Nervous and Mental Disorders, 189,* 288–295.

Moncrieff, J., Wessely, S., & Hardy, R. (1998). Meta-analysis of trials comparing anti-depressants with active placebos. *British Journal of Psychiatry, 172,* 227–231.

Morris, J., & Beck, A. (1974). The efficacy of antidepressant drugs: A review of research (1958–1972). *Archives of General Psychiatry, 30,* 667–674.

MTA Cooperative Group. (1999). A 14-month randomized clinical trial of treatment strategies for attention-deficit/hyperactivity disorder. The MTA cooperative group. Multimodal treatment study of children with ADHD. *Archives of General Psychiatry, 56,* 1073–1086.

Mufson, L., Weissman, M. M., Moreau, D., & Garfinkel, R. (1999). Efficacy of interpersonal psychotherapy for depressed adolescents. *Archives of General Psychiatry, 56*(6), 573–579.

Mulrow, C. D., Williams, J. W., Jr., Trivedi, M., Chiquette, E., Aguilar, C., Cornell, J. E., Badgett, R., Noel, P. H., Lawrence, V., Lee, S., Luther, M., Ramirez, G., Richardson, W. S., & Stamm, K. (1999). *Treatment of depression: Newer pharmaco-therapies* (Evidence Report/Technology Assessment No. 7; AHCPR Publication No. 99-E014). Rockville, MD: Agency for Health Care Policy and Research.

Murphy, J. J., & Duncan, B. L. (1997). *Practical solutions for school problems: A brief intervention approach.* New York: Guilford Press.

Murphy, J. M., Laird, N. M., Monson, R. R., Sobol, A. M., & Leighton, A. H. (2000). A 40-year perspective on the prevalence of depression. *Archives of General Psychiatry, 57,* 209–218.

Murphy, M., DeBernardo, C., & Shoemaker, W. (1998). Impact of managed care on independent practice and professional ethics: A survey of independent practitioners. *Professional Psychology: Research and Practice, 29,* 43–51.

Nathan, P. E. (1997). Fiddling while psychology burns? *Register Report, 23*(2), 1, 4–5, 10.

Nathan, K. I., Musselman, D. L., Schatzberg, A. F., & Nemeroff, C. B. (Eds.). (1995). *Textbook of psychopharmacology.* Washington, DC: The American Psychiatric Press.

National Association of Social Workers. (1999). *NASW Code of Ethics* [On-line]. Available: http:/www.naswdc.org/code/cdstan1.html.

National Institute of Mental Health (NIMH). http://www.nimh.nih.gov.

Norcross, J. (1997). Emerging breakthroughs in psychotherapy integration: Three predictions and one fantasy. *Psychotherapy, 34,* 86–90.

Norcross, J., Hanych, J. M., & Terranova, R. D. (1996). Graduate study in psychology: 1992–1993. *American Psychologist, 51*(6), 631–643.

O'Connor, E. (2001). Medicating ADHD: Too much? Too soon? *Monitor on Psychology, 32,* 50–51.

Ogles, B., Lambert, M. J., & Masters, K. S. (1996). *Assessing outcome in clinical practice.* Needham Heights, MA: Allyn & Bacon.

Olfson, M., Marcus, S. C., Weissman, M. M., & Jensen, P. S. (2002). National trends in the use of psychotropic medications by children. *Journal of the American Academy of Child and Adolescent Psychiatry, 41*(5), 514–521.

Orlinsky, D. E., Grawe, K., & Parks, B. K. (1994). Process and outcome in psychotherapy—*noch einmal.* In A. E. Bergin & S. L. Garfield (Eds.), *Handbook of psychotherapy and behavior change* (4th ed., pp. 270–378). New York: Wiley.

Orlinsky, D. E., Ronnestad, M. H., & Willutzki, U. (2004). Fifty years of process-outcome research: Continuity and change. In M. J. Lambert (Ed.), *Bergin and Garfield's handbook of psychotherapy and behavior change* (5th ed., pp. 307–390). New York: Wiley.

Parker, I., Georgaca, E., Harper, D., McLaughlin, T., & Stowell-Smith, M. (1995). *Deconstructing psychopathology.* Thousand Oaks, CA: Sage.

Parloff, M. B. (1982). Psychotherapy research evidence and reimbursement decisions: Bambi meets Godzilla. *American Journal of Psychiatry, 139,* 718–727.

Pelham, W. (1999). The NIMH multimodal treatment study for attention-deficit hyperactivity disorder: Just say yes to drugs alone. *Canadian Journal of Psychiatry, 44,* 981–990.

Rabasca, L. (1999). Find the right niche in new market. *APA Monitor, 30*(2), 1, 10–12.

Robinson, L. A., Berman, J. S., & Neimeyer, R. A. (1990). Psychotherapy for the treatment of depression: A comprehensive review of controlled outcome research. *Psychological Bulletin, 108,* 30–49.

Rosenhan, D. L. (1973). On being sane in insane places. *Science, 179,* 250–258.

Rosenzweig, S. (1936). Some implicit common factors in diverse methods of psychotherapy. *American Journal of Orthopsychiatry, 6,* 412–415.

Salovey, P., & Turk, D. (1991). Clinical judgment and decision making. In C. R. Snyder & D. R. Forsyth (Eds.), *Handbook of social and clinical psychology: The health perspective* (pp. 416–437). New York: Pergamon.

Saltzman, N., & Norcross, J. (Eds.). (1990). *Therapy wars: Contention and convergence in differing clinical approaches.* San Francisco: Jossey-Bass.

Sanchez, L., & Turner, S. (2003). Practicing psychology in the era of managed care: Implications for practice and training. *American Psychologist, 58,* 116–129.

Sanderson, W. C., Riley, W. T., & Eshun, S. (1997). Report of the working group on clinical services. *Journal of Clinical Psychology in Medical Settings, 4*(1), 3–12.

Sasich, L. D., Lurie, P., & Wolfe, S. M. (2000). The drug industry's performance in finishing postmarketing research (Phase IV) studies: A Public Citizen's health research group report. *Health Research Group* [On-line]. Available: http://www.citizen.org/publications/release.cfm?ID=6721.

Schappert, S. (1994). National ambulatory medical care survey: 1991 summary. *Vital Health Statistics, 13,* 1–110.

Scott, J. (2000). Treatment of chronic depression. *New England Journal of Medicine, 342,* 1518–1520.

Shadish, W. R., Matt, G. E., Navarro, A. M., & Phillips, G. (2000). The effects of psychological therapies under clinically representative conditions: A meta-analysis. *Psychological Bulletin, 126,* 512–529.

Shea, M., Elkin, I., Imber, S., Sotsky, S., Watkins, J., Collins, J., Pilkonis, P., Beckham, R., Glass, D., Dolan, C., & Parloff, M. (1992). Course of depressive symptoms over follow-up: Findings from the National Institute of Mental Health Treatment of Depression Collaborative Research Program. *Archives of General Psychiatry, 49,* 782–787.

Sluzki, C. (1998). In search of the lost family: A footnote to Minuchin's essay. *Journal of Marital and Family Therapy, 24*(4), 415–417.

Snyder, S. (1986). *Drugs and the brain.* New York: Scientific American Library.

Sparks, J. (2000). The deconstruction of magic: Rereading, rethinking Erickson. *Family Process, 39,* 307–318.

Sparks, J. A. (2002). Taking a stand: An adolescent girl's resistance to medication. *Journal of Marital and Family Therapy, 28*(1), 51–58.

Sparks, J. A., & Duncan, B. (2003). The ethics and science of medicating children. *Ethical Human Sciences and Services, 6,* 36–47.

Stiles, W., & Shapiro, D. (1989). Abuse of the drug metaphor in psychotherapy process-outcome research. *Clinical Psychology Review, 9,* 521–543.

Strosahl, K. (2001). The integration of primary care and behavioral health: Type II change in the era of managed care. In N. A. Cummings, W. O'Donahue, S. C. Hayes, & V. Follette (Eds.), *Integrated behavioral healthcare: Positioning mental health practice with medical/ surgical practice* (pp. 45–69). San Diego, CA: Academic Press.

Tallman, K., & Bohart, A. (1999). The client as a common factor: Clients as self-healers. In M. A. Hubble, B. L. Duncan, & S. D. Miller (Eds.), *The heart and soul of change: What works in therapy.* Washington, DC: American Psychological Association.

Thase, M. E., Greenhouse, J. B., Frank, E., Reynolds, C. F., III, Pilkonis, P. A., Hurley, K., Grochocinski, V., & Kupfer, D. J. (1997). Treatment of major depression with psychotherapy or psychotherapy-pharmacotherapy combinations. *Archives of General Psychiatry, 54*(11), 1009–1015.

Tomiak, M., Berthelot, J., & Mustard, C. (1998). A profile of health care utilization of the disabled population in Manitoba. *Medical Care, 36,* 573–585.

Torrey, E. (1972). *The mind game: Witchdoctors and psychiatrists.* New York: Emerson Hall.

Valenstein, E. (1998). *Blaming the brain.* New York: Free Press.

Vermeersch, D. A., Lambert, M. J., & Burlingame, G. M. (2000). Outcome questionnaire: Item sensitivity to change. *Journal of Personality Assessment, 74*(2), 242–261.

Vitiello, B. (1998). Pediatric psychopharmacology and the interaction between drugs and the developing brain. *Canadian Journal of Psychiatry, 43*(6), 582–584.

Walkup, J. T. (2003). Pediatric psychopharmacology update. *Family Therapy Magazine, 2*(2), 34–36.

Walter, J., & Peller, J. (1992). *Becoming solution-focused in brief therapy.* New York: Brunner-Mazel.

Walter, J., & Peller, J. (2000). *Recreating brief therapy: From preferences to possibilities.* New York: Norton.

Wampold, B. E. (1997). Methodological problems in identifying efficacious psychotherapies. *Psychotherapy Research, 7,* 21–44.

Wampold, B. E. (2001). *The great psychotherapy debate: Models, methods, and findings.* Hillsdale, NJ: Erlbaum.

Wampold, B. E., Mondin, G. W., Moody, M., Stich, F., Benson, K., & Ahn, H. (1997). A meta-analysis of outcome studies comparing bona fide psychotherapies: Empirically, "all must have prizes." *Psychological Bulletin, 122,* 203–215.

Watzlawick, P. (1976). *How real is real?* New York: Vintage.

Watzlawick, P., Weakland, J., & Fisch, R. (1974). *Change: Problem formation and problem resolution.* New York: Norton.

Weiner-Davis, M., de Shazer, S., & Gingerich, W. (1987). Building on pretreatment change to construct the therapeutic solution: An exploratory study. *Journal of Marital and Family Therapy, 13,* 359–364.

Whipple, J. L., Lambert, M. J., Vermeersch, D. A., Smart, D. W., Nielsen, S. L., & Hawkins, E. J. (2003). Improving the effects of psychotherapy: The use of early identification of treatment and problem-solving strategies in routine practice. *Journal of Counseling Psychology, 50*(1), 59–68.

Whitaker, R. (2002). *Mad in America: Bad science, bad medicine, and the enduring mistreatment of the mentally ill.* Cambridge, MA: Perseus Books.

White, M., & Epston, D. (1990). *Narrative means to therapeutic ends.* New York: Norton.

Wile, D. (1977). Ideological conflicts between clients and psychotherapists. *American Journal of Psychotherapy, 37,* 437–449.

Wilford, J. (1986). *The riddle of the dinosaur.* New York: Knopf.

Williams, J., Gibbon, M., First, M., Spitzer, R., Davies, M., Borus, J., Howes, M., Kane, J., Pope, H., Rounsaville, B., & Wittchen, H. (1992). The structured clinical interview for *DSM-III-R* (SCID)II: Multi-site test-retest reliability. *Archives of General Psychiatry, 49,* 630–636.

Williams, J., Rost, K., Dietrich, A., Ciotti, M., Zyzanski, S., & Cornell, J. (1999). Primary care physicians' approach to depressive disorders. *Archives of Family Medicine, 8,* 58–67.

Wolfe, B. E. (1993). Psychotherapy research funding for fiscal years 1986–1990. *Psychotherapy and Rehabilitation Research Bulletin, 1,* 7–9.

Woolston, J. L. (1999). Combined pharmacotherapy: Pitfalls of treatment. *Journal of the American Academy of Child and Adolescent Psychiatry, 38*(11), 1455–1457.

Zeig, J. K. (1980). *A teaching seminar with Milton H. Erickson.* New York: Brunner-Mazel.

Zito, J. M., Safer, S. J., dosReis, S., Gardner, J. F., Boles, M., & Lynch, F. (2000). Trends in the prescribing of psychotropic medications to preschoolers. *JAMA, 283*(8), 1025–1030.

Zito, J. M., Safer, S. J., dosReis, S., Gardner, J. F., Magder, L., Soeken, K., Boles, M., Lynch, F., & Riddle, M. A. (2003). Psychotropic practice patterns for youth: A 10-year perspective. *Archives of Pediatric & Adolescent Medicine, 157*(1), 17–25.

Zito, J., Safer, D., dosReis, S., & Riddle, M. (1998). Racial disparity in psychotropic medications prescribed for youths on Medicaid insurance in Maryland. *Journal of the Academy of Child Adolescent Psychiatry, 37,* 179–184.

ᜪ About the Authors

Barry L. Duncan, trainer, therapist, and dreamer with over 17,000 hours of clinical experience, received his Psy.D. in clinical psychology from Wright State University School of Professional Psychology. Duncan is codirector of the Institute of the Study of Therapeutic Change (ISTC) and is in an outcome-informed private practice in Coral Springs, Florida. He has over one hundred publications, including twelve books. His collaborations with Scott Miller and Mark Hubble have culminated in four books, two of which are *Psychotherapy with "Impossible" Cases* (Norton, 1997) and *The Heart and Soul of Change* (American Psychological Association, 1999). Most recently, he coauthored, with Jacqueline Sparks, *Heroic Clients, Heroic Agencies: Partners for Change* (ISTC Press, 2002). Because of his self-help books, he has appeared on *Oprah, The View,* and several other national television programs and has been featured in *Psychology Today, USA Today,* and *Glamour.* Duncan conducts seminars internationally in client-directed, outcome-informed therapies in hopes of inciting insurrection against practices that diminish clients and encouraging therapists to establish their own identity. He can be reached at barrylduncan@cs. com, http://www.heroicagencies.org or http://www .talkingcure.com.

ᜪ

Scott D. Miller, lecturer and trainer on client-directed, outcome-informed clinical work, received his Ph.D. in counseling psychology from the University of Utah. For three years he codirected Problems to Solutions, Inc., a clinic specializing in the treatment of the homeless and other traditionally underserved populations. Most recently, Miller cofounded the Institute for the Study of Therapeutic Change and works gratis at a clinic dedicated to serving the underserved. He is the author of many papers and seven books including *The Heart and Soul* *of Change* (American Psychological Association, 1999), *Escape from Babel* (Norton, 1997), *Psychotherapy with "Impossible" Cases* (Norton, 1997), *Handbook of Solution-Focused Brief Therapy* (Jossey-Bass, 1996), *The Miracle Method* (Norton, 1995), and *Working with the Problem Drinker* (Norton, 1992). His latest book is a humorous self-help book couched in the culture of surfing, *Staying on Top and Keeping the Sand Out of Your Pants* (Health Communications, 2003). Miller can be reached at http://www. talkingcure.com.

—◠◠◠—

Jacqueline A. Sparks received her Ph.D from the Nova Southeastern University (NSU) Department of Family Therapy, and she is a licensed marriage and family therapist (LMFT). Sparks is coauthor of *Heroic Clients, Heroic Agencies: Partners for Change* (ISTC Press, 2002) with Barry Duncan, and author of recent articles and book chapters on resistance to mental health business as usual. She is the former director of special projects at the Center for Family Services of Palm Beach County and formerly in practice with Barry Duncan in Coral Springs, Florida. She is an assistant professor of marriage and family therapy at the Department of Human Development and Family Studies at the University of Rhode Island, where her interests are critical theory and the social construction of mental illness. A clinical member of the American Association for Marriage and Family Therapy (AAMFT), she has worked as a therapist, trainer, supervisor, and administrator in the field of family-based services and community mental health for eighteen years. Sparks offers consultation and training for agencies desiring to become effective partners with clients and communities. She can be reached at jsparks@ctrfam.org or http://www.heroicagencies.org.

In Order of Contribution

Lynn Johnson received his Ph.D. from the University of Utah. He created and directed the Brief Therapy Center of Utah and has written articles and taught seminars in tracking psychotherapy outcomes and processes. Johnson's book, *Psychotherapy in the Age of Accountability* (Norton, 1995), outlined client-centered methods of improving psychotherapy outcomes and introduced the Session Rating Scale. He now divides his time between consulting to health care and other organizations about improving performance and his clinical practice at the Brief Therapy Center. Johnson can be reached at ljohnson@ solution-consulting.com.

G. S. (Jeb) Brown, a licensed psychologist, received his Ph.D. from Duke University. He joined United Behavioral Systems as the executive director for Utah in 1987, a position he held for almost six years. In 1993 he accepted a position as the corporate clinical director for Human Affairs International (HAI), one of the largest managed behavioral health care companies in the country. Brown was the primary driver behind HAI's successful outcomes management initiative. In 1998 he left HAI to found the Center for Clinical Informatics. His present projects include the development of the ALERT outcomes management system for PacifiCare Behavioral Health. He continues to see clients for psychotherapy a few hours a week, and he does measure his own outcomes. He can reached at jebbrown@ clinical-informatics.com.

Morten Anker, a psychologist and specialist in clinical psychology and family psychology, was trained at the University of Oslo and received an advanced diploma in family therapy from the University of Oslo in collaboration with the Regional Centre for Child and Adolescent Psychiatry. He is currently a therapist at the Family Counseling Office in Vestfold, Norway, where he also has a private practice. Anker is an associate member of the ISTC and regularly conducts workshops across Norway about integrating the Outcome Rating Scale (ORS) and SRS into clinical practice. He can be reached at morten200@everyday. com.

Susanne Coleman is a doctoral candidate in the department of family therapy at NSU, from which she received her master's degree. Coleman has published two articles describing applications of the concept of the client's theory of change and is completing her dissertation, a qualitative analysis of the perceptions and experiences of children growing up with gay parents.

Lisa Kelledy is currently completing her dissertation as a doctoral candidate in the department of family therapy at NSU. She recently contributed to *Heroic Clients, Heroic Agencies: Partners for Change* (ISTC Press, 2002). Kelledy can be reached at kelledyl@bellsouth.net.

Steven Kopp is a licensed marriage and family therapist and a licensed mental health counselor for Psychology Associates in Davenport, Iowa. He received his doctoral degree in family therapy from Nova Southeastern University, and his dissertation focused on batterer's perspectives of their violence. Kopp works primarily with individuals and families experiencing difficulty with domestic violence and/or anger management. He can be reached at koppsteve@ yahoo.com.

Grace Jackson received her M.D. from the University of Colorado School of Medicine and is a former Navy psychiatrist. She also holds degrees in political science and biology, as well as a master's degree in public administration. Jackson completed her psychiatry internship and residency in the U.S. Navy, with subsequent assignment to Bethesda Navy Hospital as a staff physician. Since transitioning out of the military in spring 2002, she has lectured widely in Europe and the United States, speaking about the limitations of biological psychiatry and the unintended consequences of emerging technologies. She is currently pursuing a second residency in family medicine and can be reached at grace.e.jackson@worldnet.att.net.

Roger P. Greenberg received his Ph.D. in clinical psychology from Syracuse University and is professor and head of the psychology division in the department of psychiatry and behavioral science at SUNY Upstate Medical University in Syracuse. He has authored or coauthored more than 140 publications and delivered scores of presentations in the United States and abroad. His six books include *The Scientific Credibility of Freud's Theories and Therapy* (Wiley, 1995) (which both the National Library Association and *Psychology Today* selected one of the ten best books in the behavioral sciences) and *From Placebo to Panacea: Putting Psychiatric Drugs to the Test* (Wiley, 1997) (both coauthored with Seymour Fisher). Articles about his work have appeared in the *New York Times, Newsweek,* and *Scientific American;* and he has appeared on NBC's *Today* show and ABC's *20/20* to discuss aspects of his work. Greenberg can be reached at GreenbeR@ upstate.edu.

Karen Kinchin is a Ph.D. candidate at NSU, an LMFT, and a member of AAMFT. Kinchin has published numerous articles in the popular press about attention deficit hyperactivity disorder (ADHD) and is also the clinical coordinator of a home-based family therapy program in West Palm Beach, Florida. The master of the heroicagencies.org listserv, Kinchin can be reached at Karen@heroicagencies.org.

Ronald Bassman. (See Appendix I for Dr. Bassman's biography.)

—ᴧᴧ— Name Index

A

Addis, M. E., 40, 41
Aesop, 1
Aguilar, C., 171
Ahn, H., 32, 40
Albee, G., 21
Alimohamed, S., 41
Anastasi, A., 92
Anderson, H., 122
Anderson, T., 114
Andrews, A. A., 87
Angell, M., 154
Anker, M., 93, 108, 109, 111
Anthony, S. B., 18
Antonuccio, D. O., 156, 168, 171
Arcona, A., 156
Arneill, A. B., 88
Arnow, B., 162
Arthus, N. M., 23
Asarnow, J. R., 156
Asay, T. P., 9, 33–35, 37, 38, 51, 63

B

Bachelor, A., 35, 36, 64, 65, 85, 89, 193
Badgett, R., 171
Barber, J., 90, 92
Barends, A. W., 90, 91
Barley, D. E., 84
Barondes, S., 166, 167
Barrett, W., 120
Barry, E., 148
Bassman, R., 213, 217
Beck, A., xviii
Beckham, R., 173
Belar, C., 7

Benson, K., 32, 40
Berg, I. K., 58
Bergin, A. E., 42, 93
Bergstrom, D., 28
Berman, J. S., 173, 174
Berman, P., 2
Berthelot, J., 4
Beutler, L. E., 26, 27, 29, 41, 172
Bevilacqua, L. J., 183
Birmaher, B., 151, 156, 162
Blaske, D., 43
Blatt, S. J., 89
Bohart, A., 34, 51, 198
Boles, M., 148
Bordin, E. S., 35, 64, 90
Borduin, C., 43, 44
Bornstein, R. F., 152, 171
Borus, J., 24
Bosely, S., 162
Breggin, P., 158–162
Brent, D. A., 151, 156
Brickman, P., 121
Brill, P. L., 83, 84, 108, 109
Brown, E., 151
Brown, G. S., 85
Brown, J., 2, 14, 26, 32, 47, 83, 85, 86, 88–90, 92–94, 96, 99, 117
Browne, T., 1
Burlingame, G. M., 86–88
Burr, R., 49

C

Carlsson, A., 166, 167
Carlson, G., 162
Carroll, K. M., 36, 89
Carroll, L., 32

Carson, R. C., 24
Castonguay, L. G., 40
Cervantes, M., 81
Chalk, M., 14, 47, 94, 96, 117
Chiquette, E., 171
Ciotti, M., 5
Clarke, G. N., 156
Clarkin, J., 26, 27, 229
Claud, D., 88, 89, 92, 93, 94
Cleeland, C. S., 88
Clement, P. W., 14
Clouse, G. C., 86, 88
Coates D., 121
Cohen, D., 156, 161, 162
Cohn, E., 121
Coleman, S., 119
Collins, J. F., 26, 32, 72
Cone, L., 43
Connors, G. J., 36, 89
Conrad, J., 182
Conte, H. R., 174
Cornell, J. E., 5, 171
Cross, H., 28
Crowley, S. L., 156
Cummings, N. A., 2, 5
Curry, J. F., 156

D

Daley, D., 90, 92
Dannon, P. N., 88
Danton, W. G., 168
Dardennes, R. M., 153
Dattilio, F. M., 183
Davies, M., 24
de Shazer, S., 11, 56, 57, 96, 143
DeBernardo, C., 28
DeNelsky, G. Y., 168
DeRubeis, R. J., 172
Devlin, A. S., 88
Dewey, J., 117
DiClemente, C., 36, 89
Dietrich, A., 5
Diller, L. H., 148, 149
Dobson, K., 40
Docherty, J. P., 26, 32, 72
Dolan, C., 173
Dolberg, O. T., 88

Donovan D. M., 36, 89
dosReis, S., 30, 148, 163
Dreis, S., 2, 26, 32, 83, 85–86, 96,
    98, 117
Duncan, B. L., 7, 9, 15, 19, 27, 28, 31–34,
    38, 47, 51, 52, 65, 71, 72, 78, 88–90,
    92–94, 96–99, 108–111, 114, 117,
    118, 121, 127, 128, 152, 183
Dunner, D. L., 162
Duriez, S., 1

E

Elkin, I., 26, 32, 36, 72, 89
Emslie, G. J., 151–155, 161, 175
Epston, D., 127
Erickson, M. H., 10–12, 121, 125, 126
Ernest, D. E., 151
Eron, J., 127
Eshun, S., 15
Evan, C., 153

F

Fiester, S. J., 26, 32, 72
Finch, A. E., 15
First, M., 24
Fisch, R., 121
Fisher, R. L., 151, 162
Fisher, S., 151–153, 162, 171–173
Flexner, J. T., 13
Fogel, B., 169
Frank, A., 90, 92
Frank, E., 174
Frank, J. B., 121
Frank, J. D., 29, 33, 121
Freud, S., 7, 23, 37, 117, 187
Fucci, B., 43

G

Garb, H. N., 24
Gardner, J. F., 148
Garfield, S., 26
Garfinkel, R., 156
Gaston, L., 71, 90
Gelenberg, A. J., 162
Geller, B., 162
Georgaca, E., 187
Ger, L. P., 88

Gergen, K. E., 179
Gesten, E. L., 3
Gibbon, M., 24
Gilman, A. G., 168
Gingerich, W., 56, 57, 96
Glass, D. R., 26, 32, 72
Goldfried, M. R., 40
Goldman, A., 43
Gollan, J., 40
Goolishian, H., 122
Gordon, J. S., 168
Gortner, D., 40
Grawe, K., 36
Greenberg, L. S., 43, 90
Greenberg, M. D., 152, 171
Greenberg, R. P., 147, 152, 153, 168, 170–173
Greenhouse, J. B., 174
Grochocinski, V., 174
Grube, J., 28
Grunhaus, L., 88

H

Haas, E., 83, 84
Hagino, O. R., 162
Hales, R., 169
Haley, J., 127, 198
Hansen, N. B., 83, 86, 88
Hanych, J. M., 2
Harding, C., 27
Hardman, J. G., 168
Hardy, R., 172
Hargrave, G. E., 14
Harper, D., 187
Harwood, T. M., 41
Hatcher, R. L., 90, 91
Hatgis, C., 41
Hawkins, E. J., 15, 83, 84, 95, 117
Hayes, A. M., 40
Healy, D., 29, 167, 169
Heaton, K., 64
Heiligenstein, J. H., 151
Held, B. S., 121, 122
Henggeler, S., 43
Heracleitus, 56
Hiatt, D., 14
Hill, C. E., 64, 87, 108, 110

Hill, R. D., 83, 84
Ho, S. T., 88
Hoch, P., 120
Hollon, S. D., 172
Holloway, J. D., 29
Hoog, S. L., 151
Horvath, A. O., 35, 36, 65, 85, 89, 90, 193
Howard, K. I., 83–85, 108, 117, 83, 109
Howes, M., 24
Hubble, M. A., 2, 7, 9, 12, 19, 27, 28, 31, 33, 34, 38, 71, 72, 78, 79
Hughes, C. W., 153
Hunsley, J., 43
Huxley, T. H., 21, 31

I

Iancu, I., 88
Imber, S. D., 173

J

Jackson, G., 147
Jacobson, J. G., 151
Jacobson, N., 40
Jaycox, L. H., 156
Jensen, P. S., 148, 159
John Paul, Pope, 77
Johnson, L. D., 3, 15, 85, 89, 90, 93, 117
Johnson, S. M., 42, 43, 90–92

K

Kadera, S. W., 87
Kane, J., 24
Karasu, T. B., 174
Karon, B., 198
Karuza, J., 121
Kaspar, 178
Kaufman, J., 151
Kaye, J., 179
Kelledy, L., 119
Keller, M. B., 162, 174
Kelly, G., 120
Kendell, R., 25
Kennedy, J. F., 3
Kesey, K., 181

Kidder, L., 121
Kiesler, C., 4, 5
Kinchin, K., 147
Kipras, A., 156
Kirk, S. A., 24, 25, 28–30, 187
Kirsch, I., 168, 171, 172
Klein, D. N., 162
Klein, R. G., 162
Kline, N., 165, 166
Koerner, K., 40
Koplewicz, H., 162
Kopp, S. G., 119
Kopte, S. M., 83, 84, 96, 117
Kowatch, R. A., 153
Krause, M. S., 83, 84, 96, 117
Kremer, T. G., 3
Krupnick, J. L., 36, 89
Kupfer, D. J., 174
Kusumakar, V., 162
Kutcher, S. P., 162
Kutchins, H., 24, 25, 28–30, 187

L

Laird, N. M., 171
Lambert, M. E., 42, 93
Lambert, M. J., 9, 14, 15, 33–35, 37, 38, 41, 51, 63, 83–88, 95, 96, 108, 110, 117
Lawrence, V., 171
Lawson, D., 56, 96
Leber, W. R., 26, 32, 72
Lee, L., 82
Lee, S., 171
LeFever, G., 156, 159, 160
Leighton, A. H., 171
Leo, J., 156, 160
Levitt, T., 81–83
Lewisohn, P. M., 156
Limbird, L. E., 168
Lincoln, A., 12
Longabaugh, R., 36, 89
Luborsky, L., 32, 90, 92
Lueger, R. J., 84
Lund, T., 127
Lurie, P., 155
Luther, M., 171

Lutz, W., 83, 85, 108, 109
Lynch, F., 148

M

Mackey, P., 156
Madigan, S., 127
Magder, L., 148
Malik, M., 41
Maling, M. S., 84
Mann, B., 43
Marcus, S. C., 148
Markowitz, J. C., 162
Martinovich, Z., 83–85, 108, 109
Masters, K., 86, 110
Matt, G. E., 41
McCafferty, J. P., 162
McCall, R., 91
McCullough, J. P., 162
McGuire, W., 7
McLaughlin, T., 187
Melton, G., 43
Messer, S., 37, 42
Meyer, G., 50
Michael, K. D., 156
Mill, J. S., 145
Miller, L., 28
Miller, S. D., 2, 7, 9, 15, 19, 27, 28, 31, 33, 34, 38, 47, 51, 58, 71, 72, 78, 79, 88–90, 92–94, 96–98, 117, 152, 183
Mitka, M., 163
Mohl, D. C., 185
Moncrieff, J., 170, 172
Mondin, G. W., 32, 40
Monson, R. R., 171
Moody, M., 32, 40
Moore, T. J., 168, 172
Moras, K., 83, 85, 108, 109
Moreau, D., 156
Morrell, B., 83, 84
Morris, J., xviii
Moyer, J., 36, 89
Moynihan, D., 121
Mufson, L., 156
Mulrow, C. D., 171
Murphy, J. J., 128

Murphy, J. M., 171
Murphy, M., 28
Musselman, D. L., 167
Mustard, C., 4

N

Nace, D. K., 2, 26, 32, 83, 85–86, 96,
    98, 117
Najavits, L., 90, 92
Nathan K. I., 167, 168
Nathan, P. E., 39
Navarro, A. M., 41
Neimeyer, R. A., 173, 174
Nemeroff, C. B., 162, 167
Nicholls, S. S., 172
Nielsen, S. L., 15, 83, 84, 95, 117
Nies, A., 168
Nilsson, M., 151
Noble, S., 41
Noel, P. H., 171
Norcross, J., 2, 119, 120
Nutt-Williams, E., 64

O

Oakes, R., 162
O'Connor, E., 159
Ogles, B., 14, 41, 86, 96, 110
Okiishi, J. C., 15
Olfson, M., 148, 149
Orlinsky, D. E., 36, 83, 84, 96, 117
Orwell, G., 10, 44
Osler, W., 164
Ostrom, J., 50

P

Papatheodorou, G., 162
Parker, I., 187
Parks, B. K., 36
Parloff, M. B., 9, 26, 32, 72
Pascal, B., 126
Pelham, W., 157–159
Peller, J., 58, 127
Phillips, G., 41
Pilkonis, P. A., 26, 32, 36, 72, 89
Plutchik, R., 174
Polak, D., 88
Pope, H., 24

Q

Quinlan, D. M., 89

R

Rabasca, L., 2
Rabinowitz, V., 121
Rall, T., 168
Ramirez, G., 171
Rao, S., 169
Raue, P., 40
Reynolds, L., 90, 92, 93
Rhodes, R. H., 64
Richardson, W. S., 171
Riddle, M., 30, 148, 163
Riley, W. T., 15
Rintelmann, J., 40, 153
Robinson, L. A., 173, 174
Ronnestad, M. H., 36
Rosenhan, D. L., 27
Rosenzweig, S., 32, 33, 52
Rossi, E. L., 121
Rost, K., 5
Rounsaville, B., 24
Rush, A. J., 40, 153
Rusk, G., 65, 79
Russell, J. M., 162
Ryan, N. D., 151, 162

S

Sack, W. H., 162
Safer, S. J., 30, 148, 163
Salovey, P., 27
Saltzman, N., 120
Sanchez, L., 3–5
Sanderson, W. C., 15
Sapirstein, G., 171, 172
Sasich, L. D., 155
Schappert, S., 5
Schatzberg, A. F., 167
Schiffer, R., 169
Schindler, D., 43
Scoboria, A., 168, 172
Scott, J., 7
Segal, L., 121
Shadish, W. R., 41
Shaha, S. H., 3, 85, 117
Shapiro, D., 40

Shea, M., 173
Shea, T., 26, 32, 72
Shelton, R. C., 172
Shoemaker, W., 28
Simmens, S., 36, 89
Singer, B., 32
Siobud-Dorocant, E., 153
Siqueland, L., 90, 92
Sluzki, C., 179
Smart, D. W., 15, 83, 84,
    95, 117
Smith, L., 43
Snyder, S., 166
Sobol, A. M., 171
Soeken, K., 148
Solovey, A., 65, 79
Sorrell, R., 14, 47, 94,
    96, 117
Sotsky, S. M., 89, 173
Sparks, J. A., 11, 19, 88, 89, 92, 93, 94,
    97–99, 108, 110, 114, 118, 152,
    183, 200
Spitzer, R., 24
Stamm, K., 171
Stich, F., 32, 40
Stiles, W., 40
Stowell-Smith, M., 187
Strauss, D., 27
Strober, M., 162
Strosahl, K., 4
Sun, W. Z., 88
Swank, H., 22
Sweeney, M., 162
Symonds, B. D., 36

T

Talbott, J., 169
Talebi, H., 41
Tallman, K., 34, 51, 198
Taylor, P., 168
Terranova, R. D., 2
Thase, M. E., 162, 174
Thompson, B., 64
Tomiak, M., 4
Tompson, M. C., 156
Torrey, E., 120, 121
Trivedi, M. H., 162, 171

Truax, P., 40
Turk, D., 27
Turner, S., 3–5

U

Umphress, V., 6, 88

V

Valenstein, E., 169
Vanderbos, G., 198
Vandiver, W. D., 97
Vermeersch, D. A., 15, 83, 84, 86–88,
    95, 117
Vitiello, B., 161

W

Wade, W. A., 41
Wagner, K. D., 149, 151, 154, 162
Walkup, J. T., 150, 160–163
Walter, J., 58, 127
Wampold, B. E., 9, 32, 34, 36–38, 40, 42,
    43, 47, 63
Wang, M. S., 88
Washington, G., 12–14
Watkins, J. T., 26, 32, 36, 72, 89
Watzlawick, P., 23, 121, 127
Weakland, J., 121
Weinberg, W. A., 40, 153
Weiner-Davis, M., 56, 57, 96
Weiss, B., 172
Weissman, M. M., 148, 156
Weller, E. B., 162
Wessely, S., 172
Whipple, J. L., 15, 83–84,
    95, 117
Whitaker, R., 187, 198
White, M., 127
Wild, K. V., 174
Wile, D., 121
Wilford, J., 50
Williams, J., 24
Williams, J. W., Jr., 5, 171
Williams, R., 43
Williamson, D. E., 151
Willutzki, U., 36
Winters, N. C., 162

Wiser, S., 40
Wittchen, H., 24
Wolfe, B. E., 6
Wolfe, S. M., 155
Wong, E., 41
Woolston, J. L., 149

Y

Yanchar, S. C., 86, 88
Yudosky, S., 169

Z

Zablansky, A., 25
Zajecka, J., 162
Zanuck, D. F., 82
Zborowski, M. J., 171
Zeig, J. K., 10, 11
Zito, J. M., 30, 148, 163
Zubin, R., 27
Zuroff, D. C., 89
Zyzanski, S., 5

—ᴡᴡ— Subject Index

A

Aceylcholine, 166
ADHD. *See* Attention deficit hyperactivity disorder (ADHD)
Advil, 51
Aesop, 1, 5
Agency for Health Care Policy and Research, 171
Agitation, 166
Agoraphobia, 115–117
AIDS, 66–68
Alcoholism, 36
Alice's Adventures in Wonderland (Carroll), 32
Allegiance, 37, 42, 43
Alliance factors, 35–37
Alliance monitoring, 64–65
Alzheimer's Disease, 39
American Association of Marriage and Family Therapy (AAMFT), 13, 149
American Counseling Association (ACA), 13
American Healthcare Institute, 6
American Journal of Psychiatry, 25
American Psychiatric Association, 29, 39
American Psychological Association (APA), 2, 6, 7, 13, 15, 23, 24, 33, 39, 83, 159, 214
American Psychologist, 84
Amphetamine, 149. *See also* Medication
Amy (client), 44, 45
Antidepressant Era, The (Healy), 29
Antidepressants, 160, 164, 165, 170–175; and children, 151–152; and drug research, 152–156

Anxiety, 166
Assessment, client-directed, outcome-informed therapy, 186–192
Attention deficit hyperactivity disorder (ADHD), 149, 156, 157, 159, 160
Attribution creep, 27, 28
Axis II diagnosis, 29

B

Barbara (client), 112–113
Beck Depression Inventory, 152
Bible, 115
Bill (client), 138
Bioamine theories, 167–169
Biochemical imbalance, 165–167
Biogenic amine theory, 167
Biological fundamentalism, 180
Biological markers, 167–169
Biomine theories, 167–169
Bipolar disorder, 39
Blaming the Brain (Valenstein), 169
Bloodletting, 10
Bob (client), 126
Borderline personality disorder (BPD), 8, 25, 30, 44
Boston Globe, 148
Boulder conference, 21
Bowen family therapy, 36, 37
Boys Don't Cry (cinema), 22
BPD. *See* Borderline personality disorder (BPD)

C

California Psychotherapy Alliance Scales, 90
Case writing, 192

Catecholamine depletion, 166
CBSC. *See* Change-by-session curve
    (CBSC)
CBT. *See* Cognitive behavioral therapy
    (CBT)
Celexa, 164
Change, client's theory of, 19, 71–73;
    conversation, content, and change
    in, 122–124; learning and honoring,
    73–75; and privileging client's voice,
    126–145; and selection of content,
    124–126; in tradition, 120–126;
    trusting, 145–146
Change focus: and becoming change
    focused, 56–63; and expanding
    change into heroic stories, 58–63;
    and listening for change, 56–58
Change-by-session curve (CBSC),
    108–111
Child Outcome Rating Scale
    (CORS), 224
Child Session Rating Scale (CSRS), 225
Chlorpromazine, 166, 167
Cincinnati Bengals, 69
Circular causality, 187–188
Citalopram, 156
Client: accepting goals of, 68–70; as
    agent of change, 34–35, 51; casting,
    in heroic roles, 51–55; *versus* clini-
    cian ratings, 152; as critic of therapy
    performance, 63–71; engagement in
    therapy process, 16; feedback, 15,
    19; Kim, 125–126; language of, 73;
    Linda, 111; Mike, 75–78; Molly, 49;
    partnering with, 97–117;
    self-report, 14
Client directed: becoming, 10–12,
    49–80; *versus* theory driven, 19
Client-directed, outcome-informed
    therapy: and assessment, 186–192;
    goals for therapy, 192–194; inter-
    ventions of, 194–198; model for,
    184–186
Clients: Amy, 44; Barbara, 112–113; Bill,
    138; Bob, 126; Emma, 201–211; Jan
    and Mark, 182–199; Joan, 59–63;
    Liz and Bob, 142–145; Maria, 16–18;

Pat, 128–132; Robyn, 115–117; Sam,
    65–68; Sarah, 69; Sean, 51; Stacy,
    132–138; Steven, 113–115
Clinical trials, 31, 32
Clonidine, 148, 149. *See also* Medication
Coassessment, 190, 191
Cognitive behavioral therapy (CBT),
    26, 32, 41, 44, 147
Common cause, 39
Common factors, 52; evolution and
    dangers of applying, 79–80
Competency, 13; client, 52, 53, 133; and
    effectiveness, 13; orientation, 127,
    138; *versus* outcome, 14
Conflict avoidance pattern, 188, 189
Content, 122–124; selecting, 124–126
Continuing education requirement, 14
Conversation, 122–124

D

Deinonychus, 50
Depression: adolescent, 156; biogenic
    amine theory of, 167; genetic,
    127–132; major, 39; serotonin
    theory of, 168
Destigmatization, 160–164
Dexamethasone suppression test
    (DST), 167
*Diagnostic and Statistical Manual of
    Mental Disorders (DSM)*, 22, 23, 25,
    28, 29, 44, 118; *DSM-III*, 24;
    DSM-IV, 6, 9, 10, 18, 22
Diagnostic classification, 21
Diagnostic disorder, 23–28; and cultural
    bias, 29–30; as flawed extension of
    medical model, 30; and labeling,
    27–28; and reliability, 24–25; and
    validity, 25–26
Dialectical behavior therapy
    (DBT), 44
Diathesis-stress paradigm, 130
Disability, paradigm of, 198
Disrupted homeostasis, 169
Division of Clinical Psychology, 39
Dodo bird verdict, 32, 33, 38, 42, 43, 51
Dopamine, 166, 167
Dose-effect relationship, 108

"Dose-Effect Relationship in
  Psychotherapy" *(American
  Psychologist)*, 84
Drug companies, 29
Drug Enforcement Administration, 148
Drug research, four flaws of,
  152–156
DST. *See* Dexamethasone suppression
  test (DST)

E

Eating disorders, 39
Eclecticism, 119, 120
Effectiveness: and competence, 13;
  Human Affairs International study
  of, 32; in medical health provider
  organizations, 13; proof of, 12;
  psychotherapy, 8; and Treatment of
  Depression Collaborative Research
  Project, 26
Elavil, 152
Eli Lilly and Company, 154, 155
Emma (client), 201–211
Emotionally focused therapy (EFT),
  42–44
"Emperor's New Drugs" (Kirsch,
  Moore, Scoboria, and Nicholls), 172
Epinephrine, 166
ESPN, 70
Ethical codes, 13
Evaluation, 187
Evidence-based practice, 3, 7, 21; and
  alliance factors, 35–37; and client
  factors, 34–35; and model or
  technical factors, 37–38; myth of,
  31–47; reliability and validity of,
  46–47; as ultimate silver bullet,
  38–47
Expectancy factors, 37
Expertise, 190

F

Family Counseling Office (Vestfold,
  Norway), 108
Family Therapy Magazine, 149
FDA. *See* Federal Drug Administration
  (FDA)

FDA Talk Paper (FDA Press Office),
  155, 162
Federal Drug Administration (FDA),
  150, 154, 155, 162, 172
Federal Drug trials, 39
First-session formula task, 143
Fluoxetine (Prozac), 151, 152, 155, 156.
  See also Medication
French psychiatrists, 166
From Placebo to Panacea (Greenberg
  and Fisher), 156

G

Genetic depression, 127–132
Geodon, 161, 202
GlaxoSmithKline, 162
Global Assessment Scale, 152
Goals, 192–194
Godzilla, 49, 50

H

Hamilton Depression Scale,
  152, 174
Harding study, 27
Harvard University, 81
Hay Group, 3
Heart and Soul of Change (Hubble,
  Duncan, and Miller), 34
Helping Alliance Questionnaire II
  (HAQ), 90, 92
Heraclites, 56, 57
Heroic stories: creating new, 56–63;
  expanding change into, 58–63;
  listening for, 52–55
HIV, 67
Hollywood, 82
Homosexuality, 29
Human Affairs International, 32

I

Imipramine, 168
IMS Health, 148, 149, 164
India, 165
Interpretation, 185
Intervention, 194–198
Interview, conversation *versus,* 122
I-statement strategies, 195

J

Jan and Mark (clients), 182–199
Joan (client), 59–63
*Journal of Consulting and Clinical
    Psychology,* 6

K

Killer D's, 35, 127
Kim (client), 125–126

L

Lilly. *See* Eli Lilly and Company
Linda (client), 111, 112
Linear causality, 187–188
Linear regression, 110. *See also* Simple
    linear regression (SLR)
Liz and Bob (clients), 142–145

M

Magic pill, myth of, 9. *See* Medication
Major depressive disorder (MDD),
    155, 162
Manuals, 41
Maria (client), 16–18, 27, 53–55
Massachusetts Medicaid program, 148
MDD. *See* Major depressive
    disorder (MDD)
Medicaid, 163
Medical model, 7, 8, 10; diagnostic
    disorder as extension of, 30; myth
    of, 21–48; relational model *versus,*
    19; script for, 180
Medication: and antidepressants for
    children, 151–152; and bioamine
    theories, 167–169; and biochemical
    imbalance, 165–167; and demystify-
    ing magic pill, 170–173; and des-
    tigmatization, 160–164; and ethics
    of medicating children, 148–164;
    and medicated nation, 164–175;
    overview of, 147–148; *versus*
    therapy, 173–175
Medicine and Healthcare Products
    Regulatory Agency (United
    Kingdom; MHRA), 162
Mental disease, concept of, 21
Mental health care benefits, 82

Mental health practice: and
    client-directed, outcome-
    informed therapy assessment,
    186–192; future of, 3–10; medical
    model applied to, 5, 6, 8; models
    and, 184–186; neurology of,
    179–181; and paradigm of
    disability, 198–199; and pathology,
    181–182; relational model for, 19;
    and responsibility, 199–200; state
    of, 1–3
Mental health practitioners, 1, 2; ethical
    codes of, 13
Mental Research Institute (MRI),
    121, 127
*Merriam-Webster's Collegiate Dictio-
    nary,* 184, 195
Methylphenidate (Ritalin), 148, 149.
    See also Medication
Mike (client), 75–78
Models, 37–38, 184–186
Molly (client), 49, 63, 71, 79
Montana, 50
MRI. *See* Mental Research Institute
    (MRI)
MTA Cooperative Group, 157, 158, 175
Multimodal Treatment Study of
    Children with ADHD (MTA
    Cooperative Group), 157
Multisystemic therapy (MST), 43, 44

N

Narcotics Anonymous (NA), 65, 67
National Action Agenda for Children's
    Mental Health (NAACMH), 163
National Anxiety and Depression
    Awareness Day, 6
National Association of Rights
    Protection and Advocacy, 213–214
National Association of Social Workers
    (NASW), 11
National Institute of Mental Health
    (NIMH), 22, 25, 26, 149, 161, 173
New England Journal of Medicine,
    7, 154
New Freedom Commission of Mental
    Health, 29

New York Times, 63
Nicotine dependence, 39
NIMH. *See* National Institute of Mental
  Health (NIMH)
Norepinephrine, 166, 167
Norway, 93, 108, 111

O

One Flew Over the Cuckoo's Nest
  (Kesey), 181
Outcome: and future, 117–118;
  informed, becoming, 12–16;
  prediction of, 26; from process to,
  83–85; research, and Erickson's
  observations, 11, 12; successful,
  versus competent service, 19;
  tracking, 86–96
Outcome management, 15
Outcome Questionnaire 45.2 (OQ),
  86–88, 92, 94
Outcome Rating Scale (ORS), 87–89,
  91, 110–113, 222; in action, 94–96;
  and checking for change, 102–107;
  and conversation, 124; and drug
  research, 156; experimental version
  of, for children, 224; experimental
  version of, for young children, 226;
  incorporating, in first meeting,
  99–100; introduction of, in first
  meeting, 98–99; reliability, validity,
  and feasibility of, 91–94

P

Paroxetine, 156, 162
Participation, client, 36, 182
Pat (client), 128–132
Pathology, 8, 29; and pathological
  labels, 15; swimming in, 181–182
Paxil, 162, 164, 165
Pedophilia, 138–142
Peer ratings, 14
Personal construct theory, 120
Pharmaceutical marketing, 163–165
Pittsburgh, Pennsylvania, 174
Placebo, 151–156, 171, 172, 175
Platelet-binding assays, 168
Position, concept of, 121

Pretreatment change, 56
Problem focus, 189
Project MATCH, 89
Prozac (fluoxetine), 151–155, 161, 164,
  171, 175, 181. *See also* Medication
Psychiatric diagnoses, myth of, 9,
  23–30; and diagnostic disorder,
  23–28
Psychopharmacology, 166
Psychosis, 166
Psychotherapy Bulletin, 213
Psychotropic medications, 148, 149,
  160, 164. *See also* Medication
Psychotherapy, and medical model, 5

R

Randomized clinical trial (RCT), 22,
  39–41, 46
RCI. *See* Reliable change index (RCI)
RCT. *See* Randomized clinical
  trial (RCT)
Relational bond, cementing, 64–65
Relationship factors, 35–37
Reliability, and diagnosis, 24–25
Reliable change index (RCI), 110, 111
Religious beliefs, 78, 115
Reserpine, 165–168
Risperdal, 148, 164
Ritalin (methylphinidate), 148, 156, 216.
  See also Medication
Robyn (client), 115–117

S

Sam (client), 65–68
Sarah (client), 69, 70
Schizophrenia, 27, 28, 165–167, 201,
  202, 213, 214
Science, 27
Sean (client), 51, 56
Serotonin, 167, 168
Seroxat (paroxetine), 162
Session curve, change by, 108–110,
  109*fig.*4.2
Session Rating Scale (SRS), 89–91, 223;
  in action, 94–96; and checking for
  change, 102–107; and conversation,
  124; experimental version of, for

Session Rating Scale (SRS) (*continued*)
children, 225; experimental
version of, for young children,
227; incorporating, 101–102;
introducing, 100–101; reliability,
validity, and feasibility of, 91–94
Session-by-session evaluation, 16
Silver-bullet cure, myth of. *See*
Evidence-based practice
Simple linear regression (SLR),
110–111; in action, 111–112
SLR. *See* Simple linear regression (SLR)
SSRIs, 148, 151, 152, 154–156,
161, 162, 167, 168, 171. *See also*
Medication
Stacy (client), 132–138
Star Trek (science-fiction series), 5, 10
Steven (client), 113–115
Stimulants, 148, 149, 160; and children,
156–160. *See also* Medication

T

Talk therapy approach, 7
Television, 82
The Guardian, 162
Theory, formal *versus* informal, 121,
122
Theory-driven practice, client-directed
versus, 19
Therapeutic alliance, 72*fig.*3.1
Therapeutic relationship, 16
Therapist allegiance, 122
Therapy: consumer tips for, 219–212;
client-directed, outcome-informed
therapy's goals for, 192–194; drugs
versus, 173–175; factors arguing for
change in, 33*fig.*2.1; from process to
outcome in, 83–85; and randomized
clinical trials, 41; tailoring tasks of,
70–71
Third-party payers, 15

Treatment of Depression Collaborative
Research Project (TDCRP), 26, 32,
36, 42, 71, 72, 89
Tricyclic antidepressants, 148, 151.
See also Medication
Tylenol, 51

U

University of Southern Mississippi, 213
"Using the Outcome Rating Scale with
Couples" (Anker and Duncan),
109*fig.*4.2
Utilization (Erickson), 121

V

Validation, 65, 131
Validity, in diagnosis, 25–26
Valium, 180
Vermont hospitals, 27

W

Working Alliance Inventory (WAI),
90, 94
World Health Organization, 168
World Series (1999), 165
World War II, 21

X

Xanax, 180

Y

Yale University, 50
Young Child Outcome Rating Scale
(YCORS), 226
Young Child Session Rating Scale
(YCRS), 227

Z

Zelmid (zimelidine), 167
Zoloft, 6, 7, 161, 164, 165, 170
Zyprexa, 164